# Implementing the U.N. *Convention on the Rights of the Child*

# Implementing the U.N. *Convention on the Rights of the Child*

## A Standard of Living Adequate for Development

Edited by
ARLENE BOWERS ANDREWS
and
NATALIE HEVENER KAUFMAN

Foreword by GARY B. MELTON

Westport, Connecticut
London

**Library of Congress Cataloging-in-Publication Data**

Implementing the UN Convention on the Rights of the Child : a standard
   of living adequate for development / edited by Arlene Bowers Andrews
   and Natalie Hevener Kaufman ; foreword by Gary B. Melton
     p.  cm.
   Includes bibliographical references and index.
   ISBN 0–275–96265–2 (alk. paper)
   1. Children (International law)   2. Children—Legal status, laws,
etc.   [1. Convention on the Rights of the Child (1989)]
   I. Andrews, Arlene Bowers.   II. Kaufman, Natalie Hevener.
   K639.A41989I49      1999
   341.4'81'083—dc21      98–21661

British Library Cataloguing in Publication Data is available.

Library of Congress Catalog Card Number: 98–21661
ISBN: 0–275–96265–2

First published in 1999

Praeger Publishers, 88 Post Road West, Westport, CT 06881
An imprint of Greenwood Publishing Group, Inc.

Printed in the United States of America

The paper used in this book complies with the
Permanent Paper Standard issued by the National
Information Standards Organization (Z39.48–1984).

10 9 8 7 6 5 4 3 2 1

This book is dedicated to our children,
*Carrollee, Brook, Emily,* and *Athey*

# Contents

**Part II:  The Relationship Between Standard of Living and Specific Developmental Domains**

**Part III:  Community Context**

**Part IV:  Implementing Article 27 in Various Contexts**

# Foreword

## Gary B. Melton

In 1989, after a decade-long drafting period, the U.N. General Assembly unanimously adopted an extraordinary document, the *Convention on the Rights of the Child*. The *Convention* is unprecedented in its universality and rapidity of ratification and accession. Almost every nation of the world has ratified or acceded to the *Convention*. (At this writing, only the United States—a signatory but not a party to the *Convention*—and Somalia are exceptions.) One might argue that this near-unanimity is indicative only of the ease in attracting prochild sloganeering, no matter what the cultural differences may be in how those slogans are understood. Although such an observation undoubtedly has some power in explaining the politics of ratification in many countries, one should not assume that ratification is meaningless or that it is the product of purely cynical motives.

Two facts weigh against such an interpretation. First, the drafters of the *Convention* established a system of monitoring implementation that is of unprecedented scope. Each state party to the *Convention* is obligated to produce a periodic report for review by a U.N. committee of experts serving in their personal capacity. Although the Committee on the Rights of the Child does take this responsibility seriously, the important structural innovation is that the *Convention* provides that U.N. agencies, expressly including UNICEF, and "other competent bodies" may offer "expert advice" or technical assistance in the process of monitoring and implementation (Art. 45).

This provision mirrors the unusual history of the drafting of the *Convention*, in which nongovernmental organizations (NGOs) were granted a seat in the working group to draft the *Convention*. Further, an ongoing caucus of NGO representatives observed the debate and advised the NGO representative, who played an influential role in the drafting. By the ultimate recognition of NGOs ("other competent bodies") in the *Convention* itself, the states parties agreed to scrutiny of their efforts by domestic citizen groups as well as international organizations. To facilitate implementation and monitoring, the states parties have an express obligation to "make principles of the *Convention* widely known, by appropriate and active means, to adults and children alike" (Art. 42). In essence, the *Convention* is structured in a manner that promotes its use as an instrument in domestic as well as international law and politics.

That fact would be unimportant but for the second fact: The content of the *Convention* is also of unprecedented scope. The *Convention* is neither narrow nor trite. Unlike many expositions of children's rights, it does not consist merely of platitudes. Not only is the number of rights recognized under the *Convention* remarkable (fifty-four articles, most with multiple sections), but their theoretical coherence is also striking—an intellectual integration that is all the more stunning when one considers the process by which the *Convention* was drafted.[1]

The authors of the *Convention* adopted a "constitutional" approach to children's rights, in which they adopted expansive language covering a broad range of domains of children's lives. More than any other global human rights treaty, the *Convention* integrates civil and political rights with social and economic rights. The common theme is the requisite of *dignity* for children—a word that appears often in the *Convention* expressly and that permeates it conceptually.

Article 27, the focus of this book, is a particularly meaningful illustration. By its adoption, "States Parties recognize the right of every child to a standard of living adequate for the child's physical, mental, spiritual, moral, and social development." Note that this provision, which seems on its face to establish an extraordinarily broad entitlement, is "constitutional" not "statutory" in form. It does not establish a checklist of mandates or prohibitions for states parties. Rather, Article 27 provides a principle to guide the global community in regard to the minimum scope—that which is by *right*—of social policies intended to promote the welfare of children.

Interpretation of Article 27, like many provisions of the *Convention*, demands both normative and empirical analysis. Normatively, explication requires a determination of what is "adequate" in an extraordinarily broad range of domains of children's lives, which must be defined. Empirically, it requires identification of the social and economic circumstances (the "standard of living") necessary for adequate development.

Definition of adequacy of development requires an analysis of the purposes of the *Convention*. In that regard, the preamble to the *Convention* offers some helpful clues. For example, the Preamble recognizes "that the child, for the full and harmonious development of his or her personality, should grow up in a family environment, in an atmosphere of happiness, love, and understanding." Besides providing an assumption about a requisite for adequate development (i.e., a loving family environment), this clause of the preamble suggests that the ultimate outcome of interest is development of the child's personality. *Personality* is a term of art in international human rights law. A word that appears in numerous instruments, its meaning is closer to "personhood" than the colloquial and psychological definitions of the word. The next clause of the Preamble, which notes the drafters' desire that "the child should be fully prepared to live an individual life in society," gives further credence to this interpretation.

In short, Article 27, when combined with the Preamble, requires states parties to ensure the availability of the requisites for children's full participation in society. Therefore, Article 27 demands a standard of living sufficient to achieve personal independence at such a level in the domains listed within the article. This interpretation is consistent with the underlying theory of the *Convention*— that children, as persons, are owed respect for their dignity. Within such a framework, it is necessary but insufficient to fulfill the rudiments of citizenship. Civil and political rights are not enough. Friendships, family relationships, work, study, play, and spirituality are all essential to the human experience. Such are the aspects of children's lives that define them as persons and that enable their development as individuals worthy of respect and respectful of others—capable of living, as the Preamble admonishes, "in the spirit of the ideals proclaimed in the Charter of the United Nations, and in particular in the spirit of peace, dignity, tolerance, freedom, equality, and solidarity." The *Convention* properly mandates states parties to guarantee children the standard of living necessary to achieve individuality in the fundamental domains of life. At the same time, the *Convention* does demand meaningful opportunities for children's civil and political involvement (the nature of that participation necessarily evolving developmentally), presumably including the education necessary to be an informed participant in democratic processes (see also Arts. 28 and 29).

This understanding must be translated in concrete criteria that may guide the U.N. Committee on the Rights of the Child as well as policymakers in each state party. Accomplishment of this objective presents difficult challenges for social scientists. Several points are noteworthy in that regard.

First, some of the topics are ones that are seldom studied. Most notably, spiritual development is a domain that is rarely given attention by social scientists. Even the conceptual foundation needed for research (What does "spiritual development" in childhood mean?) is largely lacking.

Second, to the extent that information about the linkage between standard of living and developmental outcomes is available, it is typically correlational. To set standards for compliance with Article 27, research is needed that causally relates standard of living to specific *levels* of variables of interest. For example, information is available about the relation between family income and children's educational achievement. Research does also suggest some of the mechanisms by which this relationship occurs (see, e.g., Alexander & Entwisle, 1996). However, it is not framed in a way that permits easy inferences about the relation between family income and a level of achievement sufficient for an individual life in society.

Third, the relation between standard of living and the outcomes of interest is not necessarily linear. This fact is most obvious in regard to spiritual development. Many religions regard people who have taken vows of poverty as their holiest adherents. The richness, for example, of spirituals arising from the slave churches of the antebellum U.S. South raises a question at least of the necessity of a particular standard of living for spiritual development. For other domains of development, particular experiences only loosely related to standard of living may be the most important for acquisition of skills important to "mental development" in a given culture (see, for example, Hollos, 1983, on the relation of the physical environment to cognitive development).

Further, even in terrible conditions some children are sufficiently resilient to continue their development. Almost no one would question what social scientists have learned from formal study—that poverty is generally an impediment to children's development (Duncan & Brooks-Gunn, 1997). Nonetheless, the pages of history are filled with accounts of leaders who have grown up under severely adverse conditions. Some measure of social and economic resources is obviously necessary for survival, but that level is far below what most people would regard as a decent standard of living. Although "adequacy" may be defined in terms of a standard of living that gives a child a reasonable chance of development to a level sufficient for full participation in society (not that this is absolutely necessary for such development),[2] the fact remains that the standard of living adequate even for "development" (distinguished from "survival") may be quite low.[3]

Fourth, the answer in regard to the standard of living adequate for full participation in society is historically and culturally relative. The kinds of "mental development," for example, needed for independence in an agrarian society are undoubtedly different from those necessary in a society requiring computer literacy in order to communicate easily with others and to have a reasonable range of occupational choices. In that regard, even though the *Convention* addresses *minima* required for child's development, they are relevant to industrialized as well as developing countries—even to industrialized countries that, unlike the United States, do not permit gross inequality in their citizens' standard of living.

Fifth, as already noted and as some of the preceding points illustrate, the definitions of the domains of interest and the determination of adequacy are ultimately questions of law and morality. Social scientists will need to be guided by lawyers and ethicists in framing their research questions in a manner that will be useful to policymakers who take their obligations under the *Convention* seriously and to advocates who are equally diligent in the monitoring process.

Recognizing the need for an interdisciplinary, multicultural analysis of the meaning of Article 27 and the establishment of a corollary agenda for research and monitoring, the Institute for Families in Society at the University of South Carolina convened a study group consisting of distinguished scholars of diverse professional and cultural backgrounds.[4] This book emerged from provocative discussions by that group and insightful editing by my colleagues Arlene Bowers Andrews and Natalie Hevener Kaufman.

The result is a model for a process that could be used to understand the broad language present in many other articles of the *Convention*. For example, working with partner U.S. centers in the Consortium on Children, Families, and the Law and dozens of scholars from abroad, the Institute for Families in Society undertook a similar analysis of the child's right under the *Convention* to a family environment. Some of the ideas discussed in that study group were presented in a special section of *American Psychologist* (December 1996) and a special issue of *Law and Policy* (October 1995). Among the other "constitutional" provisions of the *Convention* are the right of children separated from family members to "be dealt with . . . in a positive, humane and expeditious manner" (Art.10, sec.1), "the right of the child to freedom of thought, conscience and religion" (Art.14, sec.1), the right of children to "access to information and material from a diversity of national and international sources, especially those aimed at the promotion of . . . social, spiritual and moral well-being and physical and mental health" (Art. 17), the right of children with disabilities to "a full and decent life in conditions which ensure dignity, promote self-reliance and facilitate the child's active participation in the community" (Art. 23, sec. 1), the right of children to "participate fully in cultural and artistic life" (Art. 31, sec. 2), and "the right of every child alleged as, accused of, or recognized as having infringed the penal law to be treated in a manner consistent with the promotion of the child's sense of dignity and worth. . . ." (Art. 40, sec.1).

As the compilation of chapters reflecting a model process for understanding the *Convention on the Rights of the Child*, this book is likely to be essential to policymakers, advocates, and scholars as they undertake the intellectually, morally, and politically challenging work of protecting the dignity of children. I hope that *Implementing the U.N. Convention on the Rights of the Child* will be followed by many efforts of comparable depth and quality to explicate the meaning of the *Convention* for children around the world.

## NOTES

1. The *Convention* was drafted by consensus. Thus, the ultimate wording of the *Convention* represents, in effect, the lowest common denominator—the most stringent language that, in the judgment of the chair, the participating nations could accept unanimously.

2. The concept in psychoanalytic ego psychology (Hartmann, 1939/1958) of an "average expectable environment" may be helpful in that regard.

3. Article 6 of the *Convention* obligates states parties to "ensure to the maximum extent possible the survival *and* development of the child" (emphasis added).

4. The study group met in May 1996 at Isle of Palms, South Carolina. Shelli Charles should be recognized for her skill and diligence in handling the logistical arrangements for the meeting.

I would also like to thank Cindy and Evan Nord, whose generous endowment of the Institute permits us to undertake some groundbreaking studies like the international inquiry in this book without the constraints of grant and contract funding.

## REFERENCES

Alexander, K. L. & Entwisle, D. R. (1996). Schools and children at risk. In A. Booth & J. F. Dunn, *Family-school links: How do they affect educational outcomes?* (67–88). Mahwah, NJ: Erlbaum.

Duncan, G. J. & Brooks-Gunn, J. (Eds.). (1997). *Consequences of growing up poor.* New York: Russell Sage Foundation.

Hartmann, H. (1958). *Ego psychology and the problem of adaptation.* New York: International Universities Press. (Original work published 1939.)

Hollos, M. (1983). Cross-cultural research in psychological development in rural communities. In A. W. Childs & G. B. Melton (Eds.), *Rural psychology* (45–73). New York: Plenum.

# Preface

The United Nations *Convention on the Rights of the Child* has been adopted by almost all nations of the world. The *Convention* encompasses survival, protection, participation, and development rights. One crucial dimension to any discussion of the rights of the child is determining how to create the kind of environment most likely to enhance the child's development. Article 27 of the *Convention* states that those accepting the treaty "recognize the right of every child to a standard of living adequate for the child's physical, mental, spiritual, moral and social development." The aim of this book is to present an analysis of the nature, importance, and potential implementation strategies if societies were to take seriously the obligation they have accepted. This book is based on a symposium held in May 1996, especially to address this issue and includes original papers, revised in light of the discussions, of twenty scholars and practitioners who attended. The participants were drawn from a wide variety of fields, and their viewpoints integrate contemporary scholarship and experience across disciplines and cultures. The introduction and conclusion integrate the new insights and recommendations drawn from the extensive discussions of the meetings. The focus of this book is the total child—the physical, mental, spiritual, moral, and social development—exploring both known and newly emergent scholarship and policy in psychology, economics, law, social work, education, sociology, pediatrics, and community organization.

There has been a dramatic increase in interest in children's rights globally. One of the primary forces driving this interest is the acceptance of the *Convention on the Rights of the Child* by governments from around the world. Yet the global community and its constituent parts are only beginning to forge an un-

derstanding of how to interpret and implement the set of standards and obligations that governments have taken on by adopting the *Convention*.

The child's right to survive and develop is a fundamental premise of the
*Convention*. Arlene Bowers Andrews' chapter reviews the significance of childhood for human development and the challenge of identifying adequate living
conditions within and across cultures. She reports on the already established
indicators of child development throughout the world, with emphasis on the
threats to development. Finally, and of special significance given their salient
role in Article 27, she reviews the issues affecting parents' and governments'
capacities to fulfill their responsibilities under the article.

Article 27 reflects a rather new and holistic approach to understanding the
needs of children. Natalie Hevener Kaufman and María Luisa Blanco set forth
the origins of Article 27, reviewing the controversies during the drafting process
and the special role played by the nongovernmental organizations. The authors
also outline the procedures established for interpreting and monitoring the *Convention*. Looking at the functioning of the Committee on the Rights of the Child
and the initial country reports submitted under the terms of the treaty, they
explicate some of the patterns already emerging from this process.

Clearly the Committee efforts, however strong, cannot alone be responsible
for seeing that the *Convention*'s objectives are reached. Parallel work by public
and private groups at all levels are necessary. Asher Ben-Arieh describes current
work aimed at developing and applying statistical indicators of child well-being
within nations. Having chaired such efforts at the national level, within Israel,
he describes, as well, his work with an international group of experts aimed at
meeting the challenges of identifying feasible indicators across nations. His
chapter focuses on the selection of indicators of positive development and well-
being beyond survival. Included are the results of the international study group
and an agenda for future monitoring efforts.

Central to the developing agenda on children's rights is the recognition that
children are human beings entitled to dignity and respect of their own. As the
global community begins to fully adopt an attitude toward children based on
their integrity as human beings, not human becomings, we also need to see
childhood as a state in itself and see children as more than potential adults. Jens
Qvortrup explains the implications of accepting childhood as a time and space
of life that is important in its own right and argues that indicators of quality
childhood should be comparable to indicators of quality adulthood, that is, children should be considered as partners and autonomous units in distributive justice.

The drafters of Article 27 identified five specific developmental domains that
they assumed are dependent on an adequate standard of living. The first is the
child's physical development, addressed here by Francis E. Rushton and Robert
E. Greenberg, two pediatric specialists. The authors carefully and thoroughly
present the increasingly strong evidence linking poor physical development to
low socioeconomic status.

Mental and physical development are also linked. Nutrition, health, safety, and positive stimulation for learning are associated with the child's intellectual functioning and academic achievement. Patricia Y. Hashima and Susan P. Limber present their analysis of this research and also report on the current evidence that the child's mental development is extensively influenced by the home environment and the schools.

The Holy See was instrumental in seeing that the child's spiritual development was added to the list of domains included in Article 27. Ross A. Thompson and Brandy Randall, while noting the relative scarcity of research on children's spiritual development, create their own framework for discussing the crucial domain of the child's spirituality. The authors discuss the importance of the family, community, and early childhood experiences that promote trust and security, contributing to the ability of the child to understand and appreciate the spiritual domain.

The moral domain has been the subject of more research providing us with the tools to understand how children learn social conventions and standards of morality. Judith Torney-Purta has helped to lead the formulation and investigation of extensive cross-cultural studies of civic education. She discusses findings that children learn standards of morality through natural groups in their environment, and she reports on research about children's perceptions of human rights and citizenship.

The child's social development, although beginning in the family, requires positive involvement in groups beyond the family in schools and with peers. If children learn socially responsible behavior, they are in a position to make a positive contribution to their social environment. Malfrid Grude Flekkøy and Natalie Hevener Kaufman discuss the current literature on social development and the importance of the child's participation. When participation provides experience with decision-making, children learn a sense of control over their own lives and acquire skills necessary for any well-functioning democracy.

The child's development requires more than an adequate standard of living within individual families. Varying levels of community wealth, measured in a variety of ways, are also part of the context within which children grow and develop. Frank D. Barry explores the concept of "community wealth" including relationship factors such as adult-child interaction time as well as economic resource level. The author also describes the complexity of community wealth and considers the community as potential mediator between government and families and the limitations of responsibility for child development.

The gap between rich and poor is not only an issue of nation-state dispute. It also has serious effects on the development of children within nations. Leroy H. Pelton explores the plight of poor children and their families relative to the nonpoor. He raises the issue of community responsibility to address the needs of the poor if poor children are genuinely to have the opportunity to develop and thrive.

From an important and different perspective, Allen M. Parkman considers

how human capital theory applies to Article 27. He argues that from this perspective, parents fulfill their responsibility under the *Convention*, in part, by
investing in their child's human capital, thereby making the child more productive. Investments per child can be higher when parents have more resources,
fewer children, freedom from discrimination, and long-term relationships with
the child.

The universality of the adoption of the *Convention* does not, of course, mean
universality of interpretation. Clearly different cultures will choose to select
different elements to emphasize and different provisions to implement first. For
Article 27, the very concept of "standard of living" must be interpreted within
a cultural context. Virginia Murphy-Berman explores the various conditions and
contexts that might influence cross-cultural interpretations of Article 27. Cultural
beliefs about how environments influence child development also influence these
interpretations. Therefore, as implementation measures are designed, cross-
cultural policy differences will need to be considered.

Finally, the *Convention* is only effective to the extent that it is fully understood, meaningfully interpreted, and seriously implemented. As the most politically and economically powerful nation in the world, the United States can play
a major role in advancing the needs of children globally. U.S. nonratification of
the treaty does not mean that the treaty lacks importance for the United States.
The U.S. signing of the treaty—which formally requires that the country not act
contrary to the treaty's requirements—the customary law status of the *Convention*, and the continuing international child advocacy of the U.S. government
and nongovernmental organizations means that the *Convention* has to be understood by those within the United States. Robin Kimbrough reviews the U.S.
law that applies to Article 27 and raises questions about how the treaty might
be interpreted here. She also considers how current policies, such as welfare
reform, might be examined in light of the responsibilities set forth in Article
27.

Are there critical issues for implementing Article 27 in countries that are in
transition to more democratic and more open economic systems? Jiří Kovařík
of the Czech Republic discusses the many ways that his government is involved
in steps that may affect the responsibilities the government accepted under Article 27 when ratifying the *Convention*. He reviews many dimensions of the
child's environment, including the environment of children in institutions, and
points to success and shortcomings in the country's work thus far.

One special cultural issue arises for children within Africa and of the African
Diaspora. The people of Africa have nurtured living conditions that produced
civilizations where children thrived. Since colonization, the standard of living
has virtually collapsed in some areas of Africa, leaving children dangerously
threatened. As the people of Africa have dispersed across the globe, their children have confronted challenging circumstances. Barbara Morrison-Rodriguez
reviews the implications of Article 27 for changing their plight, promoting standards that would assure that children of African descent fully develop. She

provides a wealth of information about a particular case study—that of African American children in South Carolina, indicating the great divergences between the developmental environments of black and white children in one state within the United States.

The editors' concluding chapter draws attention to the ongoing need for research about Article 27 and the important areas of policy formulation. They also explore current efforts to create global means of measuring and monitoring the child's well-being aimed at promoting adequate living conditions for the child's development.

# Acknowledgments

We would like to thank the Institute for Families in Society of the University of South Carolina, especially its director, Gary B. Melton, for supporting this project. Most of the chapters in the volume were initially written for a conference on Article 27 of the U.N. *Convention on the Rights of the Child*, led by Dr. Melton and sponsored by the Institute. We thank Shelli Charles, in particular, for her fine organizational skills in arranging the conference and compiling the original papers. Sheila Heatley and María Luisa Blanco have provided capable technical assistance as we prepared this manuscript.

Arlene Bowers Andrews offers these acknowledgments: Thank you, mother, Elfriede Traeger Bowers, for how you have shown me that adults can strive to promote a child's standard of living even in the face of imminent threats. You and Dad gave me a childhood that makes me at home among people of different nations and cultures. Stuart Andrews, my life partner, you help me try to live according to the global principles of the children's *Convention* in our daily lives and community. I am also ever grateful for your insights as I probe greater legal understanding. Brook and Emily, you are the models for how children can contribute to the quality of an adult's standard of living, for you have surely enriched mine. And I am especially grateful to all those other Bowers and Andrews children who never let me forget what the world is like through the eyes of a child: Ainsley, Jillian, Matheson, Colin, Kelley, Andrew, Annie, Jonathan, Brian, Matthew, Melanie, Jason, Lori, Brandon, Heather, and Chris.

Natalie (Lee Jane) Hevener Kaufman acknowledges: I thank my sister, Susan Kaufman, for her enthusiasm and encouragement of so many of my endeavors. I would also like to thank my brother-in-law, Peter Waldron, for so many stimulating, diverting conversations, and Miranda and Jacob Kaufman-Waldron for filling our visits with bottomless fun. I am grateful for the loving support of my parents, my sister, Helene Kaufman, and my brother, Ted Kaufman. My life is enriched in very many different ways by my women friends: Robyn Newkumet, Sue Rosser, Malfrid Flekkøy, Deb Valentine, Sara Schoeman, Jan Love, Anita Floyd, Sarah Fox, Ann Cargill, Angela Nordmann, and Francie Close. Finally, I want to thank my partner, David Whiteman, whose endless creativity and humor always gets us through, and my daughters Carrollee Kaufman Hevener and Athey Whiteman Kaufman for their caring love of me and one another.

# Abbreviations

| | |
|---|---|
| ABA | American Bar Association |
| AFDC | Aid to Families with Dependent Children |
| CACFP | Child and Adult Care Food Program |
| CATCH | Community Access to Child Health |
| CDF | Children's Defense Fund |
| CRC | *Convention on the Rights of the Child* |
| EIC | Earned Income Credit |
| GAO | General Accounting Office |
| GDP | Gross Domestic Product |
| GNP | Gross National Product |
| IEA | International Association for the Evaluation of Educational Achievement |
| JOBS | Job Opportunities and Basic Skills program |
| KDS | Christian Democratic Party (Czech Republic) |
| KDU-CSL | Christian and Democratic Union, plus Czech People's Party |
| NACLA | North American Congress on Latin America |
| NGOs | Nongovernmental organizations |
| OBE | Outcome-based education |
| ODA | Civic Democratic Alliance (Czech Republic) |
| OECD | Organization for Economic Co-operation and Development |
| ODS | Civic Democratic Party (Czech Republic) |
| SANPAC | South African National Plan of Action for Children |

| | |
|---|---|
| SES | Socioeconomic status |
| SSI | Supplemental Security Income |
| TANF | Temporary Assistance to Needy Families program |
| U.N. | United Nations |
| UNICEF | United Nations International Children's Fund |
| VAT | Value-added tax |
| WIC | Women, Infants, and Children program (U.S.A.) |

# PART I

# FOUNDATION

# 1

# Securing Adequate Living Conditions for Each Child's Development

## Arlene Bowers Andrews

The world has long known that childhood is the period of human development when the pace of growth and maturation is more rapid than at any other time of life. As each human develops, his or her capabilities and unique characteristics emerge, gradually enabling increased competence. The person is shaped by the interaction of genetic predisposition with nurture, stimulation, threats, and other environmental influences. Life experiences during infancy and early childhood profoundly affect the physical, mental, social, and emotional characteristics of the person during childhood and in later years. Development continues throughout life, though the pace decelerates and the nature of maturation changes, and the opportunities to build the person's capacities are never again so ripe as in the early years.

The human's right to survive and develop is a fundamental premise of the U.N. *Convention on the Rights of the Child* (Preamble). The *Convention* charges governments to ensure to the maximum extent possible that each child survives and develops (Art. 6). Article 27 (see Figure 1.1) establishes the child's right to a standard of living adequate for the child's physical, mental, spiritual, moral, and social development and charges parent(s) or others responsible for the child to secure the living conditions, within their means and with assistance from their governments. Governments are further charged to provide material assistance and support programs, particularly for nutrition, clothing, and housing, and to secure financial support for children from their parent(s).

Article 27 contains several principles to guide promotion of positive human development. One principle, the primacy of holistic development during childhood, emerges from the specification of various domains of child development:

**Figure 1.1**
**U.N. Convention on the Rights of the Child, Article 27**

1. States Parties recognize the right of every child to a standard of living adequate for the child's physical, mental, spiritual, moral, and social development.

2. The parent(s) or others responsible for the child have the primary responsibility to secure, within their abilities and financial capabilities, the conditions of living necessary for the child's development.

3. States Parties in accordance with national conditions and within their means shall take appropriate measures to assist parents and others responsible for the child to implement this right and shall in case of need provide material assistance and support programmes, particularly with regard to nutrition, clothing and housing.

4. States Parties shall take all appropriate measures to secure the recovery of maintenance for the child from the parents or other persons having financial responsibility for the child, both within the State Party and from abroad. In particular, where the person having financial responsibility for the child lives in a State different from that of the child, States Parties shall promote the accession to international agreements or the conclusion of such agreements, as well as the making of other appropriate arrangements.

physical, mental, spiritual, moral, and social. Another establishes the significance of the child's actual standard of living, which focuses on the child and implies the child's *realization* of adequate living standards rather than simply access to opportunities through a family's or community's living standards. A third principle affirms the child's entitlement to special care and assistance within an ecological context, as reflected in the charges to parents, others responsible for the child, and states parties.

## PRIMACY OF HOLISTIC DEVELOPMENT DURING CHILDHOOD

The Preamble to the *Convention* recognizes the inherent dignity of all members of the human family and affirms that each child should be fully prepared to live an individual life in society. The emergence of worldwide recognition that children have rights establishes that each child is fully a human being, with rights and liberties to be enabled by those who care for the child and to be exercised by children themselves as their capacities evolve.

The *Convention* embraces a view of human development that is radically different from traditional approaches that regard development primarily as preparation for the future (Casas, 1997). Humans have rights to *survive and develop*, processes that reflect the current state of the human, not just the future state. Children are regarded as human *beings*, not human *becomings* (Qvortrup et al., 1994). These rights support each human's preparation to live as an individual in society *while a child*. All rights apply regardless of age, although methods to assure the rights vary by the child's age and competence. The *Convention* affirms that the child's development does have future implications, such as enabling the child to fully assume adult responsibilities within the community, but nowhere does the *Convention* suggest that such development culminates at the end of chronological childhood. Rather, the intent is clearly to promote the human's increasing competence and unique attributes during childhood at a pace that varies individually and culturally.

Article 27 addresses the condition of the child in the context of living conditions. Often reports of child well-being rely primarily on indicators of the child's potential access to resources such as nutrition, education, housing, or health care. Article 27 distinguishes the child's condition (i.e., child's developmental status) from the child's living conditions. The living conditions are a means to the end, which is development. Thus, indicators of the degree to which the right is attained should demonstrate that the living conditions are associated with such child outcomes as physical signs of nourishment, educational attainment, child's sense of home, and health status. This framework moves beyond regarding how children could be developing to stress how they actually are developing.

As a political document, the *Convention* promotes the balance of individual rights and collective interests. Developmentally, this supports the child's emerging identity, life skills, and exercise of liberties along with respect for the rights of others and promotion of public order. Ideologically, the *Convention* advocates in Article 29 that children shall be educated for development of:

- the child's personality, talents, and mental and physical abilities to their fullest potential;
- respect for human rights and fundamental freedoms and for principles of the United Nations;
- respect for parents, own culture, national values, and civilizations different from his or her own;
- responsibility in a free society, in the spirit of understanding, peace, tolerance, equality of sexes, and friendship among all peoples, ethnic, national and religious groups, and persons of indigenous origin;
- respect for the natural environment.

A holistic and harmonious approach to human development is implicit throughout the *Convention*. Within this context, Article 27 stipulates the child's right to adequate living conditions for physical, mental, spiritual, moral, and social development. Through this declaration, nations are essentially called to move beyond promoting childhood survival and subsistence to include support for fulfillment of human potential. Each of the developmental domains is unique, though related to all others.

Physical development includes wellness, disease or disability management, and exercise of physical abilities. Article 24 asserts the child's right to the highest attainable standard of health and to access to health care services. Sections address the significance of primary health care, provision of nutritious food and clean drinking water, and protection from environmental pollution. Article 23 promotes a full and decent life for the child with physical or mental disabilities and recognizes that child's right to special care. Several sections of the *Convention* assert the child's right to protection from harm that may threaten physical well-being.

Mental development includes realization of cognitive potential as well as emotional stability and mental health. The *Convention* requires recognition of the child's evolving capacities (Garbarino, 1990), particularly with regard to the child's participation in making decisions affecting his or her life, reflecting the child's increasing mental competence with age and maturity. The Preamble recognizes that the child should grow up in a family environment, in an atmosphere of happiness, love and understanding, suggesting that a child's emotional health should be promoted. Article 8 establishes the child's right to an identity, including nationality, name, and family relations. Articles 28 and 29 cover the child's right to compulsory and free primary education and access to secondary and higher education. Several articles address protection of children from harm that could induce mental problems, including illicit drug use and trafficking, sexual exploitation, inhumane discipline, and all forms of maltreatment. Article 39 requires measures to promote physical and psychological recovery for child victims of maltreatment and other trauma. Article 23 protects the interests of children with mental disabilities. Obviously, attention to a child's mental health and development pervades the *Convention*.

Spiritual development enables children to appreciate themselves in a broader context and to understand spiritual and religious matters. Article 14 asserts the child's right to freedom of thought, conscience, and religion, and requires states to respect the duties and rights of parents in directing the child to exercise this right in a manner consistent with the evolving capacities of the child. Article 30 supplements this right by prohibiting the denial of the child's right to enjoy his or her own ethnic, religious, or linguistic minority culture or indigenous community.

Moral development facilitates responsible behavior and value-based belief systems. As noted earlier, the *Convention* stipulates that children should respect one another's rights and be prepared for societal responsibility and cooperative, tolerant lives among diverse populations. Article 40 covers the rights of children who have been alleged or found to have behaved irresponsibly by breaking the penal law. States parties are required to treat these children in a manner that promotes the child's sense of dignity and worth and reinforces the child's respect for the human rights and fundamental freedoms of others, thus promoting the child's moral development.

Social development promotes healthy and productive connections among the child and other people. References to parents, family, others responsible for the child, group affiliation, culture, and community permeate the *Convention*. The child's rights to developmentally appropriate social activities such as leisure and play, art and cultural life, and work are protected. Article 32 asserts the child's right to be protected from work that may be harmful to the child's health or physical, mental, spiritual, moral, or social development. Article 15 recognizes the child's right to form social groups through freedom of association and peaceful assembly. In many ways, the essence of the *Convention* addresses the critical relation of self and other as the individual develops throughout childhood. By promoting and protecting the particular individual rights stipulated by the *Convention*, states and adults who nurture children will encourage healthy social behavior and discourage antisocial behavior that threatens humankind.

Together, the specified developmental domains signify the primacy of holistic child development. Article 27 focuses the need to move beyond traditional emphasis on physical development to regard the child as fully human, with complex needs, characteristics, and abilities that must be nurtured from birth onward.

## SIGNIFICANCE OF THE CHILD'S ACTUAL LEVEL OF LIVING

Article 27 promotes attainment of adequate and necessary living conditions for each child's development. As with the developmental status of the child, the right addresses security of actual rather than potential living conditions. In 1954, the United Nations began to reserve the term "standard of living" for reference to aspirations, or that which ought to be, and to apply the term "level of living" for actual life conditions (Hilhorst, 1985, 2). English-speaking scholars still tend to use "standard of living" in referring to living conditions, though Amatya Sen (1987) has argued for measures that reflect the life a person is actually living rather than the resources and means a person has for living conditions. Sen's approach takes into account personal choices, constraints, circumstances, and abilities to achieve living conditions. Applying Sen's approach to assessment of a child's living conditions requires focus on the child, rather than the household or community, as the unit of observation. Additionally, what the child or the child's caregiver does with material goods and nonmaterial resources is more important than simple availability of such resources.

The terms "adequate" and "necessary" used in Article 27 imply the child's right is to minimal, not optimal, living conditions that support holistic development. Article 29 contains bolder language, stating that the child's education shall be directed to the development of the child's personality, talents, and mental and physical abilities to their *fullest* potential (emphasis added). Likewise, Article 24 recognizes the right to the highest attainable standard of health. As a practical matter, establishing standards for what constitutes adequate living conditions will be determined by various states, communities, and cultures. Notions of adequacy, need, and child development vary across nations and habitats and within societal groups. In effect, the U.N. has issued a challenge to nations through Article 27 that requires them to discover what conditions are adequate and necessary for their children's development and to secure, to the extent possible, those conditions for each child. This process requires scientific research, political discourse, and value-based decisions about child development.

Though standards for child development may vary across jurisdictions, the children of the world will benefit from cross-cultural action to attain appropriate living conditions. Children's rights belong to each and every child, not children as a collective class or group, and are intended to be secured equally across groups. Children should be able to secure adequate living conditions simply because of their human dignity, not because of their national or any other group affiliation. Neither should merit, productivity, accomplishment, nor any other standard of implied worth affect realization of any child's rights.

Substantial research exists to support the selection of standards for adequate childhood levels of living in many areas. For example, studies of U.S. children indicate that positive child development, as evidenced by academic achievement, social adjustment, and physical health, is associated with:

• adequate nourishment;

• dependable attachments to parents or other adult caregivers;

• adult-child nurturing interaction through holding, touching, smiling, talking;

• available, responsive, consistent caregiver behavior in response to child;

• protection from physical and psychological harm;

• cognitively stimulating physical and social environment;

• firm, consistent, flexible discipline strategies;

• social support and guidance when faced with adversity;

• play activities and opportunities to explore;

• more than one consistently involved adult who provides economic resources, support, regulation, and positive role modeling to the child. (See Amato, 1995; Bronfenbrenner, 1979; Halpern, 1990; Hamburg, 1996.)

Material resources such as nutritious food, safe water, clothing, and housing are necessary but insufficient for holistic development. Stable, nurturing social relationships and safe, stimulating environments are also essential (Hutton, 1991).

The *Convention* has been introduced into a world where childhood living conditions vary dramatically across and within nations. Resources and opportunities have never been equitably distributed among children. Disparities between those who "have" and those who "have not" can be vast. A child's fortune is substantially determined by circumstances of birth; national origin; familial, social, racial, or ethnic identity and socioeconomic class; geographic location; gender; physical and mental ability; or other factors. Across the world, classes of children are excluded, marginalized, and exploited. The Preamble to

**Figure 1.2**
**According to the United Nations' Report, *The State of the World's Children—1997*:**

Children in some areas of the world thrive while the very survival of children is threatened elsewhere:

- In 26 countries, more than 1 in 10 babies fail to survive to their first birthday.
- In 28 developed countries, babies are 10 times more likely to survive to their first birthday than children in the most challenged developing countries.
- In 47 countries, more than 1 in 10 babies fail to survive to their fifth birthday.

Child development is threatened by malnutrition:

- In 12 countries, more than 1 in 5 babies is born with low birth weight.
- In 38 countries, more than 1 in 3 children under age 5 suffer from stunted growth.
- In 20 countries, almost 1 in 10 children under age five is severely underweight.

Families and communities cannot adequately support children's health and educational needs:

- In 21 countries, more than half the population has no access to safe water.
- In 41 countries, more than half the population has no access to adequate sanitation.
- In 16 countries, over half the population has inadequate access to health services.
- In 13 countries, at least half of all children fail to reach 5 grades in school.

Poverty threatens millions of children and their families:

- In 24 countries, about a third or more of the urban population lives below the absolute poverty level.
- In 28 countries, over half the rural population lives below the absolute poverty level.

the *Convention* recognizes that "in all countries of the world there are children living in exceptionally difficult conditions, and that such children need special consideration." Figure 1.2 summarizes data from U.N. sources that illustrates these conditions. Circumstances often change during a child's development, but many confront persistent deprivation while others are indulged by privilege.

A 1992 study illustrates the discrepancy in living conditions across nations (Jordan, 1993). Using data from the annual UNICEF report on the condition of the world's children, the study estimated the quality of life for children in 122 countries based on selected variables: mortality rate for children under age 5, intake of daily caloric requirements, secondary school enrollment, life expectancy, percentage of females in the work force, literacy rate, and GNP per capita. The differences between the top and bottom deciles (12 countries in each group) are extensive. For example, the mean under-5 mortality rate was 10.33 for the top decile, 231.33 for the bottom. Mean female secondary school enrollment was 97.45 percent for the top decile, 6.27 percent for the bottom. The countries where children had the highest quality of life according to these indicators were economically developed and in the northern hemisphere. Most of the countries in the bottom decile were in Africa or southern Asia.

Similarly, vast differences can exist within a nation. In the United States, the Annie E. Casey Foundation Kids Count reports annually rank states according to critical indicators of child well-being (e.g., low birth weight babies; infant, child, and youth mortality; teen birth rate; juvenile crime; teen school dropouts; children in poverty). By summing standard scores across measures, composite scores are created for each state, and state scores are ranked, using the mean for all states as the standard. In 1996 Louisiana and Mississippi were lowest with scores between −10 and −15 below the mean. New Hampshire and North Dakota ranked highest with scores just above 10 over the mean. The status of children in the District of Columbia was a shocking −40 points below the mean.

The gap between advantaged and disadvantaged children is growing worldwide and within nations. Positive indicators of exceptional development are not monitored as are threats to survival and development. Two examples, though, illustrate the increasingly privileged positions of those who are advantaged. In the United States between 1921 and 1997, the average height of men increased by two inches; for women the increase was 1.5 inches (Samaras & Steckel, 1997). In just two generations, nutrition, disease containment, and wellness promotion have contributed to physical growth at a rate unprecedented in human history. Second, fewer children in a family is an indicator of more resources and opportunities per child. Lower fertility rates are associated with higher standards of living. Across the world, women with higher educational attainment have lower fertility rates, so their children have the double advantage of increased educational opportunity and smaller family size (Burns & Scott, 1994). Thus, those who have an advantage gain even greater advantage.

Living conditions include innumerable factors that potentially enable or inhibit healthy child development. Children are particularly developmentally threatened when they face persistent economic poverty, social isolation, discrimination based on characteristics they possess, or a primary parent who copes with certain types of mental illness, intellectual disability, chemical dependence, or propensity for violence (Schorr, 1988). War, political persecution, environmental pollution, natural disasters or resource depletion, community deterioration, family instability, famine and water shortages, and political neglect of children and their families also induce less than adequate living conditions for child development. The effects of threatening living conditions can be mediated by protective factors in the child's life. For example, parents who create nurturant, protective home environments under difficult life experiences tend to have strong extended families. Such families provide practical assistance, consistent emotional support, and family pride, have parental personal history that includes at least one special figure, and demonstrate beliefs and values that regard life as manageable (Amato, 1995; Halpern, 1990).

Of all developmental threats, economic poverty receives the most attention. Economic poverty is associated with dangerous neighborhoods, unsafe and overcrowded housing or homelessness, unstable and poor quality child care, insufficient learning materials, and geographic and social isolation (Anderson &

Armstead, 1995; Halpern, 1990; Klerman, 1991). Poverty can induce chronic stress and high rates of parental depression, thus creating obstacles to parental attention and nurture. The developmental effects on children are well documented: infant mortality and morbidity, acute and chronic health problems, hunger and malnutrition, withdrawal or aggression, speech and motor delays, sleep disorders, depression, anxiety, behavioral problems, and academic underachievement (Chafel, 1993; Huston, McLoyd, & Coll, 1994; Korenman, Miller, & Sjaastad, 1995; Pollitt, 1994; Rafferty & Shinn, 1991; Sampson & Laub, 1994; Scarborough, 1993). Malnourished children tend to be less social, active, playful, and happy, and their caregivers are relatively unresponsive (McDonald et al., 1994). Childhood poverty affects human development so severely that unless compensatory factors exist in the child's life, upon maturation the human is likely to produce children who will also live in poverty, perpetuating an intergenerational cycle (Hill & Sandfort, 1995).

Researchers studying standard of living formerly relied on income level as the key indicator, with minimum income to sustain physical existence as the most common measure to mark a minimum standard of living (Blackwood & Lynch, 1994; Duncan, Brooks-Gunn, & Klebanov, 1994). This focus assumed adequate income can purchase a minimally adequate standard of living (Bianchi, 1993; Scarborough, 1993). Although children whose parents have adequate income tend to have higher standards of living, not all aspects of a child's living conditions can or must be purchased. As Italian sociologist Giuseppe Carbonaro (1993) notes, "The poor lack many things: goods and services, but also opportunities, social relations, perhaps self-respect and happiness, and so on" (11). Some children whose parents have adequate income suffer inadequate living standards because of parental choices or extraordinary circumstances that place demands on the family income. For example, a child may be malnourished because of meager food intake related to poverty or a diet of "junk food" made available through wealth. Also, income alone fails to reflect other resources available to the family through social and physical environments, such as income transfers from extended family, child care, schools, or neighborhood resources. Income also fails to reflect longevity of the deprivation; family circumstances may be temporarily deprived. Children exposed to chronic deprivation suffer the most severe developmental consequences.

Poverty analysts now construct indices using multiple factors to describe poverty. Studies that focus on child socioeconomic status generally include parental level of education, occupational attainment, and head of household. Across the world, female-headed household, parental unemployment or underemployment, and low educational attainment are associated with chronic deprivation (Burns & Scott, 1994).

Cross-culturally, no consistent definitions of socioeconomic status or equality have yet emerged as best indicators of child well-being (Blackwood & Lynch, 1994; Carbonaro, 1993). The choice of a measure depends upon its intended use. Some measures focus on deprived segments of a population while others reflect the condition of the society as a whole. Some reflect physical resources (e.g., food, health care, shelter) while others include social or other aspects of life, such as social networks and participation in civic life. The advent of the *Convention on the Rights of the Child* has stimulated several international efforts to develop appropriate indicators to monitor the status of children within and across countries (Ben-Arieh & Wintersberger, 1996; Black, 1994).

States and communities that seriously pursue the child's right to actual living conditions adequate for development must assess how living conditions and child development are linked within their own countries and determine what is adequate. Implementing the right requires attention to justice and equity so that historical discrepancies among groups of children can be eradicated.

## CHILD'S ENTITLEMENT TO SPECIAL CARE AND ASSISTANCE WITHIN AN ECOLOGICAL CONTEXT

Clearly, a child's realization of living conditions for holistic development depends upon caregivers who mediate the child's access to and use of resources and opportunities. The existence and accessibility of social, material, and economic resources and opportunities for children depends upon familial, community, and governmental conditions and choices.

The *Convention on the Rights of the Child* explicitly recognizes that childhood is entitled to special care and assistance, affirms the U.N.'s determination to promote social progress and better standards of life, and acknowledges the importance of international cooperation for improving the living conditions of children in every country, in particular the developing countries (Preamble). Article 6 creates a duty for states parties to the treaty to ensure to the maximum extent possible the survival and development of the child. Article 27 charges parents, others responsible for the child, and states parties to secure the child's right to a standard of living adequate for development. As a tool for social and political action to assertively improve the plight of children, the *Convention* serves as a framework for mobilizing families, communities, and societies to promote positive child development.

Article 27 builds on the principles of Article 18, which asserts that both parents have common responsibilities for the upbringing and development of the child, that parents or legal guardians have primary responsibility, and that state parties shall render appropriate assistance to parents and legal guardians in their child-rearing responsibilities, including development of institutions, facilities, and services for the care of children, particularly child care services for working parents. Article 27 assigns primary responsibility for living conditions to the family, with specific charges to states parties to provide material assistance, support programs, and recovery of parental financial maintenance for the child. Article 26 specifically declares the child's right to benefit from social security.

The phrase ''others responsible for the child'' is interpreted differently in various countries and with various cultural groups. The term "responsible" carries legal and social connotations in different contexts. Among some groups, the child's extended family, tribe, religious group, or resource persons (e.g., teachers, social workers) share responsibility. Each can be held accountable. Among other groups, the nuclear family or single head of household has sole "responsibility" for the child. Others may assist or "serve" the child and family, but accountability lies with the parental figure. Who is included among "others responsible" also varies by culture or political jurisdiction. For example, social welfare states assign responsibility for children to the state. Other countries resist attribution of responsibility to governments, assigning the state a support role or residual responsibility when the family fails or cannot be responsible.

The principles of the *Convention* are grounded in an ecological approach to child development that regards the child as an active participant in the environment (Bronfenbrenner & Neville, 1994; Brooks-Gunn, Klebanov, & Liaw, 1995). If adequate environmental resources and opportunities exist and are accessible, the child will do his or her development. The child's capacity to exercise the right to develop is bounded by living conditions that include conditions of the parent or primary caregiver, home, neighborhood, community, natural environment, and broader society. The *Convention* implicitly advocates the continuous improvement of childhood living conditions that require attention to context far beyond the immediate residential domain of the child.

Article 27 stipulates that states parties are to "take appropriate measures" to assist parents and others responsible for the child. Like others, this phrase is subject to wide interpretive variations and will be associated closely with the availability of resources within the country and political values regarding the relation of the state to the child and family. The assistance is to be offered to the caregivers, although some countries will essentially bypass the parents and give assistance directly to the child through material and financial entitlement programs. Most states provide some form of cash or material benefits (e.g., sickness insurance, unemployment insurance, food or housing allowances, child allowances) to families with children who are living in difficult circumstances. Some provide benefits regardless of circumstances. Research indicates that nations where families with children receive such benefits have lower poverty rates than those without benefits, regardless of the nation's general economic wealth or status (Rainwater, 1995).

Increasingly, states also offer noncash assistance such as family leave, family life education, and facilitation of social support. Many states have traditionally offered residual aid after a child has been harmed by difficult living conditions. The U.N.'s designation of 1994 as the International Year of the Family aimed to stimulate local, national, and international actions as the starting point for sustained long-term efforts to strengthen the family as the basic unit of society (United Nations General Assembly, 1989). The international family resource movement aims to improve childhood living conditions to *prevent* developmental problems rather than primarily respond to them (Kagan & Weissbourd, 1994; United Nations, 1991).

Throughout the *Convention*, the rights of the child in special circumstances are asserted. Such factors include disabilities, family separation, penal system involvement, minority or indigenous group status, traumatization, exposure to armed conflict, or refugee status. Assuring living conditions adequate for the development of children confronted by extraordinary challenges requires focused, situation-relevant action by those who care for the child and the state.

The realization of the child's right to develop is related to the exercise of choice by the child, parental figures, and state regarding resources and opportunities in the environment. Throughout the world, the ecological context in which the child develops varies considerably. In various degrees, a child's social environment may include many familiar persons or few, substantial affection and attention or little, and exposure to antisocial influences or prosocial responsibility. The natural environment may be splendid whether hot or cold, dry or wet, high or low. It may also be resource poor or contaminated. The political and economic environments may actively attend to the needs of children or ignore them altogether. Macroenvironmental factors exert powerful influences on the microenvironments in which children live. Article 27 essentially charges nations to shape environments in ways that enable families to create living conditions that support their children.

## CONCLUSION

Social learning theorists maintain that humans learn in part by observing the behaviors of others: their family members, peers, neighbors, and representatives of the larger community and society (Bronfenbrenner, 1979). Children learn and grow wherever they may be. Article 27 calls upon nations and people who care for children to design environments that promote holistic, positive child development. By working to create and persistently improve such conditions, people will model for children the type of healthy, caring behaviors that are the essence of positive development.

A child's living conditions include many complex factors. The work of implementing Article 27 requires the identification of the most critical factors within each cultural context that promote child well-being, protect children from harm, or threaten the child. Families, communities, and states must also discover the most effective and efficient ways within their means to influence the conditions with particular attention to justice and equity. The vision behind Article 27 is that each child in the world is nested in conditions that nurture whole, healthy development—physically, mentally, spiritually, morally, and socially.

## REFERENCES

Amato, P. R. (1995). Single-parent households as settings for children's development, well-being, and attainment: A social network/resources perspective. *Sociological Studies of Children, 7,* 19–47.

Anderson, N. B. & Armstead, C. A. (1995). Toward understanding the association of socioeconomic status and health: A new challenge for the biopsychosocial approach. *Psychosomatic Medicine, 57*, 213–225.

The Annie E. Casey Foundation. (1997). *Kids count data book: State profiles of child well-being, 1996*. Baltimore, MD: Author.

Ben-Arieh, A. & Wintersberger, H. (1996). *Monitoring and measuring the state of children—Beyond survival*. Vienna, Austria: European Centre for Social Welfare Policy and Research.

Bianchi, S. M. (1993). Children of poverty: Why are they poor? In J. A. Chafel (Ed.), *Child poverty and public policy* (91–125). Washington, DC: The Urban Institute.

Black, M. (1994). *Monitoring the rights of children—Innocenti Global Seminar: Summary Report*. Florence, Italy: UNICEF.

Blackwood, D. L. & Lynch, R. G. (1994). The measurement of inequality and poverty: A policy maker's guide to the literature. *World Development, 22*(4), 567–578.

Bronfenbrenner, U. (1979). *The ecology of human development: Experiments by nature and design*. Cambridge, MA: Harvard University Press.

Bronfenbrenner, U. & Neville, P. (1994). America's children and families: An international perspective. In S. L. Kagan & B. Weissbourd (Eds.), *Putting families first: America's family support movement and the challenge of change* (3–27). San Francisco: Jossey-Bass.

Brooks-Gunn, J., Klebanov, P. K., & Liaw, F. (1995). The learning, physical, and emotional environment of the home in the context of poverty: The infant health and development program. *Children and Youth Services Review, 17*(1/2), 251–276.

Burns, A. & Scott, C. 1994. *Mother-headed families and why they have increased*. Hillsdale, NJ: Lawrence Erlbaum Associates.

Carbonaro, G. (1993). On defining and measuring poverty. *Revue internationale de sociologie, 1–2*, 9–36.

Casas, F. (1997). Children's rights and children's quality of life: Conceptual and practical issues. *Social Indicators Research*, 1–16.

Chafel, J. A. (Ed.). (1993). *Child poverty and public policy*. Washington, DC: The Urban Institute.

Duncan, G. J., Brooks-Gunn, J., & Klebanov, P. K. (1994). Economic deprivation and early childhood development. *Child Development, 65*, 296–318.

Garbarino, J. (1990). The child's evolving capacities. In C. P. Cohen & H. A. Davidson (Eds.), *Children's rights in America: U.N. Convention on the rights of the child compared with United States law* (19–32). Washington, DC: American Bar Association.

Halpern, R. (1990). Poverty and early childhood parenting: Toward a framework for intervention. *American Journal of Orthopsychiatry, 60*(1), 6–18.

Hamburg, D. A. (1996). *A developmental strategy to prevent lifelong damage*. New York: Carnegie Corporation of New York.

Hilhorst, J. G. M. (1985). Social indicators: A general introduction. In J. G. M. Hilhorst & M. Klatter (Eds.), *Social development in the third world: Level of living indicators and social planning* (1–16). London: Croom Helm.

Hill, M. S. & Sandfort, J. R. (1995). Effects of childhood poverty on productivity later in life: Implications for public policy. *Children and Youth Services Review, 17*(1/2), 91–126.

Huston, A. C., McLoyd, V. C., & Coll, C. G. (1994). Children and poverty: Issues in contemporary research. *Child Development, 65*, 275–282.

Hutton, S. (1991). Measuring living standards using existing national data sets. *Journal of Social Policy, 20*(2), 237–257.

Jordan, T. E. (1993). Estimating the quality of life for children around the world: NICQL '92. *Social Indicators Research, 30*, 17–38.

Kagan, S. L. & Weissbourd, B. (Eds.). (1994). *Putting families first: America's family support movement and the challenge of change.* San Francisco: Jossey-Bass.

Klerman, L. V. (1991). *Alive and well? A research and policy review of health programs for poor young children.* New York: Columbia University, National Center for Children in Poverty.

Korenman, S., Miller, J. E., & Sjaastad, J. E. (1995). Long-term poverty and child development in the United States: Results from the NLSY. *Children and Youth Services Review, 17*(1/2), 127–151.

McDonald, M. A., Sigman, M., Espinosa, M. P., & Neumann, C. G. (1994). Impact of a temporary food shortage on children and their mothers. *Child Development, 65*, 404–415.

Pollitt, E. (1994). Poverty and child development: Relevance of research in developing countries to the United States. *Child Development, 65*, 283–295.

Qvortrup, J., Bardy, M., Sgritta, G. B., & Wintersberger, H. (Eds.). (1994). *Childhood matters: Social theory, practice, and politics.* Vienna: Avebury.

Rafferty, Y. & Shinn, M. (1991). The impact of homelessness on children. *American Psychologist,* 1170–1179.

Rainwater, L. (1995). Poverty and the income package of working parents: The United States in comparative perspective. *Children and Youth Services Review, 17*(1/2), 11–41.

Samaras, T. & Steckel, R. (1997). As quoted in *Newsweek,* June 2, 10.

Sampson, R. J. & Laub, J. H. (1994). Urban poverty and the family context of delinquency: A new look at structure and process in a classic study. *Child Development, 65*, 523–540.

Scarborough, W. H. (1993). Who are the poor? A demographic perspective. In J. A. Chafel (Ed.), *Child poverty and public policy* (55–90). Washington, DC: The Urban Institute.

Schorr, L. B. (1988). *Within our reach: Breaking the cycle of disadvantage.* New York: Anchor Press.

Sen, A. (1987). *The standard of living: The Tanner lectures, Clare Hall, Cambridge, 1985.* Cambridge: Cambridge University Press.

United Nations. (1989). *Proclamation on the International Year of the Family.* Resolution 44/82, December 8, 1989.

United Nations. (1991). *1994: International Year of the Family: Building the smallest democracy at the heart of society.* Vienna: United Nations Office.

United Nations. (1995). *The world's women, 1995: Trends and statistics.* New York: United Nations.

## 2

# Drafting and Interpreting Article 27

### Natalie Hevener Kaufman and María Luisa Blanco

## I. THE DRAFTING OF THE *CONVENTION ON THE RIGHTS OF THE CHILD*

The drafting of the *Convention on the Rights of the Child* began with a text proposed by the Polish delegation to the United Nations. The Polish representative suggested to the Director of the Division of Human Rights that the idea of a human rights treaty for children be on the agenda of the thirty-fourth session of the Commission on Human Rights.

The Polish text was based on the 1959 Declaration on the Rights of the Child and proposed a prominent place for the ideas that eventually took the form of Article 27. Article II of the Polish text read: "The child shall enjoy special protection and shall be given opportunities and facilities, by law and by other means to *enable him to develop physically, mentally, morally, spiritually and socially* in a healthy and normal manner and in conditions of freedom and dignity'' (emphasis added).

A second version of the article came in the revised Polish draft that formed the basis of the discussions of the Working Group established in 1979 by the Commission on Human Rights. The 1979 text was the basis for discussion with the Working Group and Commission, and the precursor of Article 27 and appeared as Article 15.

1. The States Parties to the present Convention recognize the right of every child to a *standard of living adequate for his healthy and normal physical, mental and moral development* in every phase of the child's development.

2. *The parents*, shall, within their financial possibilities and powers, secure conditions of living necessary for a normal growth of the child.

3. The States Parties to the present Convention shall take appropriate measures to implement this right, particularly with regard to nutrition, clothing and housing, and shall extend the necessary material *assistance to parents and other persons bringing up children*, with special attention paid to incomplete families and children lacking parental care.

One can easily observe changes from Article II of the Polish text that are fundamental and integral to the significance of Article 27. First, we can see that the article now reflects the concern with the role and importance of parents or those responsible for the child's upbringing. Second, assistance to the child is to be indirect, rather than direct; that is, assistance is to be through the channel of the parents or caregivers. The acknowledgment of the primacy of the role of the parents or caregivers and strategy of putting necessary resources in the hands of the parents or those responsible for the child, brings to the fore the centrality of parents and family to the entire spirit and orientation of the treaty.

By 1982 there were two important changes in the draft article (at that time Article 14) [A/C.3/36/6, part II]. First, the opening paragraph refers to the child's right to a standard of living that "*guarantees* his normal physical, mental and moral development" (emphasis added). The earlier draft had used the term "adequate" to describe the standard of living, a less demanding legal requirement. Also, in the third paragraph, which requires states parties to implement the right by extending "material assistance to parents," the limiting phrase "within their means" could be interpreted as substantially reducing the obligation of states to provide such material assistance to parents.

The 1982 Working Group accepted the revised article with one significant modification. The group added broadening language to paragraph 3. In the final sentence of the paragraph that addresses children of families especially needing support, the language is more specific in identifying families that might otherwise be neglected by the system: "single parent and deprived families, whether due to the absence of one parent, to the lack of parental care, or to extreme poverty" [E/CN.4/1982/WG.1/WP.1, 5].

The nongovernmental organization (NGO) community was very active in the drafting of the CRC. Their Ad Hoc Group in 1984 proposed to the Working Group some important changes in the article. In the first paragraph, they included a provision to ensure that every child "from birth" would receive social security benefits "for which the child is eligible, including 'children who are deprived of all protection.' " In the second paragraph they added the term "basic" as a descriptor of the standard of living and added "social" to the list of domains of development, so that the child's right is "to a basic standard of living which guarantees the child's physical, mental, moral and social development."

In the third paragraph, the Ad Hoc Group expanded the states' responsibility by requiring that parties "implement *and*" give assistance to those caring for children. They expanded, as well, the group specifically in need of special help: "very poor or single-parent families and children deprived of parental care. Protection and adequate social benefits should be extended in particular to women before and after confinement to ensure their children's and their own well-being." This important addition reflects two essentially new concerns: one for the mother, herself, and the other an awareness that the health of the child is in a most fundamental way linked to the health of the mother.

Finally, the Ad Hoc Group added a paragraph stressing their belief that global measures, beyond national borders, would be necessary to realistically fulfill the objectives of the treaty. The new paragraph provided: "4. The States Parties to the present Convention shall take the necessary measures to develop the resources allocated to the launching and implementation of children's programmes at the national and international levels. Particular efforts shall be made on behalf of the poorest population of all countries" (E/CN.4/1985/WG.1/WP.1).

By 1985, the NGO Ad Hoc Group had developed additional provisions for the article. One was a separate paragraph asking that when states parties are developing support services for the family, they include "programmes that will allow the family, particularly the parents or guardians, to provide an adequate standard of living for the child." They also recommended a paragraph that requires parties to consider "the child's environment" and "access to an adequate standard of living" in "development planning and international cooperation programmes." Last, they offered a provision that would acknowledge that the state's responsibility to assist parents and others in providing financial support for the child, even "when the child is living apart from the parents or others responsible for him/her. . . ." (U.N. Center for Human Rights, 13).

Some important changes were offered at the 1985 meeting of the Working Group. With regard to paragraph one, they accepted the NGO Ad Hoc Group's recommendation to add "social" to the list of domains of development in paragraph one. The Holy See offered the addition of "spiritual" to this list. Both adjectives appear in the final form of Article 27 [E/CN.4/1985/64].

The United States argued for a limiting provision, "in accordance with national conditions" to modify the "standard of living." Opposition led to the deletion of this recommendation. A proposal from China was also rejected— that states "prevent and prohibit children from taking drugs."

In paragraph 2 there was discussion of how to describe people, other than parents, who might be responsible for the child and how to define the limits of their financial responsibility. The 1985 text as accepted read: "The parent(s) or others responsible for the child have the primary responsibility to secure, within their abilities and financial capacities, the conditions of living necessary for the child's development."

For paragraph 3, most discussion centered on the issue of how to word the limitations on state responsibility. The United States reintroduced the language "in accordance with national conditions," and the United Kingdom suggested the addition to the U.S. phrase of the words "within their means." After much discussion, a Canadian proposal was offered including both these phrases, and it was adopted (U.N. Center for Human Rights, 14–15).

The main developments on Article 27 in 1986 were two comments from the representative of Bangladesh. One emphasized the need for sensitivity to the limited funds available for implementation of the article within developing states. The representative pointed out that support for the convention might be minimized if the treaty did not reflect respect for the special economic problems of these states, especially the least developed. The second issue raised, one that affected the entire drafting process, was the stated demand for a provision in the convention that would "safeguard the autonomy and privacy of the Islamic family from encroachment and impingement by externally applied standards" [E/CN.4/1986/39, annex IV].

In 1987 most of the discussion on the article centered on provisions of then Article 14 referring to the obligation of parents and guardians to provide support for their children even when they were living apart from these children. Representatives from Morocco and Iraq objected to the term "legal guardian" and wondered about the true objective of the provision. Others brought up the reality of diversity among states and cultures about what guardianship meant; some states were concerned about the meaning of "support" and whether it might be limited to economic support and how long it was assumed to last. Since the original proposal had come from a member of the Finnish delegation, they were asked to rework the proposal in light of the discussion and submit a new provision, which they did in 1988 (U.N. Center for Human Rights, 18–19).

The 1988 proposal emphasized the need for states to negotiate and accede to international agreements for recovery of maintenance abroad. The main argument of the Finnish delegation was that a child's welfare should not be jeopardized because the parents happened to be living in another state. This concept was viewed favorably by the Working Group, but there was some difference of opinion over the implementation, including the desire by some to cover recovery of maintenance from those residing in the same country as the child. The new proposal for addition to paragraph 4 of Article 14 was: "States Parties to the present Convention shall take all appropriate measures to secure the recovery of maintenance for the child from the parents or other persons having financial responsibility for the child, both within the State Party and from abroad. In particular, where the person having financial responsibility for the child lives in a State different from the child, States Parties shall promote the accession to international agreements or the conclusion of such agreements as well as the making of other appropriate arrangements."

In 1988 the text of the Convention was submitted to the Secretary-General for a technical review of the draft prior to the second reading [E/CN.4/1988/ para. 248]. The purpose of the review was to identify repetition among articles, inconsistencies between articles, inaccuracies within the text, and to compare the standards set by the convention to those of other major human rights treaties.

The technical review normally also involves a set of recommendations for addressing any problems uncovered by the review. The Working Group was then provided with the results of the review [E/CN.4/1989/WG.1/CRP.1 and Add.1].

UNICEF was one of the groups that commented on the text during the technical review process. They pointed out that the language "in accordance with national conditions" and "within their means"—language proposed by the United States and United Kingdom, respectively—departs significantly from the language of the International Covenant on Economic, Social and Cultural Rights, which uses the phrases "appropriate steps to ensure the realization" and "to the maximum of their available resources."

During the second reading, there was discussion of a continuing major concern—the effort to strengthen the family [E/CN.4/1988/WG.1/WG.17]. Senegal brought up the provisions of Article 5, which at the time referred both to the family as "the natural environment of the child" and the need for the state to assist "the family with a view toward helping it assume its responsibilities for the harmonious development of the child." An NGO called the Four Directions Council also stressed the need for language on the strengthening of the family. They pointed out that the draft article (then 14) was not as strong as the analogous provision in the Covenant on Economic, Social and Cultural Rights, which demands the "widest possible protection and assistance" be given to families. As a result, they recommended the following: "In the allocation of resources for the progressive realization of economic, social and cultural rights, States Parties to the present Convention shall give priority to measures for strengthening families and communities as environments for the growth and development of children" [E/CN.4/1988/WG.1/NGO/2].

At the 1989 discussions of the technical review, the Working Group determined which recommendations to accept or reject. They accepted a number of technical language modifications, but, most significantly, rejected a UNICEF proposal to strengthen the responsibility of states parties for enhancing the child's standard of living. UNICEF had suggested the addition of the phrase "to the maximum of their available resources" after the words "appropriate measures" in paragraph 3, which lays out the state's obligation to support parents and others responsible for the child to meet the child's basic needs of food, clothing, and shelter [E/CN.4/1989/WG.1/CRP.1].

The Working Group ultimately accepted the following language for Article 14, which became Article 27 in the *Convention* as adopted.

1. States Parties recognize the right of every child to a standard of living adequate for the child's physical, mental, spiritual, moral and social development.

2. The parent(s) or others responsible for the child have the primary responsibility to secure, within their abilities and financial capacities, the conditions of living necessary for the child's development.

3. States Parties, in accordance with national conditions and within their means, shall take appropriate measures to assist parents and others responsible for the child to

implement this right and shall in case of need provide material assistance and support programmes, particularly with regard to nutrition, clothing and housing.

4. States Parties shall take all appropriate measures to secure the recovery of maintenance for the child from the parents or other persons having financial responsibility for the child, both within the State Party and from abroad. In particular, where the person having financial responsibility for the child lives in a State different from that of the child, States Parties shall promote the accession to international agreements or the conclusion of such agreements, as well as the making of other appropriate arrangements.

On March 8, 1989, the Commission on Human Rights adopted this text for Article 27, along with the rest of the *Convention*, by resolution 1989/57. The Economic and Social Council, on May 24, 1989, in resolution 1989/79, followed suit. And on November 20, 1989, the United Nations General Assembly, in resolution 44/25 gave final approval to the treaty.

## II. THE IMPLEMENTATION OF THE *CONVENTION ON THE RIGHTS OF THE CHILD*: THE COMMITTEE ON THE RIGHTS OF THE CHILD

### 1. Composition

The implementation procedures of the *Convention on the Rights of the Child* (CRC) are covered in part II of the *Convention*. Article 43 provides for the establishment of a Committee to oversee each ratifying nation's compliance through a country self-reporting system assessing the condition of children in their nation. The Committee consists of "ten experts of high moral standing and recognized competence in the field"[1] of children's rights. Although a larger number of members would have been preferable, the drafters of the *Convention* decided that a small fixed-membership committee would be better mainly because of financial considerations.

The members are elected by the states parties from among their nationals,[2] and membership is distributed among the United Nations' five world areas. Each state party to the *Convention* submits their nomination to the Secretary-General of the United Nations who will thereafter compile a list of nominees and submit it to the states parties two months before the elections. This period of time should be sufficient to study and reflect on the qualifications of each candidate. Members are then selected by secret ballot at a states parties meeting in which two thirds of the ratifying countries constitutes a quorum. The candidates who obtain the largest number of votes, and an absolute majority of the countries present and voting, will be the new members of the Committee.[3] This Committee will be uninstructed, which means its members serve in their personal capacity, not as government representatives. The term of office is four years and reelection is allowed.

## 2. Committee's Mandate

The Committee's mandate is to develop standards for monitoring the implementation of the CRC and to examine and consider the reports of the states parties. According to Article 44, states parties agree to submit reports to the Committee on the Rights of the Child within two years of ratification and every five years thereafter. In these reports, governments must indicate the measures they have adopted to implement the CRC, as well as "factors and difficulties, if any, affecting the degree of fulfillment of the obligations."[4] Governments are requested to undertake a review of their legislation, policies, and practices related to children and modify them where necessary to further the implementation of the CRC. The effectiveness of the system relies heavily on a positive and serious attitude toward reporting obligations. The Committee formulates "general comments" to explain its understanding of the content of an article and to recommend concrete steps that states parties should take to give full effect to a particular right.

International cooperation is also a crucial factor in the implementation of the CRC. Article 45 "encourages" cooperation among nations and special agencies and "other competent bodies," meaning NGOs. The work of NGOs, so valuable during the drafting of the CRC, continues to be essential domestically in developing and pressing for strong reports and in setting standards for children's rights and providing evidence of compliance or violations.

## 3. Usefulness of the Country Report System

In only eight years the *Convention* has been ratified by 191 out of 193 governments in the world, becoming the most rapidly accepted human rights treaty in history. The significance of the Treaty lies not only in the consensus of legal and governmental experts and child advocates on the importance of protection for children, but also as a statement of the basic principles and standards on the rights of the child. Although its implementation procedures rests on state compliance, children's advocates should not underestimate the power of the Committee on the Rights of the Child. As Melton and Kaufman (1997) remind us: "Changes in international law, like those in domestic law, provide an opportunity to change behavior" (83). The process may be slow but children's rights are now well rooted in custom and convention. The comments of the Committee will continue to develop a valuable jurisprudence on children's rights by clarifying and interpreting the language of the *Convention*. By establishing a uniform interpretation, the Committee helps the states parties develop strategies for implementing the Convention in their individual countries.

The rights protected by the CRC naturally have different levels of acceptable implementation. Not surprisingly, the first efforts by governments are often directed at the most literal interpretation. However, over time and with the help of the general standards set by the Committee, countries may address the CRC

in a wider sense, enlarging the protection of the children living in their territories. To suggest that each country interprets the content of the CRC does not
mean it can overlook the transcendent nature of the rights included. If national
circumstances permit, states parties should interpret the CRC in a broad manner;
however, in those countries where, due to poverty, children are deprived of
essential nutrition, health care, housing, or education, they should try to comply
with the Convention to the maximum of their resources. According to Melton
(1991) the CRC leaves enough room for the different countries to legislate and
carry out the Convention within their own system. Nevertheless, the CRC spells
out the contours of minimally acceptable treatment of children in sufficient detail
and with sufficiently comprehensive scope that it provides a road map for development of global children's policies. Thus, although national interpretation
will take place, the basic physical and mental needs of children are, according
to the CRC, identifiable worldwide. Every child is an individual with dignity
and the right for protection of her or his integrity, personality, privacy, and full
development without any kind of discrimination (Lopatka, 1992). The CRC sets
ambitious standards of promotion and protection of the rights of the child. In
those countries where the economic situation makes the full implementation of
Article 27 difficult, the achievement of this right should be fulfilled "in accordance with national conditions and within their means."[5] According to Adam
Lopatka, "If the national standards are higher than those set by the Convention,
they should be maintained and developed further" (51) with broad interpretation
of adequate standard of living.

The reports and the Committee's consideration of them are public,[6] providing
a fruitful source of comparative data. Through the *Convention on the Rights of
the Child*, the United Nations seeks to educate governmental officials and private
citizens in the promotion and observance of children's rights.[7] On a global scale,
the CRC Committee provides a permanent international forum that engages in
informed advocacy of children's issues. It also provides international and domestic groups with an opportunity to pressure governments to formulate more
progressive, child-centered policies.

Although the recommendations from the Committee lack binding legal force,
they often carry significant political weight. The public discussion and dissemination of a country's report is one of the most important powers of the Committee. Lack of effort by particular countries or a poor record of implementation
could bring international embarrassment and subsequent pressure for change.

The first review of reports from states parties led to the awareness of a need
for tools to "measure or assess the implementation" (Childwatch International,
1996, 2) through appropriate indicators. "Governments reporting to the Committee could not deliver adequately statistically or other quantitative information
that would provide more specific illustrations of the situation in their countries
with respect to the status of children's rights" (ibid., 3). One Childwatch International project has the objective of the development of a method for measuring
and monitoring the state of the world's children. The results of the study would

serve as useful tools to the Committee, individual countries, and any child rights advocacy groups.

One positive venture of the Committee took place in Quito in 1992. Representatives of states and various organizations of the Latin American region met with the Committee to analyze the particular problems affecting children in the Western Hemisphere. Children actively participated in the meetings, providing their views of the problems they face in their countries. Regional initiatives such as this one enable the Committee to address cross-cultural issues affecting the rights of the child. Furthermore, they help develop a more effective and coordinated regional response for agencies working at the field level. The Committee can, therefore, play a major role in bringing together the needs of a particular country and the resources available through international organizations.

A further significant initiative undertaken by the Committee was the development of Rule 76 of the Provisional Rules of Procedure (CRC/C/4, 14 November 1991), which established the holding of "general discussions" on particular issues or articles of the CRC.[8] The problem of children in armed conflict, which has caused 2 million deaths in the last ten years, was the topic chosen for the first of such meetings. The discussion took place between various U.N. agencies and NGOs working in this field, including the Red Cross.

The determination of the Committee to use the *Convention* genuinely to protect children was signaled by the decision to adopt an urgent action procedure to be used in cases where gross violations of children's rights occur. Communications from the Committee will be forwarded to the state party, and the situation will be monitored for signs of improvement. Action may include on-site visits from international observers to the country in search of more information. The implementation of the CRC is the key to the improvement in the lives of children worldwide. As Malfrid G. Flekkøy notes: "Laws, national and international, are, after all, words on paper. They may codify attitudes, but the real result depends upon how they are implemented, what is done to follow up and to reach the ideals" (*A Voice for Children*, 218).

## 4. An Overview of the Committee's Work

The unparalleled number of ratifying states to the CRC has generated a tremendous workload for the Committee that now must proccess an immense number of reports in a short amount of time. Moreover, Article 45 (a) of the CRC encourages the Committee to keep updated on studies, reports, articles, or any other source of information from scholars and NGOs related to children's rights issues. These updates should provide a stronger basis for the drafting of recommendations. Local advocates may communicate to the Committee when they think the state party report might be incomplete, or draw attention to areas of special concern. To review reports thoroughly and prepare for subsequent meetings with governments to discuss the reports requires an immense amount of work in a short period.

In addition, the Committee does not work full-time, but meets annually.[9] In view of this amount of work, the Committee has adopted a new method for a more complete consideration of the reports. The work is distributed into small Working Groups months before the meetings of the full Committee. States parties are notified of the additional information the Committee requires and are invited to attend the session in which their country report will be considered, to answer questions or address areas of special concern the Committee might have.

## III. REPORTS SUBMITTED BY STATES PARTIES TO THE CRC: LOOKING AT ARTICLE 27

### 1. Article 27, Paragraphs 1–3

Under the guidelines for initial reports provided by the Committee and UNICEF, states parties are requested to provide: "Relevant information, including the principal legislative, judicial, administrative or other measures in force; the institutional infrastructure for implementing policy in this area, particularly monitoring strategies and mechanisms; and factors and difficulties encountered and progress achieved in implementing the relevant provisions in respect of standard of living (Article 27, paras. 1–3)" (CRC/C/5, para. 19).

Furthermore, the Committee continues providing countries with guidelines for the drafting of their subsequent periodic reports, which should include the following information: the relevant indicators used to assess an adequate standard of living among children without discrimination; the criteria established to assess the ability and financial capacity of parents to secure the set standard; detailed information on the measures taken by the state to assist parents; and the measures adopted to follow-up the Declaration and Plan of Action adopted by the United Nations Conference on Human Settlements (Habitat II)(CRC/C/58, paras. 103–4).

On the eighth anniversary of the CRC, UNICEF released data to the World Bank on children's poverty around the world. More than 650 million children live in absolute poverty, and in some areas of the Third World, the situation is expected to become worse. As Toope acknowledges, one major problem with the *Convention* is its implication for resources (Toope, 1996). If the *Convention* is to be taken seriously by the ratifying countries, it will cost a great deal of money. Moreover, the issue of any substantial resource allocation from the North to the South raises not only economic concerns, but moral and ethical ones as well.

The Committee has frequently expressed deep concern about "the impact on children of structural adjustment policies in countries dependent on international aid, and of transition to a market economy in many countries, particular in post-communist eastern Europe." A recent recession "has also brought restraints on public expenditure everywhere. The result has been an increasing, often catastrophic impoverishment of children from population groups dependent on state aid for their survival.''

In its response to the government of Honduras, the Committee noted that ''the social inequalities existing in the country, including through the unequal distribution of income and land, have contributed to the considerable problems facing children in Honduras.'' Moreover the Committee recommended that the government consider the matter of the ''availability of resources for implementation of the rights recognized in the Convention, including within the framework of international cooperation'' (Honduras CRC/C/15/Add. 24, paras. 8 and 29).

Another example of international cooperation is the government of Pakistan's report to the Committee demanding increased involvement of NGOs to ensure full achievement for the survival, protection, and development of the child: ''Planned efforts shall be made to further mobilize the NGOs to play a greater and more effective role in supplementing government programmes, especially those designed to serve the child population of the country in a more systematic and holistic manner. . . . Such an approach would, indeed, open up new vistas of service for the survival, protection and development of children'' (CRC/C/3/Add. 13, p. 42).

The vast majority of the country reports enumerate the provisions in their national legislation regarding programs aimed at providing resources such as food, clothing, health services, and housing. Most countries tend to ignore other factors essential for the development of the child such as stable, nurturing social relationships and safe, stimulating environments (Hutton as cited by Andrews, 1999).

The Committee's response has been to request an analysis of the multiple issues related to child development. For example, the Committee, recognizing Germany's commitment to undertake measures to improve the situation of children in their country, believed that ''greater priority should be given to an analysis of the occurrence of child poverty. Such analysis should be undertaken from a holistic perspective, taking into account the possible linkages between such matters as housing conditions, family support to the child at home and in school, and the risk of dropping out of school. The results of this research could serve as a vehicle for discussion of these matters both in Parliament and with the relevant authorities as well as for the development of a more comprehensive and integrated approach for responding to the problem'' (Germany CRC/C/15/Add. 43, para. 31). Nevertheless, we do find examples of countries such as Norway (CRC/C/8/Add.7, p. 35) and Poland (CRC/C/8/Add.11, p. 39) who include assistance such as family leave, family life education, secure environment within neighborhoods or communities, or facilitation of social support as part of their programs to implement Article 27.

Barry argues in his contribution to this book that identifying basic needs for children is hard because standards and expectations vary across time, among societies, and even between groups within a society. Such cross-cultural differences within a given country are exemplified by the aboriginal populations in New Zealand and Canada. Canada acknowledges the need for a better information base concerning aboriginal children living on reserves. However, the government's Action Plan for Children provides no detailed measures or substantial resources devoted to accomplishing that goal. In their response the Committee, while recognizing the steps already taken, noted "the special problem still faced by children from vulnerable and disadvantaged groups, such as aboriginal children, with regard to the enjoyment of their fundamental rights, including access to housing and education" (Canada CRC/C/15/Add. 37, para. 17).

When dealing with state aid it is important to look at the treatment of alien children by the government and their access to benefits. Germany and Belgium, for example, have broadly interpreted governmental responsibilities to include all children in their country despite their status. Under the Federal Social Assistance Act in Germany, the government provides assistance for children to lead a life in a manner consistent with human dignity "regardless of his or her residency status" (CRC/C/11/Add.5, para. 30). The government of Belgium states a belief that since the goal of social assistance is to "enable everyone to live a life in keeping with human dignity . . . no criteria of nationality or race are needed to avail oneself of this right" (CRC/C/11/Add.4, p. 87).

## 2. Article 27, Paragraph 4

The payment of maintenance for children is one crucial way in which parents can fulfill their legal and moral obligation to care for their children. The Committee emphasizes the importance of "the best interest of the child" and "respect for the views of the child" as guidelines countries should follow when dealing with this issue. States parties should include in their reports to the Committee the measures taken "to secure the recovery of maintenance for the child from the parents or other persons having financial responsibility for the child, both within the State and from abroad, including in cases of the separation or divorce of the parents" (CRC/C/ 58, para. 79). Information should be provided on measures taken to ensure the maintenance, respect for the principles of the *Convention* related to this article, and any relevant international agreements.

Many countries in their reports to the Committee address only paragraph 4 of Article 27. Even those reports that address paragraphs 1 through 3 devote an exclusive title to the recovery of maintenance payments for the child. In most cases, the states parties simply cite their national legislation on maintenance. By national law Costa Rica can garnish salaries and even allows imprisonment for those parents who do not meet their financial obligations to their children. Japan provides enforcement measures to secure child maintenance from the parents. The Nordic countries drafted and ratified a specific convention on March

23, 1962, enabling the signatory nations to more easily recover maintenance payments abroad.

The maintenance of children is complicated when father refuses to pay custody awards to the mother. According to a report in 1988, as many as 75.4 percent of the mothers in Japan have never received any payments from the ex-husband. In most of the cases the money is never paid because the means of enforcement are ineffective. In cases of divorce by mutual consent, there is no provision for enforcement. On the other hand, Namibia, which has a large number of female-headed family households, has taken action to ensure a simple, low-cost, and effective system for mothers to pursue maintenance awards and has reported a high volume of success by unmarried women in urban areas (Namibia CRC/C/15/Add.24, para. 160).

The legal definition of maintenance may indicate the extent of parental obligation and encourage parents to play a more active role in their children's upbringing. For instance, the Committee was informed that in Argentina parents are legally obligated to provide maintenance, which is defined as including meeting the child's needs for sustenance, education, leisure, clothing, housing, assistance, and expenditure on account of illness (Argentina CRC/C/8/Add.2, paras. 56–58). In the case of Bolivia, parents have a defined legal duty to ensure that children acquire a trade or profession for the future and, if necessary parents must cover the cost of training (Bolivia CRC/C/15/Add.4, para. 99). Costa Rica has defined a familial order for the financial responsibility for the child. Within the family, parents, elder siblings, grandparents, and great-grandparents are financially liable for the child (Costa Rica CRC/C/15/Add.11, para. 155).

## IV. RECOMMENDATIONS

The CRC is a practical and ever-expanding resource tool for children in the world. The *Convention* provides child advocates with the means to make a major impact on all levels of society, moving toward a world in which children may develop their physical, mental, spiritual, moral, and social capacities. Steps that would advance this goal include:

1. Appeal to national and local legislative bodies to pass laws consistent with the CRC standards.

2. Attempt to influence business leaders and media representatives who can, in turn, influence public policy.

3. Encourage governmental and nongovernmental agencies to incorporate the *Convention*'s norms into their programs.

4. Include the views of children in the country reports to the Committee. As Melton (1987) points out, child advocates sometimes make the mistake of speaking for children before they actually speak with them.

5. Take seriously the obligations to children about their rights.

6. Implement Article 45 applying principles of planning, managing, and monitoring to international cooperation. Develop and coordinate joint efforts of U.N. agencies, governments, NGOs, and other intergovernmental initiatives.

## V. CONCLUSIONS

The language of Article 27 was discussed and debated by NGOs, national governments, and the U.N. Drafting Committee. Although some serious controversy arose, consensus was reached on the domains of concern, the focus on the family as the preferred and primary unit for meeting the child's needs, and the desire for international cooperation. The Committee charged with monitoring the reports of states parties has taken an active role in interpreting and pressing for expanded implementation of Article 27. The Committee has not been satisfied with simple citations of national legislation, but has pressed for a deeper review to direct governments to meet the social and economic obligation incumbent in Article 27.

National and regional efforts to foster implementation of Article 27 and the other provisions of the Convention will continue to be of primary importance, but the Committee's evolving interpretation and implementation recommendations will also play a significant role in establishing a climate in which the child's rights to an adequate standard of living is taken seriously.

## NOTES

The authors wish to especially thank John Defede for his research for this chapter. We would also like to thank Rachel Hodgkin and Peter Newell as well as Leslie Miller of UNICEF for providing us with a prepublication draft of their *Implementation Handbook for the Convention on the Rights of the Child.*

1. *Convention on the Rights of the Child*, Article 43, para. 2.

2. Ibid., Article 43, para. 3.

3. Ibid., Article 43, para. 5.

4. Ibid., Article 44, para. 2.

5. Ibid., Article 44, para. 2.

6. Ibid., Article 44, para. 6: "States Parties shall make their reports available to the public in their countries."

7. Ibid., Article 42: "States Parties undertake to make the principles and provisions of the Convention widely known, by appropriate and active means to adults and children alike."

8. For the most part Rules of Procedure address issues related with functions and working process of the Committee (i.e., drafting agenda of sessions, minutes, distribution of reports).

9. *Convention on the Rights of the Child*, Article 43, para. 10: "The Committee shall normally meet annually."

# REFERENCES

Andrews, A. (1999). Securing adequate living conditions for each child's development. In *Implementing the U.N.* Convention on the Rights of the Child. Westport, CT: Praeger.

Barry, F. D. (1999). Significance of community wealth for child development: Assumption and issues. In *Implementing the U.N.* Convention on the Rights of the Child. Westport, CT: Praeger.

Childwatch International. (1996). ''Indicators for children's rights. Child: updated 1996.'' Source http://childhouse.uio.no/Child watch/cwi/projects/indicators.

Flekkøy, M. 1990. *A voice for children.* London: Jessica Kingsley Press.

Fernandez-Cuesta, J. (1997, November 21). *ABC* (Spanish Newspaper).

Hodgkin, R. & Newell, P. 1998. *Implementation handbook for the* Convention on the Rights of the Child. Geneva: UNICEF.

Lopatka, A. (1992). The rights of the child are universal: The perspective of the UN Convention on the Rights of the Child. In M. Freeman & P. Veerman (Eds.), *The ideologies of children's rights.* Dordrecht: Martinus Nijhoff Publishers.

Melton, G. B. (1987). Children, politics, and morality: The ethics of child advocacy. *Journal of Clinical Child Psychology, 16,* 357–367.

Melton, G. B. (1991). Socialization in the global community. *American Psychologist, 46(1),* 66–71.

Melton, G. B. & Kaufman, N. H. (1997). Monitoring of children's rights. In A. Ben-Arieh & H. Wintersberger (Eds.), *Measuring and monitoring the state of children—Beyond survival* (81–88). Vienna: European Centre for Social Welfare Policy and Research.

Newell, P. & Hodges, R. (1998). *Implementation handbook for the* Convention on the Rights of the Child. Geneva: UNICEF.

Toope, S. J. (1996). The Convention on the Rights of the Child: Implications in Canada. In M. Freeman (Ed.), *Children's rights: A comparative perspective.* Aldershot, England: Dartmouth Publishing Co., Ltd.

United Nations Center for Human Rights. (1992). *Legislative History of the Convention on the Rights of the Child (1978–1989).* (Preliminary Draft). Geneva: United Nations.

## 3

# The International Effort to Measure and Monitor the State of Children

*Asher Ben-Arieh*

*State Parties recognize the right of every child to a standard of living adequate for the child's physical, mental, spiritual, moral and social development.*

—U.N. *Convention on the Rights of the Child*, Article 27

Few will disagree that securing an adequate standard of living for children is a desired goal. Even fewer will agree on what is an adequate standard and how it can be secured. It is easy to accept the need to reduce child mortality, to enforce immunization among children, and to aim for higher school enrollment rates, but is that enough? Article 27 clearly says it is not. Whenever speaking about an adequate standard of living for the child's *"physical, mental, spiritual, moral and social* development" (emphasis added) we are referring to a much broader issue. In fact, we are speaking beyond the child's basic needs; to use another phrase, we are speaking beyond survival. Stepping into the field of "beyond survival" is a hard task. It is stepping into a minefield of moral and social judgments, a vague and unclear field with different definitions, conceptions, and ideologies. However, the step is inevitable. If we want to secure an adequate standard of living we have to deal with issues beyond survival. The first step for any action would have to be gaining knowledge and developing tools for monitoring and learning about children's standard of living.

This chapter summarizes an extraordinary experience, the first international workshop on Measuring and Monitoring the State of Children—Beyond Survival, held in Jerusalem in January 1996. The first part of this chapter describes the history and development of children's indicators. In the second part, the Jerusalem meeting is briefly described. The third part deals with some of the meeting's outcomes and issues we should think about in any future effort to monitor children's well-being. The last part suggests an agenda for future efforts in this area. This agenda is based on the assumption that measuring the state of the child is not an end in and of itself. Rather, we can speak of measuring for monitoring or, more accurately, measuring for doing. This agenda is rooted in the many discussions and papers that were presented at the Jerusalem meeting, as well as in my own experience with monitoring the state of the child in Israel for the last six years.

## CHILDHOOD INDICATORS: BACKGROUND AND DEVELOPMENT

Although there is a long history of sociological and demographic studies of social trends using statistical indicators, it was the publication of Bauer's book entitled *Social Indicators* (1966) that prompted the widespread use of the same term. One of the key objectives of the early work on social indicators was to assess the extent to which social well-being was improved by public programs or policies. In order to monitor or evaluate changes taking place in society, emphasis was placed on the utility of social indicators in social systems models (Land, 1975).

Concerns about monitoring the situation of children are also not new. UNICEF has published its *State of the World's Children* report since 1979. This annual review of basic indicators of children's survival and development has helped to create a global awareness of the need for monitoring how children fare. Regional initiatives, such as the European Childhood Project, have focused on the need to become more specific about and accurate in describing the situation of children. Under the auspices of the Vienna Center, a group of researchers developed strategies for using the child as the unit of analysis in studying and recomputing public statistics. And certainly there have been many local initiatives to address the issue of getting better and more factual information on the actual situation of children and their well-being. These efforts have been initiated by researchers, public agencies, and NGOs within their spheres of interest or operation (Miljeteig, 1997).

Over the past decade there has been a growing interest in measuring the well-being of children. This has been partly due to a movement toward accountability-based public policy that requires increasing amounts of data to provide more accurate measures of the conditions that children face and the outcomes that various programs achieve. At the same time, rapid changes in family life also have prompted an increased demand from child development professionals, social scientists, and the public for a better picture of children's social well-being (Lee, 1997). By identifying key indicators and their relationships to specific outcome measures of social well-being, these measurement efforts place emphasis not only on the descriptive function of social indicators but also on their analytic function. By and large, the purpose is to increase understanding of the impact of changes in children's policy and shifts in sociodemographic trends on the well-being of children (Zill, Sigal, & Brim, 1982).

The recent growth of the childhood social indicators field can be seen in the publication of various "state of the child" reports. These reports have contributed to the increased level of interest in statistical descriptions of children's well-being, resulting in several ongoing data compilation and reporting efforts in various countries (see for example, Ben-Arieh, 1992; Jensen & Saporiti, 1992; Zill & Nord, 1994; U.S. Department of Education, 1988; and Center for the Study of Social Policy, 1993). A review of more than twenty "state of the child" reports (see reference list) reveals that the material is organized primarily by domains or service systems. The most common are: education, children as victims (neglect and abuse), health/nutrition, day care, family structure, economic status (poverty), housing, children as offenders, deviant behavior, sexual behavior, and family formation. Another domain that is highlighted in several reports is an explicit focus on children's rights.

The interest in advancing the art and science of children's status monitoring is reflected in three interdisciplinary projects that have recently been developed: the EuroSocial Childhood Program, the Conference on Indicators of Children's Well-Being (held at Bethesda, Maryland, in November 1994), and the Jerusalem workshop mentioned previously. Analysis of the reports and records of these projects suggests several shifts in the field of monitoring children's status.

## From "Survival" to "Beyond" or "Well-being"

Increased interest in the state of children has led to a call for new measures and indicators that extend the current body of statistical data about children. Measures such as infant and child mortality rates, school enrollment, and percentage of immunized children, while important, deal mainly with survival and the basic needs of children and are inadequate for measuring the state and quality of life of children beyond survival. Even simply using the term "well-being" contributed to this shift. Aber (1997) argues it is time to develop indicators beyond the basic needs of development and beyond the phenomenon of deviance. Pittman and Irby (1997) argue for indicators and action beyond survival and prevention in order to promote youth development. In fact, for many years, most childhood-related statistical information was about deviance. Only in recent years have we seen the development of more appropriate indicators that aim to measure and monitor the living conditions and well-being of children.

## From Negative to Positive

Thus, attention is beginning to focus on the need for positive indicators of the state of the child as much as for negative ones. Measures of the absence of risk factors or negative behaviors are not the same as measures of the presence of protective factors or positive behaviors (Aber & Jones, 1995). Most common measures of early childhood development pertain to deficiencies in achievements and problem behaviors and negative circumstances. The absence of problems or failures, however, does not necessarily indicate proper growth and success. Realizing this was the basis of a shift toward recognizing the importance of "positive" indicators for children's well-being (Aber, 1997). I agree with Resnick (1995) that "children's well-being indicators are on the move from concentrating only on trends of dying, distress, disability and discomfort to tackling the issue of indicators of sparkle, satisfaction and well-being" (Resnick, 1995, 3).

### From "Traditional" to "New" Domains

The two shifts described earlier ultimately contributed to a third one. Until recently, when measuring the state of the children, we occupied ourselves with measuring children's basic survival needs and focused primarily on the deviant and the negative aspects of their lives. Looking beyond survival and at positive indicators of child well-being naturally brought into focus new domains. I would argue that moving from education and health domains to those that indicate child well-being here and now, and especially life skills, is the result of the shifts already mentioned: from "survival" to "well-being" and from "negative" to "positive," leading to the shift from the "traditional" to the "new" domains.

To sum up, I would say that the effort to develop and learn from and about children has come a long way since the seventies when the first steps were taken. Recent years have brought new shifts and directions for developing children's well-being indicators. There is now also enthusiastic recognition of the need for measuring and monitoring the state of children. The benefits to be gained from the use of good measurement tools are becoming increasingly evident. In the following sections I will try to lay the basis for an agenda for future work in the field.

### THE JERUSALEM WORKSHOP

The focus of the Jerusalem Workshop was to develop innovative ways to measure and monitor the state of children beyond survival. A group of thirty five experts from various disciplines related to children's well-being, representing sixteen countries, came together in Jerusalem in January 1996. The meeting was the first in a series to facilitate development of indicators that permit comparison of the condition and well-being of children beyond survival. During the meeting an effort was made to break down into several stages the huge task of developing the desired indicators.

First, the "state of the art" and the rationale for measuring and monitoring the state of children were summarized. An attempt was also made to learn from the experience of other efforts, such as the Social Impact Assessment Movement and the Childwatch International project for monitoring the implementation of the *Convention on the Rights of the Child*. A lengthy discussion was held about the various domains of the state of children, as well as about a possible conceptual framework. Many of the participants accepted that the minefield of cross-cultural value judgments had already been crossed by the almost universal acceptance and ratification of the *Convention*. Even so, finding specific indicators that reflected the *Convention*'s principles proved to be a task fraught with problems. This continuous discussion about a conceptual framework for measuring and monitoring the state of children was the background to several sessions dealing with overlapping areas of interest. In this workshop an effort was made to avoid the traditional areas of concern regarding the state of children (e.g., health and education). Instead, the discussion went on to issues such as the status of children within families, communities, and society. Special emphasis was given to studying possible ways of measuring the development of both personal and civil life skills among children. The discussion also dealt with measuring and monitoring the self-fulfillment of children, as well as issues of the costs and benefits of children's lives. Finally, a special session was devoted to looking into possible data sources and measurement issues. Sources such as administrative data, census, and surveys were considered along with quantitative research and data bases. A majority of participants agreed that there is a need for qualitative data and for rearranging existing data in order to learn more about children and their lives.

During the four days of this initial meeting, a number of problems were raised and discussed. Not the least of these was that suggestions for monitoring specific indicators were constantly inhibited by sparse data availability. Another important problem was the general uneasiness regarding the conceptual framework for constant and reliable measuring and monitoring of the state of children.

Although, as mentioned earlier, this meeting was only a first stage in a continuous effort to deal with measuring and monitoring the state of children, progress was made. In general, the conference yielded an impressive discussion of the form and use of new indicators, and the importance and scope of the overall task. The following points highlight some of the issues that were discussed and agreed upon in the meeting.

### On the Rationale, Importance, and Urgency of the Task

Almost all attendees agreed that thinking about and measuring the state of children in both facets—survival and beyond—is critical for monitoring children's conditions and countries' resources. The task was recognized as an urgent one, though there were some disputes over priorities and goals. One group hoped to develop better indicators for both survival and beyond-survival factors in a parallel effort. The other argued that the survival side was more or less covered, and that the first priority should therefore be to develop indicators that measure the state of children beyond survival—the truly neglected facet.

Thinking of survival and especially of factors beyond survival is complex. It is not simply a matter of identifying new indicators. It requires basic work to define relevant outcomes beyond survival that must be grounded within cultures. Then, of course, the major obstacle one would have to overcome is the variety of cultures and different concepts of children's well-being. The complexity of the task requires us to broaden some assumptions and to avoid others. The assumption that quantitative data is better than qualitative must be reexamined, as must the assumption that an indicator is valid only if it can be applied, with identical meaning, across countries. The need for beyond-survival indicators should promote a commitment to their development. The excuse that we cannot monitor because there are no adequate indicators or no comparable data should not be acceptable.

Naturally all the participants agreed that social indicators are a powerful tool for change, but only if those in a position to change policies and resources accept them as valid indicators of conditions and make use of them. To have an impact, the search for indicators will need to be concerned about definition and measurement as well as implementation. Measuring the state of children is a tool and not an end in and of itself; bearing this in mind is critical. The resulting indicators may be less "scientific" but more powerful as tools for change.

### On the Possible and Desired Uses of "Beyond Survival" Indicators

The meeting participants reiterated the importance of collecting data and reanalyzing existing data with focus on the child as the unit of observation and analysis. Mutual agreement was reached that collecting data on children could and should be done not only through looking at the family or parents, but also at the child as an individual.

Besides the need for cross-country comparisons, there is an equally important comparison that can be made within each country—measuring the disparity between those at the lower rung of the economic ladder and those at the top. Creative measures of equity could and should be devised using existing data sources and indicators.

Matters beyond survival vary with the life stages between early childhood and early adulthood. Outcomes in one stage become inputs in the next. There is a need to reaffirm development by monitoring progress within key transition stages from birth to adulthood. Otherwise, the ideas of development and of the importance of continuous, appropriate supports, get lost.

Monitoring beyond survival requires defining a purpose. Why monitor? Who is the audience? Who are we trying to educate, convince, inform, persuade? Cost benefit analyses should be done, but must be done in a holistic way. What are the costs/benefits to the family, the immediate environment/community, the dominant society/culture, the economy? From a political perspective, decisions about investment in youth may be very much determined by who benefits and who pays. If it is perceived that youth and families benefit but the larger society pays, there may not be strong political support for diverting additional resources to youth.

Thinking of survival and beyond is not important just because we, as adults, are concerned with the outcomes of childhood and adolescence. We must be equally concerned with the quality of childhood and adolescence in "real time." What are the costs and benefits of being a child or youth?

## SEVERAL ISSUES THAT SHOULD BE CONSIDERED

Any effort to devise indicators for measuring the state of children will have to consider the following points. Based on the Jerusalem discussion here is a short description of the issues and some thoughts regarding the appropriate way to deal with them.

### Sources of Information

The scope of possible domains to describe children's well-being, as well as the variety of proposed indicators, is in many ways both a reason for hope and a reason for despair. One of the most vital components regarding the feasibility of the indicators is the existence of data, or at least the possibility of identifying an adequate source of information. The diversity of children's lives leads to the conclusion that any single source of information will fail to deliver the goods. Any attempt to develop children's well-being indicators will have to be built upon a range of sources. The three major sources are: administrative data, census and surveys, and primary social research.

Administrative data may be the best option for quickly developing community-based indicators of children's well-being. Given the cost of new or continuing social surveys, and given that administrative data already exist, this source is ideal for the short-term development of indicators that can be used to inform the public and policymakers (Goerge, 1995; Goerge, 1996).

Census or survey data can provide the indicators that describe the contexts in which children live. Census data provide a powerful background for this type of analysis because they provide population counts for most demographic sub-groups in all areas. The census data on socioeconomic conditions and family composition can be introduced into the analysis of the children's well-being. By combining data at the level of individuals with information about the contexts in which children live, we can improve our understanding of the influence of macro factors on outcomes for children. This approach can also be used to examine how the effect of a macroindicator on children's well-being varies across different contexts. For example, how does the effect of poverty on infant mortality vary across communities and how do different measures of poverty affect this relationship?

Primary social research is needed because we still do not know enough about various aspects of children's lives. Enriching our knowledge is a priority task in order to devise and shape appropriate indicators to measure and monitor children's well-being. Qualitative research, one aspect of primary social research, is immensely important for measuring and understanding the state of children, particularly their subjective well-being. If we agree that our knowledge about children is not good enough (Furstenberg & Hughes, 1995; Furstenberg, 1997; Frones, 1997; Qvortrup, 1994; Ben-Arieh, 1997), then we must accept the importance of enriching this knowledge, which could also be used to plan better census and survey efforts and make better use of administrative data.

## Costs and Benefits

There are potentially expensive costs involved in measuring children's well-being. High cost alone is enough for some people to discard the effort. This chapter opposes such reasoning. The measurement of children's indicators is not necessarily more sophisticated or expensive than the measurement of other economic or social factors and is likely to be of significant benefit to society.

We should avoid going to extremes. Some researchers may prefer indicators that try to capture the whole complexity of the well-being of children. In doing so, they drown in an ocean of details, indicators, and subindicators. The result is a totally impractical effort to measure the state of the child. On the other hand, and due partly to the economic problem, there is a tendency to look for easily accessible, existing data when devising indicators—rather like looking for the coin under the lamp instead of where it really is (see Haveman, 1995).

## Enhancing Knowledge

Measuring the state of children can expose new and important information that would otherwise remain hidden. This information should enhance professional knowledge concerning childhood and children. Knowing about the state of children may enable us to identify specific groups of children, for example, those who are in distress or who are deprived, as well as those who are well-to-do. It is important to know about the state of various groups of children. Knowing about the deprived groups may help to develop new policies and ideas to promote their well-being, while knowing the state of those children who are well-to-do can enable us to enrich knowledge regarding what works in giving children better lives. Data collected by measuring the state of children should be used to help us build a basis for discussion about the needs, programs, priorities, achievements, and directions for the future.

## Providing Tools for Better Planning

Knowledge and information are the bases for planning any service or policy. Such knowledge, when dealing with children, cannot be obtained without making children the focus of the data and information collection process. Measuring the state of children may provide planners with new perspectives. For example, it can provide a view of children's living conditions different from that represented by adults. It can also help illuminate the relative position, and needs, of children in comparison to other age groups in society. Finally, it can highlight children's contributions to society and, by doing so, can provide an "economic" rationale for investing more resources in children (Jensen & Saporiti, 1992; Wintersberger, 1994).

Measuring the state of children is the first step in planning services, programs, and policies that will be directed to the specific needs of different children's groups. A good example is knowledge about the state of children in different geographical areas within nations and internationally, and within different population groups. Good planning can result in differential resource allocation that addresses the problems and needs of each city or population group. Monitoring the state of children can enable us to compare their well-being across different time periods. Such comparison is essential if we want to know if children's well-being has improved or worsened, and in order to plan policy in accordance with those trends.

### Making Monitoring Possible

Knowing the state of children and even planning the best policy and services for children is not enough. Constantly monitoring the implementation of policies, programs, and services is no less important. When routinely published, the information can shed light on the progress being made in society. Child well-being indicators will enable us to check more precisely than in the past the consequences of policy on the national and local level, and may enable us to compare the situation of children in different places and societies. Doing so may make possible the necessary adjustments and changes each policy and plan needs in order to remain relevant and adequate to meet the ever changing needs of children.

### Enabling Better Evaluation

Good indicators for children's well-being are essential for evaluating policies, services, and programs for young children. The importance of evaluation is widely accepted. A good reliable set of indicators for the well-being of young children could enable us to set goals for any early childhood intervention program, to evaluate the program's outcomes and achievements, and to make the necessary adjustments in the next stage in order to achieve our overall goals.

## AN AGENDA FOR THE FUTURE

Any attempt to shape and influence social policy is contingent on the pressure and political power that can be manifested by those wanting to influence change. Influencing children's policy is no different. Efforts to improve the living conditions of children must be based on a general perception of children as a separate and deserving population group. Focusing on children is vital for improving their lives. Those who seek to best utilize the benefits gained from measuring the state of the children should bear in mind four points.

## Enhancing Public Awareness

Making the best of the effort to measure the state of the children should include an effort to raise public awareness. This can be achieved if we use simple and clear indicators, and if we publish those indicators and information regarding the state of children (Miringoff & Opdycke, 1993). Regularly publishing a "state of the children" report is a first and important step on the road to rising public awareness. Finally, working closely with the media will assure that children are a public issue (Adamson, 1996).

## Using Measurement as a Tool for Advocacy

Dealing with public pressure and especially with political arguments requires the use of advocacy. Child policy, as any other policy, is an outcome of political power. Measuring and publishing the state of children can shed light on the situation of children in different communities and nations. Making those differences visible can provide a strong weapon for advocating changes and improvement in the state of children.

The Fordham Institute for Innovation in Social Policy in New York has gone a long way in this direction through an effort to build a single composite indicator for the state of children. Doing so should enable the comparison of the state of children in different geographical areas, communities and nations. The comparison will be clear and visible; such a comparison can be a powerful tool for any advocacy effort (Miringoff, 1990; Miringoff & Opdycke, 1993).

But one does not have to build a single composite indicator for the state of children in order to use the advocacy benefits of measuring the state of children. A good example is the North Carolina Advocacy Institute's annual report on the well-being of children in the different regions of that state. The comparison uses sixteen indicators, divided into four main domains: health, education, social security, and physical security (Citizens' Committee for Children, 1993; North Carolina Child Advocacy Institute, 1993). In fact, most of those who are involved in an effort to measure the state of children around the world tend to agree on the need to use measurements as an advocacy tool for and on behalf of children in order to improve their living conditions (Adamson, 1996; Barnhorst & Johnson, 1991; Citizens' Committee for Children, 1993; Miringoff, 1990; Miringoff & Opdycke, 1993; North Carolina Child Advocacy Institute, 1993).

### Measuring for Monitoring

Closer monitoring of children's indicators should allow society to see its achievements and to compare different policies, services, and programs. In a time of budget difficulties, we can make wiser investments in our children's well-being. The indicators should enable us to ensure that services and programs for children are cost-efficient and effective in goal attainment.

### Change-focused Measurement

Measuring for the sake of knowing, planning, and even monitoring is not enough. Measuring the state of children is and should be done for the sake of improving the state of children. The knowledge gained from such an effort should primarily be action focused. The Israeli experience, for example, has shown that by publishing an annual "State of the Children" report, one can attract public awareness that will lead to practical actions on behalf of children.

## CONCLUSION

Measuring the state of the child is a small but important aspect of accepting children as a significant population group with its own rights, needs, and contributions to make. Children should be a major focus of data collection as part of the effort to develop improved social policies. The primary goal should be improving children's well-being. Realizing this leads us to accept that measuring the state of children is not an end in itself, but a means for monitoring and improving the children's well-being. Therefore, future efforts should not be about measuring and monitoring, but rather, measuring for *doing*.

As complex as the concept of children's well-being is, one can identify which aspects or domains are already covered and which are neglected. Without underestimating the importance of monitoring the survival factors of children's well-being, an emphasis on the neglected domains and factors beyond survival is urgently needed and strongly recommended.

## REFERENCES

Aber, J. L. & Jones, S. (1995). Indicators of positive development in early childhood: Improving concepts and measures. In *Indicators of children's well-being: Conference papers* (Vol. 3). Madison: University of Wisconsin-Madison, Institute for Research on Poverty Special report series (60c).

Aber, J. L. (1997). Measuring child poverty for use in comparative policy analysis. In A. Ben-Arieh & H. Wintersberger (Eds.), *Measuring and monitoring the state of children—Beyond survival*. Vienna: European Centre for Social Welfare Policy and Research.

Adamson, P. (1993–1995). *The progress of nations*. New York: UNICEF.

Adamson, P. (1996). *The state of the world's children 1995*. New York: UNICEF.

Barnhorst, R. & Johnson, L. C. (Eds.). (1991). *The state of the child in Ontario.* Toronto: Oxford University Press.

Bauer, R. A. (Ed.). (1966). *Social indicators.* Cambridge, MA: MIT Press.

Ben-Arieh, A. (1992–1995). *The state of the child in Israel—A statistical abstract.* (Hebrew). Jerusalem: The National Council for the Child.

Ben-Arieh, A. (1992, 1994). *The state of the child in Israel—A statistical abstract.* (English). Jerusalem: The National Council for the Child.

Ben-Arieh, A. (1997). Why bother? The rationale for measuring the state of children (9–26). In A. Ben-Arieh & H. Wintersberger (Eds.), *Measuring and monitoring the state of children—Beyond survival.* Vienna: European Centre for Social Welfare Policy and Research.

Center for the Study of Social Policy. 1993. *Kids Count data book 1993.* Washington, DC: Center for the Study of Social Policy.

Children's Defense Fund (CDF). (1991). *The state of America's children.* Washington, DC: Author.

Children's Defense Fund. (1992). *America's children falling behind: The United States and the* Convention on the Rights of the Child. Washington DC: Author.

Citizens' Committee for Children. (1993). *Keeping track of New York City's children.* New York: Citizens' Committee for Children.

Frones, I. (1997). Children in modern families: A Scandinavian perspective (115–126). In A. Ben-Arieh & H. Wintersberger (Eds.), *Measuring and monitoring the state of children—Beyond survival.* Vienna: European Centre for Social Welfare Policy and Research.

Furstenberg, F. F. & Hughes, M. E. (1995). The influence of neighborhoods on children's development: A theoretical perspective and a research agenda. In *Indicators of children's well-being: Conference papers Vol. III.* Madison: University of Wisconsin-Madison, Institute for Research on Poverty Special report series.

Furstenberg, F. F. (1997). The political and social context of children's well-being: The evidence gap (187–192). In A. Ben-Arieh & H. Wintersberger (Eds.), *Measuring and monitoring the state of children—Beyond survival.* Vienna: European Centre for Social Welfare Policy and Research.

Goerge, R. M. (1995). Potential and problems in developing indicators on child well-being from administrative data. In *Indicators of children's well-being: Conference papers Vol. III.* Madison: University of Wisconsin-Madison, Institute for Research on Poverty Special report series (60c).

Goerge, R. M. (1997). The use of administrative data in measuring the state of children (277–286). In A. Ben-Arieh & H. Wintersberger (Eds.), *Measuring and monitoring the state of children—Beyond survival.* Vienna: European Centre for Social Welfare Policy and Research.

Haveman, R. H. (1995). Assessing children's well-being: How many and which indicators, and at what cost? In *Indicators of children's well-being: Conference papers Vol. I.* Madison: University of Wisconsin-Madison, Institute for Research on Poverty Special report series.

Hobbs, F. & Lippman, L. (1988). *Children's well-being: An international comparison.* Washington DC: U.S. Department of Commerce, Bureau of the Census.

Jensen, A. M. & Saporiti, A. (1992). *Do children count?* Vienna: Eurosocial.

Land, K. (1975). Social indicators models: An overview. In K. Land & S. Spilerman (Eds.), *Social indicators models* (5–35). New York: Russell Sage Foundation.

Lee, B. J. (1997). The use of census and surveys: Implications for developing childhood social indicator models (301–308). In A. Ben-Arieh & H. Wintersberger (Eds.), *Measuring and monitoring the state of children—Beyond survival*. Vienna: European Centre for Social Welfare Policy and Research.

Miljeteig, P. (1997). The international effort to monitor children's rights (55–62). In A. Ben-Arieh & H. Wintersberger (Eds.), *Measuring and monitoring the state of children—Beyond survival*. Vienna: European Centre for Social Welfare Policy and Research.

Miringoff, M. L. (1990). *The index of social health 1990: Measuring the social well-being of New York City—focus: The children of New York*. New York: Fordham Institute for Innovation in Social Policy.

Miringoff, M. L. & Opdycke, S. (1993). *The index of social health: Monitoring the social well-being of children in industrialized countries: A Report to UNICEF*. New York: Fordham Institute for Social Innovation.

North Carolina Child Advocacy Institute. (1993). *Children's index 1993: A profile of leading indicators of the health and well-being of North Carolina's children*. Raleigh, NC: Author.

Norwegian Commissioner for Children. (1990). *Facts about children in Norway*. Oslo: Author.

Pittman, K. & Irby, M. (1997). Promoting investment in life skills for youth: Beyond indicators for survival and problem prevention (239–246). In A. Ben-Arieh & H. Wintersberger (Eds.), *Measuring and monitoring the state of children—Beyond survival*. Vienna: European Centre for Social Welfare Policy and Research.

Prout, A. (1997). Objective vs. subjective indicators or both? Whose perspective counts? (89–100). In A. Ben-Arieh & H. Wintersberger (Eds.), *Measuring and monitoring the state of children—Beyond survival*. Vienna: European Centre for Social Welfare Policy and Research.

Qvortrup, J., Bardy, M., Sgritta, G., & Wintersberger, H. (Eds.). (1994). *Childhood matters: Social theory, practice and politics*. Vienna: Avebury.

Qvortrup, J. (1994). Childhood matters: An introduction. In J. Qvortrup et al. (Eds.), *Childhood matters: Social theory, practice and politics*. Vienna: Avebury.

Resnick, M. (1995). Discussant's comments. In *Indicators of children's well-being: Conference papers Vol. II*. Madison: University of Wisconsin-Madison, Institute for Research on Poverty Special Report Series.

Shamgar-Handelman, L. (1990). *Childhood as a social phenomenon. National report: Israel: Eurosocial Report 3615*. Vienna: Eurosocial.

Testa, M. & Lawlor, E. (1985). *The state of the child 1985*. Chicago: Chapin Hall.

U.S. Department of Education. (1988). *Youth indicators 1988: Trends in the well-being of American youth*. Washington, DC: U.S. Government Printing Office.

U.S. Department of Health and Human Services. (1991). *The feasibility of linking research-related data bases to federal and non-federal medical administrative data bases: A report to Congress*. Washington, DC: U.S. Government Printing Office.

Wintersberger, H. (1994). Costs and benefits—The economics of childhood. In J. Qvortrup et al. (Eds.), *Childhood matters: Social theory, practice and politics*. Vienna: Avebury.

Zill, N. & Nord, C. W. (1994). Running in place: How American families are faring in a changing economy and an individualistic society. Washington, DC: Child Trends, Inc.

Zill, N., Sigal, H., & Brim, O. G. (1982). Development of childhood social indicators. In E. Zigler, S. L. Kagan, & E. Klugman (Eds.), *America's unfinished business: Child and family policy* (188–222). New York: Cambridge University Press.

*4*

# The Meaning of Child's Standard of Living

## *Jens Qvortrup*

My discussion of the *meaning* of "child's standard of living" begins by challenging the value, status, and position of widespread and ingrained notions such as child "quality," child "success," and child "outcome." I am not sure we need these notions—indeed, I'm afraid they are counterproductive. I wonder if they do justice to children and their life conditions, or if they embody a children's perspective. I fear that they rather are representations of reifying or teleological displacements of the perspective from children/childhood toward adulthood/society.

Obviously, growing up and becoming adult is a reality for most of us. The question is, however, if outcome measurements are good indicators of child well-being and child welfare. In my view, notions of child outcome, quality, and success as they are currently used are potentially dangerous for children. As a matter of fact, they seem to justify any type of life for children, provided the end result—that is, the adult person—exhibits positive values on a set of success criteria, which are either highly normative or comply with our society's achievement ethos.

Child outcome, quality, and success, as I read about them, appear to have obtained an undisputed or, indeed, indisputable status; nobody really asks about their relevance or importance. Are they for children or adults? The latest version I heard comes from western Australia, where one speaks of "outcome-based education" (OBE). The use of the acronym shows that it has become a standard in administrative procedures.

I shall restrict my discussion to one prominent example of the use of outcome-

perspectives, emphasizing what it signals; afterward I shall mention positive alternatives to its use.

The examples are legion (see, for instance, Haveman & Wolfe, 1993, 1995). I shall, by way of illustration, use Judith Blake's study of family size (Blake, 1989). My reference here is to the shorter version (Blake, 1981). By child "quality" she means "some objective measure of human capital such as educational or occupational attainment" (Blake, 1981, 422), and her main finding is that being an only child is less deleterious than having siblings. She is advocating the so-called dilution thesis, which suggests that having more children attenuates parents' attention. If you have only one child, you are able to concentrate your attention on that child, and the probability that you will produce a successful outcome increases in terms of cognitive ability, intelligence, and educational attainment. The relation between "sibsize" (number of siblings) and attainment is inverse.

Blake notes, "Increasing sibsize is an important negative influence on a person's educational attainment. Moreover, our results suggest that there is no family size that is too small for the production of quality" (433). Sibsize seems to be even stronger than socioeconomic status (SES): "it may not be so easy to avoid the negative consequences of large families, even if one is well-off" (441). Indeed, "Large families are considerably more deleterious to a child's educational attainment than are broken homes, suggesting that, on average, a simple nostrum of famialistic traditionalism—stable marriages and high fertility—is not the ticket to producing quality offspring." Blake noted that her results are associated with other outcomes: "for intelligence and educational attainment, appear to extend to other dependent variables in our work such as life satisfaction, social adjustment, alienation and occupation achievement" (440). She concludes by saying, "Personally, I doubt whether, on average, any country, or any ethnic or racial group, can meet the human capital demands of the modern world and simultaneously maintain a statistical norm of large families" (441).

If we are to become wiser about understanding children's life conditions while they are still children, we must question whether a reduction of child issues to human capital questions does not amount to instrumentalising children for purposes that lie beyond their lives as children? At least, one is obliged to ask if child-quality, as defined by Blake, coincides with quality childhood or children's quality of life? Reading much of contemporary literature about children (and Blake is only one prominent representative of the mainstream), it seems to me that we have not moved much ahead of Davis' standpoint almost six decades ago, namely that childhood is merely a preparatory stage, a savings account, and that taking children as seriously as adults is a sociological anomaly (Davis, 1940, 217).

There are a number of problems that I believe we should reflect upon before embarking on an "outcome"-model.

The first is linguistic—or rather metaphorical. Talking about children as "resources," as "next generation," as "human capital" or about child outcomes that result from a composition of "investments" in children has a reifying and productivistic tone that is hard to reconcile with ideas about children as human beings in their own right. It indicates that children are to be dealt with as mere clay in our hands, with a view to an end result that lies beyond their childhood; children are malleable to an extent that their own subjectivity and agency are slighted. Is childhood a project, the main purpose of which is to produce quality adults? The notion is echoing discussions of modern geno-technology, which again resounds eugenic views, which some of us thought our society had left behind.

Second, maximizing outcome, result, or success as the end point of childhood is in principle justifying whatever means found for achieving the desired ends. History has taught us many lessons about what children were told to endure for achieving certain goals as adults. They were told, for example, that they should be pleased with discipline and indeed corporal punishment; although they may not understand it as children, they will, later in life, come to appreciate such measures as the opposite of indifference, as signs of attention and affection. Blake, for instance, comes close to trivializing the problem of broken homes, if only that would further children's future accomplishments ("large families more deleterious than broken homes"). Can we be sure that production of "quality" children presupposes a quality childhood? I don't think so, and I am afraid that this question does not really bother outcome-oriented researchers. But if quality childhood is potentially at odds with quality children, where should we invest our resources and energy and devotion? Should we really sacrifice quality childhood? Should we prioritize outcome over process? But would an affirmation of these questions not be a version of letting the end justify the means?

Third, the outcome perspective is very much oriented toward the individual child and not toward a collectivity of children or toward childhood as such. What counts seems to be the maximization of achievement potentials in the individual child, without any consideration of implications for or value of, for instance, children's present welfare or being together with each other, for the cultural climate in society, for the future of childhood. Blake, for instance, does not ask if children, in respects other than pure attainment, would benefit from having siblings. Perhaps it is great fun to have siblings, perhaps more siblings would constitute a much nicer family environment or change the balances of power and interests between adults and children in the family? Also, Blake does not consider an achievement-oriented environment as ambiguous for children. She is not preoccupied with an ensuing child-poor climate in locality or society, should singletons be the norm among children. She does not—strangely enough, given her productivistic concern—look forward to a society in which the median age inevitably will increase, with problems that will concomitantly accrue. And when mentioning her results' extension to other dependent variables, she has, generally speaking, not children's life-satisfaction, social adjustment, or alienation in mind.

Fundamentally, thus, I contend that outcome studies have no basic interest in children themselves. And given that such studies represent a major portion of what count as studies in children, I believe it is an important issue with which to come to terms.

It has not been my purpose to expose Judith Blake as such, but rather to regard her as a representative of a view that hardly accords with a standard of living addressed by Article 27 of the U.N. *Convention on the Rights of the Child* (the right to an adequate standard of living for development). I do not, of course, contest the idea that one should be concerned about children's adult futures. I do suggest that concern for a child's standard of living first of all must take an interest in children's lives as children, and to the extent conflicts arise between children's present and children's future (i.e., adults), then give priority to children's present lives, for two reasons. One, because childhood is a time and space of life that existentially and morally is as important in its own right as any other time and space of life (is this not, by the way, what we have been told: that children's early years are of utmost importance?). Second, because I believe that we do not run great risks for the future of children if we make childhood a time and space worth living in for children.

Therefore, I believe that in future studies about children's standard of living we should basically ignore the forward-looking studies dealing with individual attainment or achievement and forget about child outcome or child quality to the advantage of quality childhood. In my interpretation, moreover, the U.N. *Convention on the Rights of the Child* is a document that does regard children as humans in their own right, while dealing with protection, provision, and participation of children, who are still children. This is the ground upon which we must stand when expressing ourselves about children's standard of living.

It is, in a sense, trivial to suggest a number of factors as being of utmost importance, such as material resources. Adequate standards of living must necessarily be such that are conducive to nonpoverty, to proper housing, to health, to knowledge, to rest, to leisure, and so on. What proper and adequate means is more interesting and difficult, because that must partly depend on the norm and the standard in a given society. That is why I believe it is relevant to consider Article 27 of the *Convention* together with Article 4, which addresses state parties' responsibilities to undertake (to the maximum extent of their available resources) legislative, administrative and other measures to implement economic, social, and cultural rights recognized in the *Convention*. This means, first, that any nation must make sure that children's standard of living corresponds to the general welfare in the society in which they live, that is, that children get their fair share of societal resources and are considered as partners and autonomous units in distributive justice. In terms of, for instance, infant mortality, one would therefore expect the United States to do better than, say, Greece or Cuba. The three nations have the same infant mortality rates, but the U.S. GNP is more than three times higher than that of Greece, and is 21 times higher than Cuba's GNP (see Adamson, 1996). Second, it also means a claim for universalism, that is, that children are supposed to be dealt with equally within one single country. If children thus are universally claimants on a society's resources, it means that resources must be more equally distributed than what parental background allows. One would therefore not expect a dramatic variation of infant mortality rates within the United States, such as the discrepancy of from 19.6 per 1,000 births in Washington, D.C., to 5.6 in Maine. This gap corresponds to the difference between Venezuela and the Scandinavian countries (see The Annie E. Casey Foundation, 1996).

In one of the most interesting American books on childhood, de Lone (1979) has leveled a fundamental attack on what he sees as an instrumentalization of children—and in my view his arguments are in principle valid for most developed countries. Our belief, he contends, that equal access to educational opportunities for children will in the end produce equal adults, justifies our neglect of children's conditions as they presently are. However, this promise has never been met, and our insistence on its validity therefore condemns a large number of children to live in relative deprivation.

In short, a decent and equitable material condition is a claim that children have on society while they are still children. It is, however, not an absolute demand, but one that is dependent on the resources available in each single country (but it is worth noting that Article 4 of the *Convention* also encourages wealthy nations to support children in less affluent countries). Under given circumstances, that is, large economic cleavages between rich and poor, one has to think politically in terms of children. This means in practice that children's material conditions must be less dependent on their parents and more on the larger society.

I would like to go a step further and suggest additional criteria for quality childhood. Contrary to anticipatory views, which treat children as human becomings rather than human beings, it is my view that children and adults as humans share a common ontology; therefore, it is plausible to suggest, as a general rule, that children's demands do not differ basically from those of adults. Thus, it makes sense to explore the validity for children of typologies that originally were proposed for adults. One such typology is Thomas' four wishes: (1) the desire for new experience, (2) the desire for security, (3) the desire for response, and (4) the desire for recognition (1966, 119).

Compared with the United Nation *Convention on the Rights of the Child*'s three P's—protection, provision, and participation—Thomas' desire for security covers more or less protection and provision, whereas the desires for new experience, response, and recognition go further than simply the right to participate. They acknowledge, as inherent wishes in any human, needs to make one's own explorations in the world and to receive feedback and be rewarded for active involvement—that is, to be visible and to be seen as deserving. In an abstract sense such claims amount to being accepted as citizens—irrespective of age.

The question is how to translate such desires into operational devices. In any case, what I am suggesting is that exactly as adults understand it as an inalienable part of their standard of living to have access to resources and activities, to be seen in and recognized for such activities, children must have similar claims—with due respect for, of course, physical and psychological differences. There is nothing extraordinary in this reservation. Other groups may experience limitations, justified or not; for example, women do not have rights or duties to conscription and old people may be forced to retire. What is needed, without prejudice, is to have a new look at children's rights and capacities. I suspect, however, that analyses of this kind might lead to discussions about divergent interests between children and adults. But I do not regret that—I think this is necessary.

Our protective mood is, obviously, often justified and positive—but not merely and not always; it may also be unduly sentimentalizing and paternalizing. Two examples illustrate this point. One is found in British statistics, showing that from 1970 to 1992 the number of children killed in road accidents fell dramatically—from around 1,000 to just over 300 (Central Statistical Office, 1994, 52). At face value this is an extremely positive development. At the same time a study from 1971 and replicated in 1990 showed that more and more children had their license withdrawn to move around on their own. For instance, the percentage of English junior children (aged 7 to 11) who were allowed to cross roads alone fell from 72 to 51 percent and those permitted to visit leisure parks alone plummeted from 63 to 37 percent (Hillman, Adams, & Whitelegg, 1990, 131). It is hard not to conclude that the price for reducing the number of children killed on the roads was paid by children themselves. In Thomas' terminology, the wish for security was achieved at the cost of a wish for making new experiences. It was, in other words, a change in the internal bookkeeping on children's own account, without compromising adults' demands and interests. The potential conflict of interests between adults and children becomes clear when the car is seen by adults as the ultimate epitome of freedom, while for children it apparently means curfew.

Similarly, in the news in Europe we were recently told that children and young people were not permitted to be around on their own during the evening and night in Washington, and it was therefore hardly a surprise that criminality and victimization of children and youngsters decreased. The problem is that children have a right to understand the city as also their city and thus may ask adults to make sacrifices in order to leave room for children. The examples illustrate the phenomenon called status offense, for which children can be punished—not because the activity they are involved in is wrong as such, but merely because they are young.

Another example has to do with the desires for response and recognition. In the EU countries it has recently been decided that children under 13 years of age are not permitted to work gainfully after or before their school hours; the good argument for this piece of legislation is of course children's protection. On the other hand, thousands of children—as we know from studies made— are prevented, by this law, from having other experiences and from being recognized in economic terms. They are furthermore prevented from a right to be autonomous consumers. I do not deny the relevance of many valid arguments for forbidding child labor; I would, however, have preferred a more serious debate on the basis of children's own wishes and a respect for children's rights to be recognized. As long as we do not respect children's school work as valuable enough to being rewarded in monetary terms, children's only remaining path to make market experiences is to become employees.

The British author Colin Ward, well known for his excellent books *The Child in the City* (1978, 1990) and *The Child in the Country* (1988, 1990), noted:

The child as customer has a regard from the adult world quite different from that given to the child as beneficiary or supplicant, and this lesson is not lost on children. It is part of everyone's experience, that those most gratifying occasions in childhood were those when we were not treated as children, but met the adult world on equal terms. Some activity, in say, sport or music, was recognized as worthy of uncondescending respect without regard to age, and the children's self-esteem blossomed. In everyday life, this accolade is most often given to the child with a job, as important for the feeling of responsibility involved, as for the independent earnings that ensue. (Ward, 1994, 147–148)

Ward has coined three alternative R's to those obsessed with "outcome-based education": "the three R's of children's use of their environment are resourcefulness, responsibility and reciprocity" (1994, 146). Reciprocity refers to the need to create coherence between different aspects of children's experiences. For instance, many preschool experiences make life easier in primary school; responsibility for others as well as for our own behaviour is similarly "learned through interaction with others, whether they are our own age mates, older or younger children, or the adult world" (Ward, 1994, 146). But most "teasing and tantalizing of these characteristics, that most of us would like to see in children, is that of resourcefulness in making use of their environment, simply because it involves those other attributes of responsibility and reciprocity" (Ward, 147).

Resourcefulness has to do with, on the one hand, access to facilities, for instance leisure facilities, and on the other hand, pecuniary access to them. Ward notes that the distribution of facilities favours access of middle class children, which in addition makes facilities a part of their mental universe and enhances an ability to manipulate them. But he also points out that children increasingly, as we approach the end of our century, need money to pay for them.

As a last typology, one could think of Hirschman's famous exit, voice, and loyalty (Hirschman, 1970). This one—like that of Thomas invented with adults in mind—is granting adults these options for most areas of their lives, whether as producers, as consumers, or as marriage partners. Children do not, however, normally have these options. "They may 'voice' their opinions, but without the possibility of exerting power, because the choice of 'exit' is not available. They cannot leave their families, schools or other institutions in which they have been placed by their parents and the state. In practically all respects, they are left with only the 'loyalty' option'' (Qvortrup, 1985, 139).

The purpose of mentioning such typologies is to broaden the perspectives within which children's lives can be seen; to enhance our imagination as to what quality childhood may mean. First and last, we must be aware of the limits, or rather the restrictions, the *de facto* priorities of adult life worlds put on children's standard of life. The characteristic way of dealing with children is—on the side of state and municipal authorities—rather reactive or defensive, and thus at the end of the day amounts to creating protective measures that may be seen as positive, of course, but also as controlling and disciplinary. We need, therefore, to develop policies that are pro-active and assertive, while taking into account children as subjects and agents and leaving room for children's rights for movement in time and space. Such measures will—and we should make no secret of it—unavoidably provoke vested interests among adults. We must finally find solutions for compatibility between children's and adults' life worlds, but our strivings toward such solutions must include willingness also on the side of adults to make compromises. Too long, in my view, have we accepted that the adult world is something to which children must adapt and that socializing measures are directed toward children's futures as adults. This is not a fair deal for children, and I think that advocates for children should be much more conscious about and develop ideas of children's standpoint and children's priorities.

An understanding of children's standard of life must, in my view, include visions of children as citizens. This obliges us to include not only their material conditions in a rather straightforward sense; it also demands a view of children's rights in a broader sense—their rights to response, to recognition, and to making new experiences.

## REFERENCES

Adamson, P. (1996). *The state of the world's children 1995*. New York: UNICEF.

The Annie E. Casey Foundation. (1996). *1995 Kids Count data sheet*. Baltimore, MD: Author.

Blake, J. (1981). Family size and the quality of children. *Demography, 18*(4), 421–442.

Blake, J. (1989). *Family size and achievement*. Berkeley: University of California Press.

Central Statistical Office. (1994). *Social focus on children*. London: HMSO.

Davis, K. (1940). The child and the social structure. *Journal of Educational Sociology, 14*(4), 217–229.

de Lone, R. H. (1979). *Small futures: Children, inequality, and the limits of liberal reform*. New York: Harcourt Brace Jovanovich.

Haveman, R. & Wolfe, B. (1993). Children's prospects and children's policy. *Journal of Economic Perspectives, 7*(4), 153–174.

Haveman, R. & Wolfe, B. (1995). The determinants of children's attainments: A review of methods and findings. *Journal of Economic Literature, 23*, 1829–1878.

Hillman, M., Adams, J., & Whitelegg, J. (1990). *One false move . . . A study of children's independent mobility*. London: Policy Studies Institute.

Hirschman, A. O. (1970). *Exit, voice and loyalty*. Cambridge, MA: Harvard University Press.

Qvortrup, J. (1985). Placing children in the division of labour. In P. Close & R. Collins (Eds.), *Family and economy in modern society*. London: Macmillan.

Thomas, W. I. (1966). *On social organization and social personality: Selected papers*. Ed. by Morris Janowitz. Chicago: The University of Chicago Press.

Ward, C. (1978, 1990). *The child in the city*. London: Architectural Press, Penguin Books and Bedford Square Press.

Ward, C. (1988, 1990). *The child in the country*. London: Roberts Hale and Bedford Square Press.

Ward, C. (1994). Opportunities for childhoods in late twentieth century Britain. In B. Mayall (Ed.), *Children's childhoods: Observed and experienced* (144–152). London: Falmer Press.

# PART II

# THE RELATIONSHIP BETWEEN STANDARD OF LIVING AND SPECIFIC DEVELOPMENTAL DOMAINS

## 5

# The Relationship Between Standard of Living and Physical Development

*Francis E. Rushton and Robert E. Greenberg*

As part of the discussion about Article 27 of the U.N. *Convention on the Rights of the Child*, we intend to focus on the relationship between "standard of living" and "physical development." Multiple studies have previously demonstrated the relationship between social class and physical development. For instance, there is a direct relationship between socioeconomic status and height, weight, and head circumference in primary school children in England (Wright et al., 1992). The more affluent children were significantly taller and had larger head circumferences, while the children who were living in poor communities were noted to be markedly heavier. Similarly, a relationship between adolescent stature and poverty was recently noted in a study of Mexican American youth, although genetic factors appeared to play a significant role in explaining differences in stature in comparison to American youth of other ethnic backgrounds (Martorell, Mendoza, & Castillo, 1989).

The relationship between social class and health has similarly been recognized for centuries (Krieger et al., 1993). In 1790, Johann Peter Frank noted: "Every social group has its own types of health and diseases, determined by the mode of living. They are different for the courtiers and noblemen, for the soldiers and scholars. The artisans have various diseases peculiar to them, some of which have been specifically investigated by physicians. The diseases caused by the poverty of the people and by the lack of all goods of life, however, are so exceedingly numerous" (Frank, 1961).

This discussion addresses the following:

1. The extent of the effect of socioeconomic status on health, using several examples to indicate the profound and long-lasting impact of childhood poverty;

2. The impact of poor physical development and low socioeconomic status during childhood on the health of adults;

3. The potential significance of the concept of having an "unfair share" in society;

4. Possible mechanisms by which social class can affect health.

## STANDARD OF LIVING AND THE EFFECT OF SOCIOECONOMIC STATUS ON CHILDREN'S HEALTH

Article 27 of the *Convention on the Rights of the Child* indicates that "States Parties recognize the right of every child to a standard of living adequate for the child's physical, mental, spiritual, moral and social development" and that "the parent(s) or others responsible for the child have the primary responsibility to secure, within their abilities and financial capacities, the conditions of living necessary for the child's development." Part of the task of this discussion is to define more precisely the "conditions of living" that are necessary for the child's development.

*Socioeconomic status* represents the framework in which social class is documented. In epidemiologic research in the United States, the three indicators used as empirical measures of social class are *occupation, education,* and *family income*. Significant differences exist regarding how these markers of socioeconomic status are developed, defined, and used.

A central question, thus, focuses on what measures will be used to evaluate "standard of living" and how they will vary, if at all, from current approaches to measure "socioeconomic status." Parameters that have been linked to standard of living include: (1) income (cash flow), (2) wealth (economic reserves), and (3) education. The latter may be the best measure for studying socioeconomic disparities in relationship to health, at least in adults.

It is important to frame a broad conceptual net for the effect of socioeconomic status on the health of children. Research about the life cycle indicates the intimate relationship between events during early development and consequences, including health status, in later life. Further, the concept of "critical periods" suggests that certain phases of development have greater impact than others on the health status of adults. The following categories simply indicate some of the features of these interrelationships during time.

### Importance of Preconceptional Factors

In the United States, a greater appreciation has developed for the relationship between the preconceptional maternal condition and the outcome of pregnancy. Certainly, adequate energy reserves on the part of the mother prior to conception are critical for adequate growth of the developing fetus (Kramer et al., 1990). Preconceptional factors may also have a direct influence on disease presentation in the infant, as the current relationship between folate deficiency and skeletal development highlights. Other elements responsible for fetal growth failure that have been postulated include deficiencies in nitrogen, essential amino acids, minerals, and trace metals (Dimperio, 1990). Poverty may play a particular role in the development of these deficiency syndromes (Golden, 1991).

Geographical differences have also been described in relationship to the age of onset of pregnancy. Teen pregnancies, with potential deficiency in nutritional states and emotional capabilities for child rearing, are noted in Western populations to be concentrated in socioeconomically depressed communities. Poor teen mothers also appear less likely to abort their pregnancies, and exhibit a higher rate of taking pregnancies to term than adolescent mothers in more affluent areas (Smith, 1993).

### Poverty and the Outcome of Pregnancy

Other factors during pregnancy impact on the physical outcome of the infant, and many of these factors are related to socioeconomic status. Lack of access to prenatal care, decreased utilization of prenatal care when available, and an increase in the use of tobacco, alcohol, and other drugs among poor mothers may all be associated with a less optimal outcome of pregnancy (Poland, Ager, & Sokol, 1991).

### Long-lived Consequences of Intrauterine Growth Retardation

The deficits of poverty-induced intrauterine growth retardation are not easily overcome. Long-term neurodevelopmental abnormalities in very small infants are extensively documented, with an excess of 50 percent of very small infants having significant neuro-developmental handicaps (Calame et al., 1986). In a comparison of preterm infants with those who suffered from intrauterine growth retardation, preterm infants had higher rates of perinatal mortality. However, intrauterine growth retarded infants, during the first two years of postnatal life, were noted to be hospitalized for diarrhea at least twice as often as their age matched counterparts. Both groups of infants suffered from more frequent bouts of pneumonia than full-term infants with appropriate birth weights (Barros et al., 1992).

### Marked Increase in Chronic Conditions with Limitation of Activity in Poor Children

Children growing up in poverty appear to be at risk for a variety of chronic disease conditions. Obesity, diabetes, and disability secondary to accidental injury have, for example, all been shown to have an inverse relationship with socioeconomic status (Olvera-Ezzell et al., 1994).

### Marked Increase in Perceived Poor or Fair Health in Poverty

Poverty can have an adverse effect on the ability of the family to provide a consistent supportive environment for children, especially if the parents themselves are seriously debilitated by the impacts of poverty. The resulting psychological stress can compound the severity of chronic conditions and adversely affect health status (McLoyd, 1990).

In a study of infants in New York City, poverty was associated with lower maternal ratings of the health status of their infants. Lower ratings of infant health were also associated with problems in the neonatal period, rates of hospitalization, and frequency of illness. Such ratings were also associated with mothers' rating of their own health. Perception of poor health status resulted in greater utilization of hospital services than those who perceived their health status to be good (McCormick et al., 1989).

### Marked Increase in Bed-disability Days in the Poor

A study performed in Boston indicated that patients from lower socioeconomic groups, whether defined by occupation, education, or income, had substantially longer hospital stays than patients from groups with higher socioeconomic status. Health care costs were also increased in patients from lower socioeconomic groups, although the increase was not statistically significant (Epstein et al., 1988).

## THE IMPORTANT EFFECT OF STANDARD OF LIVING FOR THE YOUNG ON HEALTH STATUS AS AN ADULT

An ever-increasing body of information, primarily from investigators in England, has identified a relationship between early health status and health of adults. Intrauterine growth retardation, for example, has been demonstrated to be associated with an increased incidence of type I diabetes, type II diabetes, hypertension, and coronary artery disease in adulthood. Obviously, adverse effects of standard of living on physical, cognitive, and emotional development of children will have long-term effects into adulthood. Other disease entities, studied primarily in adults, may well have their genesis during childhood. For example, the incidence of helicobacter infections, associated with peptic ulcer disease, was inversely related to socioeconomic status, with the lowest socioeconomic group having a sevenfold increase in infection (Malaty & Graham, 1994). The natural history of this entity has not been fully clarified. However, there are some suggestions that colonization during childhood may precede adult disease.

# THE SIGNIFICANCE OF HAVING AN "UNFAIR SHARE" IN SOCIETY

## The Lack of a Plateau in the Relationship Between Socioeconomic Status and Health

The Whitehall Study, developed by Marmot and colleagues (Black et al., 1988), indicated that age-standardized mortality was inversely related to socioeconomic status. Health was demonstrated to be worse (i.e., mortality rates were higher) for those on the lower rung of the socioeconomic "ladder," *regardless* of how high the next lower rung actually was. In other words, there was no plateau of socioeconomic status, above which there was no further linkage between socioeconomic status and health. If one is in poverty, one's health status is clearly worse; however, even if one is, for example, a businessman, one's health status is still worse than those higher in the socioeconomic scale. Extensive studies have reinforced the significance of this observation: The relationship between socioeconomic status and health persists over time, exists across the life span of the individual, and has been observed in every country where data enable analysis. Health care may alter the slope of the relationship, but the overall gradient is not significantly modified by the nature of health care (Evans, Barer, & Marmar, 1994). Further, the gradient has persisted even though the specific diseases that produced either morbidity or mortality have changed over time. In other words, there are some factors associated with socioeconomic status that affect health as a general phenomenon, beyond consideration of the biology of specific disease processes. The potential importance of socioeconomic status of children is exemplified by other studies from England in which childhood socioeconomic position was a better predictor of heart disease in middle-aged men than was their adult socioeconomic status, even after being adjusted for other risk factors (Kaplan & Salonen, 1990).

## The Importance of the Gradient Between Rich and Poor in Determining Health Status of a Population

A striking and potentially crucial finding is that it appears to be the *gradient* between rich and poor (i.e., income distribution) that is the most significant feature in the relationship between socioeconomic factors and health, rather than the average standard of living. Wilkinson demonstrated that, in developed countries, standard measures of health correlate with the discrepancy between rich and poor; the greater the gradient, the worse the health status of the population (Wilkinson, 1996). Thus, life expectancy is greatest and infant mortality less where the divergences between rich and poor are less, regardless of the average standard of living (among developed countries). Where there is greater relative poverty, health status is worse. In the United States during the last fifteen years, the rise in wealth inequality has been striking (Wolff, 1995). Virtually all of the growth in wealth has accrued to the top 20 percent of households, with the bottom 40 percent experiencing a decline in their wealth in absolute terms; the difference between the income of the top 5 percent and the bottom 20 percent has markedly widened. While the specific mechanisms by which this gradient is reflected in health status remain unclear, it seems possible that the primary effect centers on "psychosocial welfare," on the consequences of the feeling that one has an "unfair share" in society.

## SOME MECHANISMS BY WHICH SOCIAL CLASS AFFECTS HEALTH

### Shaping Who Has and Who Lacks Basic Material Necessities

Basic material necessities include food, clothing, sanitation, and health care. Those who have less access to such necessities will, as often demonstrated, have compromised physical health outcomes.

### Who Is Exposed to Occupational and Environmental Health Hazards

Although the relative risk of poor children to environmental hazards that may lead to poor outcome is often difficult to ascertain, certain toxins have shown a clear relationship to poverty. Lead poisoning has been noted to be much more common in poor neighborhoods, leading to recent calls to focus screening for lead poisoning in these high-risk areas (De Rienzo–De Vivio, 1992). Cigarette smoke is another environmental toxin noted to be more prevalent in poor families (Eames, Ben-Shlomo, & Marmot, 1993).

### Relationship Between Social Class and Different Behaviors and Ways of Living

Use of cigarettes represents one situation where associated behaviors have been examined. In a study of economically disadvantaged pregnant teenagers, it was noted that this population smoked for such reasons as to cope with increased weight gain, to have smaller infants and thus easier labor and less pain at delivery, to counteract anxiety arising from feelings of abandonment, and to establish a separate identity from their parents' and peers' drug abuse. Poor adolescents who were pregnant perceived short-term benefits from smoking that outweighed any perceptions of long-term health consequences (Lawson, 1994).

Similarly, many studies have noted decreased rates of breastfeeding among lower socioeconomic populations. Maternal educational levels appear to be correlated directly with this infant feeding practice, with known effects on the physical development of children (MacGowan et al., 1991). The influence of fathers, and perhaps peers, in the promotion of breastfeeding (and other health habits) is important. A study of mothers in Finland shows a direct effect of the socioeconomic status of the father and the propensity to breastfeed (Stahlberg, 1985). Yet, the usual behavioral risk factors, such as smoking, diet, and exercise, are insufficient to explain observed class-based differences in health (Krieger et al., 1993).

### Illness as a Mediator for Poor Physical Development

The individual's standard of living is recognized to result in decreased health status, increased rates of illness, and thus an ultimate negative impact on physical and cognitive development. In the United States, poor African American and Hispanic babies have been noted to have, for example, a 20 to 24 percent increase in the incidence of iron deficiency anemia. Iron deficiency, according to our current understanding, also may result in long-term cognitive defects.

The frequency of common illness between socioeconomic classes is difficult to assess because of confounding factors such as decreased availability of health services and lack of health insurance to poor families. Indirect information, however, can be illuminating: In a 1990 measles epidemic in the United States, African American and Hispanic children were noted to have infection rates seven to nine times higher than Anglo children (Pollitt, 1994). A study in Singapore noted a marked decrease in acute glomerulonephritis as socioeconomic factors improved. As the gross national product increased almost threefold between 1971 and 1985, there was over an 80 percent drop in the incidence of this potentially severe illness (Yap et al., 1990).

Clearly, the relationship between poverty, standard of living, and the incidence of disease are strongly correlated. Yet, the mechanisms by which these factors lead to compromised physical growth and health require much more intensive study. The relationship between socioeconomic status and health has been primarily investigated in adults. If the potentially long-lived effects of alterations in health status of the fetus, infant, and child are both recognized and accepted, elucidating the impact of socioeconomic status on child health is an urgent task.

## SHIFTS IN DISEASE RELATED TO SOCIOECONOMIC DEVELOPMENT

Recent demographic information from around the world indicates a shift, to some extent, in disease patterns and their relationship to socioeconomic status. In the United States, the greatest improvement in health care status has been in upper socioeconomic status groups. Although there has been an overall decline in mortality rates in the United States since 1960, lower socioeconomic groups still exhibit mortality rates much higher than those with higher incomes or better education, and this disparity actually worsened between 1960 and 1986 (Pappas et al., 1993).

Data from Australia suggest that improvement in socioeconomic status has resulted in a shift in morbidity from organic illnesses to behavioral conditions. Findings from studies of a multiethnic, lower socioeconomic status population group demonstrated an increase in behavioral disturbances, with growth failure and organic morbidity related to social disadvantage diminished in extent (Carmichael, Williams, & Picot, 1990).

In spite of dramatic improvements in the economic status of Saudi Arabians, there continues to be a high rate of short stature and anemia on the basis of nutritional deficiency. Strategies to improve health care status for children in Saudi Arabia (and elsewhere) clearly require an educational as well as an economic focus (Sebai, 1988).

These findings indicate that the relationships between ''standard of living'' and ''physical status'' are indeed complex and interrelated to children's social and mental development, if not also their spiritual and moral status. Defining ''standard of living'' must be done within the context of the surrounding society, and efforts to improve the socioeconomic quality of life may need to be carefully considered if the primary goal is the improvement of children's physical health.

## REFERENCES

Barros, F. C., Huttly, S. R., Victora, O. G., Kirkwood, B. R., & Vaughan, J. P. (1992). Comparison of the causes and consequences of prematurity and intrauterine growth retardation: A longitudinal study in southern Brazil. *Pediatrics, 90*, 238.

Black, D., Morris, J. N., Smith, C., Townsend, P., & Whitehead, M. (1988). *Inequalities in health: The Black report—The health divide*. London: Penguin.

Calame, A., Fawer, C. L., Claeys, V., Arrazola, L., Ducret, S., & Jaunin, L. (1986). Neurodevelopmental outcome and school performance of very-low-birth-weight infants at 8 years of age. *European Journal of Pediatrics, 145*, 461.

Carmichael, A., Williams, H. E., & Picot, S. G. (1990). Growth patterns, health and illness in preschool children from a multi-ethnic, poor socio-economic status municipality of Melbourne. *Journal of Pædiatric Child Health, 26*, 136.

De Rienzo–De Vivio, S. (1992). Childhood lead poisoning: shifting to primary prevention. *Pediatric Nursing, 18*, 565.

Dimperio, D. (1990). Preconceptional nutrition. *Journal of Pediatric Perinatology Nutrition, 2*, 65.

Eames, M., Ben-Shlomo, Y., & Marmot, M. G. (1993). Social deprivation and premature mortality: Regional comparison across England. *British Medical Journal, 307*, 1097.

Epstein, A. M., Stern, R. S., Tognetti, J., Begg, C. B., Hartley, R. M., Cumella, E., Jr., & Ayanian, J. Z. (1988). The association of patients' socioeconomic characteristics with the length of hospital stay and hospital charges within diagnosis-related groups. *New England Journal of Medicine, 318*, 1579.

Evans, R. G., Barer, M. L., & Marmar, T. R. (1994). *Why are some people healthy and others not?* New York: Aldine de Gruyter.

Frank, J. P. (1961). The people's misery: Mother of diseases. An address delivered in 1790. *Bulletin of the History of Medicine, 9,* 81.

Golden, M. H. (1991). The nature of nutritional deficiency in relation to growth failure and poverty. *Acta Paediatrica Scandinavica Supplement, 374,* 95.

Kaplan, G. A. & Salonen, J. P. (1990). Socioeconomic conditions in childhood and is-chaemic heart disease during middle age. *British Medical Journal, 301,* 1121.

Kramer, M. S., Olivier, M., McLean, F. H., Dougherty, G. E., Willis, D. M., & Usher, R. H. (1990). Determinants of fetal growth and body proportionality. *Pediatrics, 86,* 8.

Krieger, N., Rowley, D. L., Herman, A. A., Avery, B., & Phillips, M. T. (1993). Racism, sexism, and social class: Implications for studies of health, disease, and well-being. *American Journal of Preventive Medicine, 9,* 82.

Lawson, E. J. (1994). The role of smoking in the lives of low-income pregnant adoles-cents: A field study. *Adolescence, 29,* 61.

MacGowan, R. J., MacGowan, C. A., Serdula, M. K., Lane, J. M., Joesoef, R. M., & Cook, F. H. (1991). Breast-feeding among women attending women, infants, and children clinics in Georgia, 1987. *Pediatrics, 87,* 361.

Malaty, H. J. & Graham, D. Y. (1994). Importance of childhood socioeconomic status on the current prevalence of Helicobacter pylori infection. *Gut, 35,* 742.

Martorell, R., Mendoza, F., & Castillo, R. (1989). Genetic and environmental determi-nants of growth in Mexican-Americans. *Pediatrics, 84,* 864.

McCormick, M. C., Brooks-Gunn, J., Shorter, T., Holmes, J. H., & Heagarty, M. C. (1989). Factors associated with maternal rating of infant health in central Harlem. *Developmental Behavioral Pediatrics, 10,* 139.

McLoyd, V. C. (1990). The impact of economic hardship on black families and children: Psychological distress, parenting, and socioemotional development. *Child Devel-opment, 61,* 311.

Olvera-Ezzell, N., Power, T. B., Cousins, J. H., Guerra, A. M., & Trujillo, M. (1994). The development of health knowledge in low-income Mexican-American chil-dren. *Child Development, 65* (2 Spec No), 416.

Pappas, G., Queen, S., Hadden, W., & Fisher, G. (1993). The increasing disparity in mortality between socioeconomic groups in the United States, 1960 and 1986. *New England Journal of Medicine, 329,* 103.

Poland, M. L., Ager, J. W., & Sokol, R. J. (1991). Prenatal care, a path (not taken) to improved perinatal outcome. *Journal of Perinatal Medicine, 19,* (Germany) 427.

Pollitt, E. (1994). Poverty and child development: Relevance of research in developing countries to the United States. *Child Development, 65,* 283.

Sebai, Z. A. (1988). Nutritional disorders in Saudi Arabia: A review. *Family Practice, 5,* 56.

Smith, T. (1993). Influence of socioeconomic factors on attaining targets for reducing teenage pregnancies. *British Medical Journal, 306,* 1212.

Stahlberg, M. R. (1985). Breast feeding and social factors. *Acta Paediatrica Scandinav-ica, 74,* 36.

Wilkinson, R. G. (1996). *Unhealthy societies: The afflictions of inequality.* New York: Routledge.

Wolff, E. N. (1995). *Top heavy: A study of the increasing inequality of wealth in America.* New York: The Twentieth Century Fund Press.

Wright, C. M., Aynsley-Green, A., Tomlinson, P., Ahmed, L., & MacFarlane, J. A. (1992). A comparison of height, weight, and head circumference of primary school children living in deprived and non-deprived circumstances. *Early Human Development,* 31–157.

Yap, H. K., Chia, K. S., Murugasu, S., Saw, A. H., Tay, J. S., Ikshuvanam, M., Tan, K. W., Cheng, H. K., Tan, C. L., & Lim, C. H. (1990). Acute glomerulonephritis—changing patterns in Singapore children. *Pediatric Nephrology, 4,* 482.

*6*

# An Adequate Standard of Living Necessary for Children's Cognitive (Mental) Development

*Patricia Y. Hashima and Susan P. Limber*

Article 27 of the U.N. *Convention on the Rights of the Child* asserts that states parties must "recognize the right of every child to a standard of living adequate for the child's physical, *mental*, spiritual, moral, and social development" (emphasis added). In this chapter, we explore the question "What is the minimum standard of living necessary for a child's cognitive development?" Before attempting to answer this question, however, it is necessary to provide some clarification regarding the meaning of the term "mental development" used by drafters of Article 27.

Mental development, or the more commonly used term, cognitive development, is an extraordinarily broad concept, although as Flavell (1985) pointed out, cognition is all too frequently thought to be synonymous with intelligence, reasoning, knowledge, or other "higher mental processes." Flavell argued that mental processes intrude themselves into virtually all human psychological processes and activities, and consequently there is no really principled nonarbitrary place to stop in defining cognition. Thus, cognitive development involves the development of such abilities as perceiving, remembering, planning, evaluating others, and exchanging information. Moreover, these abilities develop in socially structured situations and therefore vary with a child's specific cultural experiences (Rogoff, 1990; Vygotsky, 1933/1978). Consequently, cognitive development must be understood within the social context in which the child is embedded (Rogoff, 1990; Rogoff et al., 1993; Vygotsky, 1933/1978). Perhaps Wechsler (1975) best captured the essence of cognition as an individual's capacity to understand his/her world and his/her resourcefulness to cope with its many challenges.

In the discussion that follows, we argue that adequate cognitive growth typically cannot occur unless children grow up in environments that are (1) healthy, (2) safe, and (3) nurturing. These conclusions are based upon findings from the voluminous research literature on cognitive development that has emerged over the last two decades. Moreover, they are consistent with Maslow's (1970) theoretical framework for human motivation, which recognized that an individual's physiological needs, safety needs, and needs for belonging and love are the most basic of all human needs and are critical to one's survival and well-being.

In recent years, numerous researchers have grappled with the challenge of documenting the effects of poverty on children's cognitive development. Perhaps not surprisingly, many studies have confirmed Sameroff's (1986) assertion that "children from poorer families have poorer intellectual outcomes" (193). For example, in a recent study that compared children in families with incomes less than half of the poverty level to children in families with incomes between 1.5 and 2 times the poverty level, researchers observed that the poorer children scored 6 to 13 points lower on standardized tests of IQ, achievement, and verbal ability (Smith, Brooks-Gunn, & Klebanov, 1997). Children in families with incomes closer to (but still below) the poverty level also fared worse than their higher-income peers, but the differences were significantly smaller. Economic conditions of neighborhoods, although less powerful than family-income effects, also are significant predictors of IQ and behavior problems in children (Duncan, Brooks-Gunn, & Klebanov, 1994).

Other researchers have revealed that duration of poverty is a critical factor in the cognitive outcomes of children. A recent longitudinal study found that long-term poverty has significantly greater effects on children's cognitive ability than short-term poverty (Korenman, Miller, & Sjaastad, 1995). Not only are the degree and duration of poverty significantly related to children's cognitive functioning, but the timing of poverty also appears to play an important role. Several studies have found a stronger correlation between poverty experienced during preschool and early school years and low rates of high school completion, compared with poverty experienced during later childhood and adolescence (Duncan et al., 1998).

Although such studies clearly illustrate the linkages between a low standard of living and poor cognitive outcomes for children, they do not necessarily shed light on the pathways through which low income affects these outcomes. What are the factors within an impoverished environment that significantly affect children's cognitive development?

Over the past two decades, a large body of research findings have confirmed that a child's cognitive development is shaped by three primary influences: (1) genetics, (2) organic influences (such as environmental toxins and other hazards), and (3) experience (see Thompson, 1997 for a review). The conditions in which a child lives do not affect his or her predetermined genetic blueprint. However, such living conditions profoundly influence the child's everyday experiences and the extent to which he or she is exposed to environmental toxins and other environmental hazards.

## ORGANIC INFLUENCES ON COGNITIVE DEVELOPMENT

Because nerve cells in the brain develop rapidly during the early months and years of life (Cowan, 1979; Morgan & Gibson, 1991), a child's developing brain is extremely vulnerable to organic influences such as malnutrition, environmental toxins, prenatal exposure to alcohol and other drugs, and disease. Children in substandard living conditions are all too likely to be exposed to multiple organic hazards.

### Malnutrition

One of the best-documented hazards to a child's cognitive development is malnutrition. Both prenatal and postnatal malnutrition have been found to seriously impair a child's physical and cognitive development (McDonald et al., 1994; Morgan & Gibson, 1991; Morgane et al., 1993; Winick, 1976; see Pollitt et al., 1996 for review).

*Prenatal malnutrition.* Autopsies of malnourished babies who died at or shortly after birth reveal fewer brain cells and a brain weight as much as 36% below average (Morgane et al., 1993). Thus, an infant who has been malnourished *in utero* frequently begins life at a serious cognitive disadvantage. Moreover, prenatal malnutrition has been observed to influence the intellectual functioning of the child later in life (Hicks, Langham, & Takenaka, 1982; Kopp, 1983; Kopp & Parmalee, 1979; Teberg, Walther, & Pena, 1988; Zeskind & Ramey, 1978, 1981). Teberg and colleagues (1988) found that compared to normal weight babies, "small-for-date-babies" (who are below their expected weight when length of pregnancy is taken into account) have lower intelligence test scores, are less attentive, and achieve more poorly in school by middle childhood. In a study of children whose mothers had participated in the WIC program, Hicks et al. (1982) found that a supplemental food program provided to mothers during the third trimester influenced the cognitive functioning of their children. Approximately five to seven years later, children who had received food supplements prenatally outperformed their siblings (who began the supplemental feeding program after one year of age) on a variety of intellectual measures.

*Postnatal malnutrition.* Although it is difficult to single out the effects of postnatal dietary deficiency from the effects of children's impoverished environment, a number of studies have demonstrated a significant relationship between nutritional status and intellectual functioning in infants (Barrett, Radke-Yarrow, & Klein, 1982; Lester, 1975; Palti, Meijer, & Adler, 1985; Wasserman et al., 1992; Wolf, Jimenez, & Lozoff, 1994) and children (McDonald et al., 1994; Sigman et al., 1991; Simeon & Grantham-McGregor, 1990; Winick, Meyer, & Harris, 1975). For example, it has been found that malnourished infants and children scored lower than a nonmalnourished control group on a wide range of psychological tests (including developmental scales, intelligence tests, and tasks of specific cognitive function) (Pollitt, 1994). Malnourished infants also have been found to exhibit lowered attention and responsiveness to other people (Brazelton et al., 1977; Lester, 1975). Moreover, the effects of postnatal malnutrition have been found to continue into the preschool and early primary school grades (Barrett, Radke-Yarrow, & Klein, 1982; Galler, Ramsey, & Solimano, 1984; Palti, Meijer, & Adler, 1985). For example, Palti, Meijer, & Adler (1985) found a significant relationship between nutritional deficiency in infancy and learning achievement in second grade.

## Environmental Toxins

In addition to malnutrition, prenatal and postnatal exposure to environmental toxins have significant influences on the development of the brain. Not surprisingly, children who grow up in disadvantaged settings are more likely than their nondisadvantaged peers to be exposed to common teratogenic agents such as environmental hazards, drugs, and infections. Intrauterine exposure to environmental hazards such as radiation and industrial pollutants (e.g., mercury, PCBs, lead) can cause significant cognitive impairment later in life. In addition to the grave health risks of radiation exposure, radiation exposure *in utero* can cause later cognitive deficits. For example, more than half of the children whose mothers were survivors of the atomic bombings of Hiroshima or Nagasaki were mentally retarded (Mole, 1987; Schull & Otake, 1986). Maternal consumption of fish from Minamata Bay, which was polluted by discharge of mercury from a manufacturing plant, was found to be associated with cerebral palsy in infants (Koos & Longo, 1980). Prenatal exposure to polychlorinated-biphenyls (PCBs), a chemical compound used in a wide range of industrial products, also has been related to slower visual discrimination processing and lower short-term memory abilities among preschool children (Jacobson, Jacobson, & Humphrey, 1990; Jacobson et al., 1992).

Although evidence of the effects of lead exposure on the cognitive functioning of humans (as measured by IQ tests) are mixed (Bellinger et al., 1991; Shaheen, 1984; Wolf, Jimenez, & Lozoff, 1994), numerous studies have found that prenatal or early postnatal exposure to lead is associated with delay in early cognitive development (Bellinger et al., 1987; Dietrich et al., 1987; McMichael et al., 1988; Wasserman et al., 1992). For example, Needleman and colleagues found that exposure to lead in childhood was associated with lower IQ scores, slower speech and language processing, attention deficit, and problems in classroom performance (Needleman et al., 1979). Moreover, exposure to low doses of lead in childhood has been found to produce long-term deficits in cognitive functioning, as measured by academic failure, reading disabilities, and lower

vocabulary and grammatical-reasoning scores, which persisted into young adulthood eleven years later (Needleman et al., 1990).

### Alcohol, Tobacco, and Illegal Drugs

Numerous studies have revealed that maternal use of tobacco, alcohol, and
illegal drugs have harmful effects *in utero* on children's cognitive development.
Although use of these substances can be found among individuals from every
socioeconomic status, use tends to be higher among those in more deprived
living conditions. For example, the National Household Survey on Drug Abuse
(U.S. Department of Health and Human Services 1993) reported significantly
higher rates of cigarette, marijuana, cocaine, and heroine use and heavy alcohol
consumption among unemployed adults than among those who were employed
full time or part time.

Maternal smoking has been found to be associated with a child's lower score
on the Bayley Scales of Mental and Motor Development (Fried & Watkinson,
1988), delay in language development (Fried & Watkinson, 1990), lower reading
and mathematics achievement (Fogelman, 1980), hyperactivity (Denson, Nanson, & McWatters, 1975), and attention deficit (Streissguth et al., 1984). Infants
born to mothers who are heavy drinkers during pregnancy are likely to suffer
from fetal alcohol syndrome, which is characterized by mental retardation, hyperactivity, and attention deficits (Streissguth et al., 1984). Although it is difficult to isolate the effects of a single drug, infants born to mothers who use
illegal substances such as opiates and cocaine also are more likely to have
damage to their central nervous systems than infants born to mothers who do
not use illegal substance (Delaney-Black et al., 1996; Fox, Calkins, & Bell,
1994; Holzman & Paneth, 1994; Kaye et al., 1989; Moroney & Allen, 1994).

### Infections

There are a number of maternal infections (viral, bacterial, and parasitic) such
as acquired immune deficiency syndrome (AIDS), chickenpox, cytomegalovirus,
genital herpes, rubella, syphilis, tuberculosis, and toxoplasmosis that increase
the child's risk for mental retardation (Chatkupt et al., 1989; Cohen, 1993; Peckham & Logan, 1993; Qazi et al., 1988; Samson, 1988; Sever, 1983; Vorhees,
1986). Although there are confounding factors such as mother's drug use and
poor prenatal care, one of the effects of pediatric human immunodeficiency virus
(HIV) infection, for instance, is neurologic abnormalities such as microcephaly,
calcification of the basal ganglia, encephalopathy, cerebral atrophy, developmental delay, and cognitive deficits (APA Task Force on Pediatric AIDS, 1989;
Chamberlain, Nichols, & Chase, 1991; Henggeler, Melton, & Rodrigue, 1992).
In addition to becoming infected *in utero*, children can acquire HIV infection
through blood transfusions. In such cases, the prognosis following the onset of
AIDS are comparable to those of children who have acquired HIV infection

prenatally (Henggeler, Melton, & Rodrigue, 1992). Another infection-causing microorganism that children can acquire postnatally is intestinal worms (e.g., hookworm, whipworm, and roundworm). Although these worms infect hosts of all ages, the prevalence of intestinal worm infection are usually highest in school-age children. The infection has been associated with deficits of memory, reaction time, attention, and school performance (Watkins & Pollitt, 1997).

## EXPERIENTIAL INFLUENCES

In addition to the genetic and organic influences that affect cognitive development, a child's everyday experiences, whether positive or negative, stimulating or deprived, shape how his or her brain matures. As we discuss below, children require not only a healthy environment in which to develop, but they also require a safe, nurturing environment that includes age-appropriate stimulation and a variety of experiences that can support their cognitive growth (Thompson, 1997).

### A Safe Environment

Children throughout the world face numerous threats to their physical safety. In alarming numbers, children are beaten and sexually abused within their homes, and they are witnesses to or victims of violent crimes within their neighborhoods. Not only do such hazardous environments threaten the physical and emotional well-being of children, but they also may seriously affect children's cognitive development. One of the most prevalent threats to children's safety is physical abuse, which is associated with decreases in children's cognitive functioning, as measured by IQ scores, language ability, and school performance (Coster et al., 1989; De Paul & Arruabarrena, 1995; Eckenrode, Laird, & Doris, 1993; Fantuzzo, 1990; Friedrich, Einbender, & Luecke, 1983; Hoffman-Plotkin & Twentyman, 1984; Salzinger et al., 1984).

Although there are numerous studies examining the adverse effects of sexual abuse on the social and emotional development of children (Browne & Finkelhor, 1986), there are only a few studies that address the cognitive development of sexually abused children. Available findings reveal that sexually abused children perform less well academically and drop out of school more frequently than those without a history of sexual abuse (Chandy, Blum, & Resnick, 1996; Eckenrode, Laird, & Doris, 1993).

Finally, a handful of research studies have investigated the relationship between children witnessing domestic violence and their cognitive functioning (Kolbo, Blakely, & Engleman, 1996). Available findings support the conclusion that children who observe partner violence are more likely to have verbal and cognitive delays and poor school performance (Kerouac et al., 1986; Moore, Galcius, & Pettican, 1981; Westra & Martin, 1981; Wildin, Williamson, & Wilson, 1991) than their peers who have not witnessed such violence.

## A Nurturing Environment

Not only is a safe environment necessary for adequate cognitive development, but research also suggests that a nurturing environment is critical to foster children's cognitive growth. Perhaps the strongest evidence for the importance of a stimulating, nurturing environment on cognitive growth comes from studies of deprivation (Thompson, 1997). For example, rats who were bred in cages with many stimulating toys developed more complex brains than did rats who were raised in bare cages (Greenough & Black, 1992). Similarly, a number of studies also suggest that children's cognitive development may suffer as a result of growing up in environments that provide little stimulation or nurturing. For example, children who grow up in circumstances that are characterized by neglect face significant deficits in cognitive abilities (language abilities, academic performance), intelligence (as measured in IQ scores), and problem-solving compared to their non-neglected peers (Eckenrode, Laird, & Doris, 1993; Egeland, Sroufe, & Erickson, 1983; Hoffman-Plotkin & Twentyman, 1984; Kendall-Tackett, 1997; Kendall-Tackett & Eckenrode, 1996; Leiter & Johnsen, 1994; Maxfield & Widom, 1996; Wodarski et al., 1990). Wodarski and colleagues (1990), for instance, found that neglected children were more likely to receive lower scores on tests of language, reading, and math skills, and to exhibit poorer school performance than a control group of nonmaltreated children. It may be argued that neglectful conditions affect children's cognitive development because such children are malnourished and grow up in unhealthy or unsafe environments. However, it also is likely that neglectful caretakers fail to provide a stimulating environment for their children (e.g., reading to them, supervising their homework, and generally being involved in their child's academic life). Such an argument is consistent, for example, with findings that neglected children demonstrate more developmental problems than any other maltreated group of children (Erickson, Egeland, & Pianta, 1989). Others who have probed the specific effects of a nurturing environment on cognitive development have observed that the affective quality of the mother-child relationship was positively associated with the school-relevant cognitive performance of children (Estrada et al., 1987). Moreover, this association was not explained by the socioeconomic status of the family or the mother's IQ.

What are the developmental pathways through which deprived, non-nurturing environments tend to stunt cognitive development? Or conversely, what are the mechanisms by which an adequately nurturing environment leads to cognitive growth? Estrada and colleagues (1987) concluded that there are three ways in which positive affective relationships may influence children's cognitive abilities: (1) by affecting parents' tendencies to engage and support children in solving problems, (2) by affecting children's social competence and, consequently, the flow of information between children and adults, and (3) by influencing children's exploratory tendencies—hence their willingness to approach and persist in tasks.

Similarly, Vygotsky (1933/1978) concluded that cognitive development proceeds through children's participation in activities slightly beyond their competence with the assistance of adults or more skilled peers. He proposed that there exists a "zone of proximal development," which is the area between the child's "actual developmental level as determined by independent problem solving" (Vygotsky, 1933/1978, 86) and the higher level of "potential development as determined through problem solving under adult guidance or in collaboration with more capable peers" (86).

In Vygotsky's view of cognitive development, language plays a critical role. As children collaborate with more mature partners, they incorporate the language of these dialogues as part of their private speech and later use it to organize their independent efforts. Thus, Vygotsky theorized that "every function of the child's cultural development appears . . . first on the social level, and later, on the individual level; first between people (interpsychological) . . . and inside the child (intrapsychological)" (57).

However, social interactions between children and their caregivers or more capable peers do not always advance individual learning. Vygotsky was not explicit about how these dialogues specifically promote transfer of cognitive processes, but Rogoff (1990) extended Vygtosky's zone of proximal development by focusing on the instructional features of social interactions between children and their caregivers. She conceptualized cognitive development as an apprenticeship. Children develop mentally as a result of "guided participation in social activity with companions who support and stretch their understanding of and skill in using tools of culture" (Rogoff, 1990, vii). According to Rogoff, a child masters a task only when the main objective of a shared activity is in the teaching and not in the accomplishment of the task.

In order for the expert to guide the novice through the activity with his/her level of ability in mind, there must be a common ground of communication between them. The concept of intersubjectivity describes a process in which two participants who begin a task with different understandings arrive at a mutual understanding (Newson & Newson, 1975). Guided participation only works when the expert and the novice adjust to the perspective of the other (Rogoff, 1990). For example, an adult, the expert, must try to help a child, the novice, in a way that the child could understand, and the child must adjust to take the adult's approach in order to master a new task.

According to Rogoff (1998), the concept of guided participation is "a perspective for examining peoples' opportunities to learn through diverse processes of participation in the valued activities of their various communities" (700). It applies across cultures and age groups (Rogoff, 1990; Rogoff et al., 1993) and indeed fosters cognitive skills (Bradley et al., 1994; Siegel, 1982). For example, Sigel (1982) found that preschool children whose parents used "high level distracting behaviors" (i.e., anticipating, proposing alternatives, and evaluating outcomes) that challenged their representational abilities out-performed children with equivalent IQ scores on various cognitive tasks. The type of assistance adults offer children varies from culture to culture, however. For example, when Rogoff and her collaborators (1993) observed adult-child interactions in four different communities, they found that parents from middle-class urban areas in Turkey and the United States helped their children accomplish a task primarily through verbal instruction whereas parents from a Mayan town in Guatemala and a tribal village in India depended less on verbal instruction and more on demonstration and gesture. Thus, verbal instruction is not the only means to foster cognitive development. Nevertheless, adult caregivers in every culture guide their children in mastering tasks of their society. Children from diverse cultures are apprentices in thinking through social play with peers, joint activities with family members (e.g., Mayan girls learning to weave through observation, instruction, and participation), and interactions with other adults (e.g., learning to manipulate a computer through structured activities and guidance from a teacher).

What particular techniques can experts use to support novices' learning? In studying the role of tutoring in problem solving, Wood, Bruner, and Ross (1976) introduced the concept of "scaffolding" (90). According to Wood et al., this scaffolding process consists of a tutor structuring the learner's activities so that the learner can focus on the tasks that are within his/her range of competence. They proposed six functions of the tutor in the scaffolding process: (1) to recruit the child's interest in the task, (2) to break down a task into manageable units, (3) to keep the learner in pursuit of the goal by motivating the learner and controlling the activity, (4) to point out important features of discrepancies between what a child has produced and the correct solution, (5) to control the learner from getting frustrated with the task and also to prevent the learner from becoming too dependent on the tutor; and (6) to demonstrate the ideal solution by incorporating what was partially executed by the learner into the solution.

According to Greenfield (1984), an effective scaffold has five characteristics: (1) it provides support, (2) it functions as a tool, (3) it extends the range of the child, (4) it allows the worker to accomplish a task not otherwise possible, and (5) it is used selectively to assist the child where needed. Thus, an "expert" provides a support for the "novice," such that the expert structures an interaction by building upon what he or she knows the novice can do. Although Wood et al. (1976) used the term "scaffolding" as a metaphor to describe an effective intervention of a tutor, the term is now used to describe a process in which an adult *continuously* guides a child's activities. Just as a worker must continue to construct a scaffold to fit the building as it is being completed, an adult must continuously provide a support that fits well with the child's current level of competence.

## Ecological Context

The work of Vygotsky and later Rogoff and her colleagues has emphasized that social experience plays a critical role in a child's cognitive development.

Although a child's family provides the setting for many of his or her social experiences, the social environment in which the family is embedded also significantly affects a child's social experiences, and hence, helps to shape a child's cognitive development—either positively or negatively.

For example, research has confirmed that violent conditions of neighborhoods are significant predictors of children's academic and behavior problems (Richters & Martinez, 1993). Richters and Martinez observed that it was not the mere accumulation of violent experiences in the community that gave rise to adaptational failure among children. Rather, it was when such adversities in the exosystem (i.e., community) eroded the quality of the child's microsystem (i.e., family) that the odds of children's adaptational failure increased. In addition to eroding the stability of the children's homes, violent conditions of communities rob children of their opportunities to play without fear. As Vygotsky (1933/ 1978) and others have argued, play experiences enable children to act in accordance with internal ideas instead of simply responding to external stimuli and thus are critical to the development of children's ability to think.

The social environment in which a family is embedded also may provide significant opportunities to enhance children's development, however. For example, research indicates that schooling may buffer the effects of early risk to children (Werner, 1990). Early child care interventions, in particular, have been found to have a strong positive impact on the development of impoverished children and appear to be efficient strategies for intervention efforts (Seitz & Apfel, 1994). Although the quality of the observed teacher-child interaction has been found to be lower in poor neighborhoods (Caughy, Di Pietro, & Strobino, 1994; Phillips et al., 1994), high quality preschool education has been found to enhance poor children's cognitive developmental outcomes (Boocock, 1995; Brooks-Gunn, Klebanov, & Duncan, 1996; Campbell & Ramey, 1994; Gorman & Pollitt, 1996; Seitz & Apfel, 1994). Early child care also can be an occasion for substantial parent education provided in a supportive, interactive manner and focusing on concrete problems of child rearing. The findings of Seitz and Apfel (1994) suggest that changes in the caregiving environment resulting from early family support lead to benefits for all children within a family. Although early intervention programs alone will not compensate for the effects of early disadvantage (Campbell & Ramey, 1994; Gorman & Pollitt, 1996; Lee et al., 1990; Ramey et al., 1992), those that combine early intervention with long-term, continuing, age-appropriate assistance produce the most significant and enduring cognitive gains (see Gomby et al., 1995, for a review).

## CONCLUSION

Research that has been compiled over the last two decades indicates that there are numerous potential hazards to cognitive growth. A child's cognitive development may be significantly impaired by organic influences such as malnutrition, disease, drug-abuse, and environmental toxins that threaten the child's health, as well as by exposure to abusive, neglectful, or deprived social environments. Unfortunately, children who grow up in deprived living conditions frequently are exposed to multiple, overlapping hazards that persist over time (Thompson, 1997). Children with serious cognitive deficits often live in environments that provide insufficient nutrition and stimulation, that are dangerous, and that expose them to drugs, alcohol, or other toxins prenatally. Any one of these hazards may affect a child's cognitive development. When they exist simultaneously and persist over time, their effects on a child's developing brain may be significantly compounded.

Although much remains to be learned about the extent to which specific negative environmental factors exert their influence on cognitive functioning and about the effects of specific early interventions, the literature points to several broad-scale efforts that are critical to prevent or minimize cognitive delays (see Thompson, 1997, for a review). Such efforts include, at a minimum,

- interventions designed to promote adequate prenatal care;
- interventions to provide supplemental nourishment to children and families living in poor communities;
- programs intended to rid communities of environmental toxins;
- home visitation and parent education programs to help to ensure that children are reared in safe, nurturing, and stimulating environments; and
- high-quality educational programs that begin early and provide age-appropriate stimulation to children over an extended period of time.

As the drafters of Article 27 recognized, failure to ensure a minimally adequate environment for children may have profound and lasting effects on children's cognitive development.

## REFERENCES

American Psychological Association (APA) Task Force on Pediatric AIDS. (1989). *American Psychologist, 44*, 258–264.

Barrett, D. E., Radke-Yarrow, M., & Klein, R. E. (1982). Chronic malnutrition and child behavior: Effects of early caloric supplementation on social and emotional functioning at school age. *Developmental Psychology, 18*, 541–556.

Bellinger, D., Leviton, A., Waternaux, C., Needleman, H., & Rabinowitz, M. (1987). Longitudinal analysis of prenatal and postnatal lead exposure and early cognitive development. *New England Journal of Medicine, 316*, 1037–1043.

Bellinger, D., Sloman, J., Leviton, A., Rabinowitz, M., Needleman, H. L., & Waternaux, C. (1991). Low-level lead exposure and children's cognitive function in the preschool years. *Pediatrics, 87*, 219–227.

Boocock, S. S. (1995). Early childhood programs in other nations: Goals and outcomes. *The Future of Children, 5*, 94–114.

Bradley, R. H., Whiteside, L., Mundform, D. J., Casey, P. H., Kelleher, K. J., & Pope,

S. K. (1994). Contribution of early intervention and early caregiving experiences to resilience in low-birthweight, premature children living in poverty. *Journal of Clinical Child Psychology, 23,* 425–434.

Brazelton, T., Tronick, E., Lechtig, A., Lasky, R. E., & Klein, R. E. (1977). The behavior of nutritionally deprived Guatemalan infants. *Developmental Medicine and Child Neurology, 19,* 364–372.

Brooks-Gunn, J., Klebanov, P. K., & Duncan, G. J. (1996). Ethnic differences in children's intelligence test scores: Role of economic deprivation, home environment, and maternal characteristics. *Child Development, 67,* 396–408.

Browne, A. & Finkelhor, D. (1986). Impact of child sexual abuse: A review of the research. *Psychological Bulletin, 99,* 66–77.

Campbell, F. A. & Ramey, C. T. (1994). Effects of early intervention on intellectual and academic achievement: A follow-up study of children from low-income families. *Child Development, 65,* 684–698.

Caughy, M. O., Di Pietro, J. A., & Strobino, D. M. (1994). Day-care participation as a protective factor in the cognitive development of low-income children. *Child Development, 65,* 457–471.

Chamberlain, M. C., Nichols, S. L., & Chase, C. H. (1991). Pediatric AIDS: Comparative cranial MRI and CT scans. *Pediatric Neurology, 7,* 357–362.

Chandy, J. M., Blum, R. W., & Resnick, M. D. (1996). Female adolescents with a history of sexual abuse: Risk outcome and protective factors. *Journal of Interpersonal Violence, 11,* 503–518.

Chatkupt, S., Mintz, M., Epstein, L. G., Bhansali, D., & Koenigsberger, M. R. (1989). Neuroimaging studies in children with human immunodeficiency virus type 1 infection. *Annals of Neurology, 26,* 453.

Cohen, F. L. (1993). Epidemiology of HIV infection and AIDS in children. In F. L. Cohen & J. D. Durham (Eds.), *Women, children, and HIV/AIDS* (137–155). New York: Springer.

Coster, W., Gersten, M., Beeghly, M., & Cicchetti, D. (1989). Communicative functioning in maltreated toddlers. *Developmental Psychology, 25,* 1020–1029.

Cowan, M. W. (1979). The development of the brain. *Scientific American, 241,* 112–133.

Delaney-Black, V., Covington, C., Ostrea E., Jr., Romero, A., Baker, D., Tagle, M., Nordstrom-Klee, B., Silvestre, M. A., Angelilli, M. L., Hack, C., & Long, J. (1996). Prenatal cocaine and neonatal outcome: Evaluation of dose-response relationship. *Pediatrics, 98,* 735–740.

Denson, R., Nanson, J. L., & McWatters, M. A. (1975). Hyperkinesis and maternal smoking. *Canadian Psychiatric Association Journal, 20,* 183–187.

De Paul, J. & Arruabarrena, M. I. (1995). Behavior problems in school-aged physically abused and neglected children in Spain. *Child Abuse and Neglect, 19,* 409–418.

Dietrich, K. N., Krafft, K. M., Bornschein, R. L., Hammond, P. B., Berger, O., Succop, P. A., & Bier, M. (1987). Low-level fetal lead exposure effect on neurobehavioral development in early infancy. *Pediatrics, 80,* 721–730.

Duncan, G. J., Brooks-Gunn, J., & Klebanov, P. K. (1994). Economic deprivation and early childhood development. *Child Development, 65,* 296–318.

Duncan, G. J., Yeung, W., Brooks-Gunn, J., & Smith, J. R. (1988). How much does childhood poverty affect the life chances of children? *American Sociological Review, 63,* 406–423.

Dwyer, J. T. (1996). Commentary: Nutrition: Essential ingredient for child development.

*Social policy report: Society for research in child development*, (Vol. 10). Ann Arbor, MI: Society for Research in Child Development.

Eckenrode, J., Laird, M., & Doris, J. (1993). School performance and disciplinary problems among abused and neglected children. *Developmental Psychology, 29*, 53–63.

Egeland, B., Sroufe, L. A., & Erickson, M. F. (1983). The developmental consequences of different patterns of maltreatment. *Child Abuse & Neglect, 7*, 459–469.

Erickson, M. F., Egeland, B., & Pianta, R. (1989). The effects of maltreatment on the development of young children. In D. Cicchetti & V. Carlson (Eds.), *Child maltreatment: Theory and research on the causes and consequences of child abuse and neglect* (647–684). New York: Cambridge University Press.

Estrada, P., Arsenio, W. F., Hess, R. D., & Holloway, S. D. (1987). Affective quality of the mother-child relationship: Longitudinal consequences for children's school-relevant cognitive functioning. *Developmental Psychology, 23*, 210–215.

Fantuzzo, J. W. (1990). Behavioral treatment of the victims of child abuse and neglect. *Behavior Modification, 14*, 316–339.

Flavell, J. (1985). *Cognitive development* (2nd ed.). Englewood Cliffs, NJ: Prentice-Hall, Inc.

Fogelman, K. (1980). Smoking in pregnancy and subsequent development of the child. *Child: Care, Health, and Development, 6*, 233–251.

Fox, N. A., Calkins, S. D., & Bell, M. A. (1994). Neural plasticity and development in the first two years of life: Evidence from cognitive and socioemotional domains of research. *Development and Psychopathology, 6*, 677–696.

Fried, P. A. & Watkinson, B. (1988). 12- and 24-month neurobehavioral follow-up of children prenatally exposed to marijuana, cigarettes and alcohol. *Neurotoxicology and Teratology, 10*, 305.

Fried, P. A. & Watkinson, B. (1990). 36- and 48-month neurobehavioral follow-up of children prenatally exposed to marijuana, cigarettes, and alcohol. *Journal of Developmental and Behavioral Pediatrics, 11*, 49.

Friedrich, W. N., Einbender, A., & Luecke, W. (1983). Cognitive and behavioral characteristics of physically abused children. *Journal of Consulting and Clinical Psychology, 51*, 313–314.

Galler, J. R., Ramsey, F., Solimano, G., Kucharski, L. T., & Harrison, R. (1984). The influence of early malnutrition on subsequent behavioral development: IV. Soft neurological signs. *Pediatric Research, 18*, 826–832.

Gomby, D. S., Larner, M. B., Stevenson, C. S., Lewitt, E. M., & Behrman, R. E. (1995). Long-term outcomes of early childhood programs: Analysis and recommendations. *The Future of Children, 5*, 6–24.

Gorman, K. S. & Pollitt, E. (1996). Does schooling buffer the effects of early risk? *Child Development, 67*, 314–326.

Greenfield, P. M. (1984). A theory of the teacher in the learning activities of everyday life. In B. Rogoff & J. Lave (Eds.), *Everyday cognition: Its development in social context* (117–138). Cambridge, MA: Harvard University Press.

Greenough, W. T. & Black, J. E. (1992). Induction of brain structure by experience: Substrates for cognitive development. In M. R. Gunnar & C. A. Nelson (Eds.), *Minnesota Symposium on Child Psychology* (155–200). Hillsdale, NJ: Erlbaum.

Henggeler, S. W., Melton, G. B., & Rodrigue, J. R. (1992). *Pediatric and adolescent*

*AIDS: Research findings from the social sciences.* Newbury Park, CA: Sage Publications.

Hicks, L. E., Langham, R. A., & Takenaka, J. (1982). Cognitive and health measures following early nutritional supplementation: A sibling study. *American Journal of Public Health, 72,* 1110–1118.

Hoffman-Plotkin, D. & Twentyman, C. T. (1984). A multimodal assessment of behavioral and cognitive deficits in abused and neglected preschoolers. *Child Development, 55,* 794–802.

Holzman, C. & Paneth, N. (1994). Maternal cocaine use during pregnancy and perinatal outcomes. *Epidemiologic Reviews, 16,* 315–334.

Jacobson, J. L., Jacobson, S. W., & Humphrey, H. E. B. (1990). Effects of in utero exposure to polychlorinated biphenyls on cognitive functioning in young children. *Journal of Pediatrics, 116,* 38–45.

Jacobson, J. L., Jacobson, S. W., Padgett, R. J., Brumitt, G. A., & Billings, R. L. (1992). Effects of prenatal PCB exposure on cognitive processing efficiency and sustained attention. *Developmental Psychology, 28,* 297–306.

Kaye, K., Elkind, L., Goldberg, D., & Tytun, A. (1989). Birth outcomes for infants of drug abusing mothers. *New York State Journal of Medicine, 89,* 256–261.

Kendall-Tackett, K. (1997). Timing of academic difficulties for neglected and nonmaltreated males and females. *Child Abuse & Neglect, 9,* 885–887.

Kendall-Tackett, K. A. & Eckenrode, J. (1996). The effect of neglect on academic achievement and disciplinary problems: A developmental perspecive. *Child Abuse & Neglect, 20,* 161–169.

Kerouac, S., Taggart, M. E., Lescop, J., & Fortin, M. F. (1986). Dimensions of health in violent families. *Health Care for Women International, 7,* 413–426.

Kolbo, J. R., Blakely, E. H., & Engleman, D. (1996). Children who witness domestic violence: A review of empirical literature. *Journal of Interpersonal Violence, 11,* 281–293.

Koos, B. J. & Longo, L. D. (1980). Mercury toxicity in the pregnant woman, fetus, and newborn infant. *American Journal of Obstetrics/Gynecology, 126,* 390–400.

Kopp, C. B. (1983). Risk factors in development. In P. H. Mussen (Ed.), *Handbook of child development: Vol. 2. Infancy and developmental psychobiology.* New York: Wiley.

Kopp, C. B. & Parmalee, A. H. (1979). Prenatal and perinatal influences on behavior. In J. D. Osofsky (Ed.), *Handbook of infant development.* New York: Wiley.

Korenman, S., Miller, J. E., & Sjaastad, J. E. (1995). Long-term poverty and child development in the United States: Results from the National Longitudinal Survey of Youth. *Children and Youth Services Review, 17,* 127–151.

Lee, V. E., Brooks-Gunn, J., Schnur, E., & Liaw, F. R. (1990). Are Head Start effects sustained? A longitudinal follow-up comparison of disadvantaged children attending Head Start, no preschool, and other preschool programs. *Child Development, 61,* 495–507.

Leiter, J. & Johnsen, M. C. (1994). Child maltreatment and school performance. *American Journal of Education, 102,* 154–189.

Lester, B. M. (1975). Cardiac habituation of the orienting response to an auditory signal in infants of varying nutritional status. *Developmental Psychology, 11,* 432–442.

Maslow, A. H. (1970). *Motivation and personality.* New York: Harper & Row.

Maxfield, M. & Widom, C. (1996). The cycle of violence: Revisited 6 years later. *Archives of Pediatric Adolescent Medicine, 150*, 390–395.

McDonald, M. A., Sigman, M., Espinosa, M. P., & Neumann, C. G. (1994). Impact of a temporary food shortage on children and their mothers. *Child Development, 65*, 404–415.

McMichael, A. J., Baghurst, P. A., Wigg, N. R., Vimpani, G. V., Robertson, E. F., & Roberts, R. J. (1988). Port Pirie Cohort Study: Environmental exposure to lead and children's abilities at the age of four years. *New England Journal of Medicine, 319*, 468–475.

Mole, R. H. (1987). Irradition of the embryo and fetus. *The British Journal of Radiology, 60*, 17–31.

Moore, J. G., Galcius, A., & Pettican, K. (1981). Emotional risk to children caught in violent marital conflict—the Basildon treatment. *Child Abuse and Neglect, 5*, 147–152.

Morgan, B. & Gibson, K. R. (1991). Nutritional and environmental interactions in brain development. In K. R. Gibson & A. C. Petersen (Eds.), *Brain maturation and cognitive development* (91–106). New York: Aldine deGruyter.

Morgane, P. J., Austin-LaFrance, R., Bronzino, J., Tonkiss, J., Díaz-Cintra, S., Cintra, L., Kemper, T., & Galler, J. R. (1993). Prenatal malnutrition and development of the brain. *Neuroscience and Biobehavioral Reviews, 17*, 91–128.

Moroney, J. T. & Allen, M. H. (1994). Cocaine and alcohol use in pregnancy. In O. Devinsky, F. Feldmann, & B. Hainline (Eds.), *Neurological complications of pregnancy* (231–242). New York: Raven Press.

Needleman, H. L., Gunnoe, C., Leviton, A., Reed, R., Peresie, H., Maher, C., & Barret, P. (1979). Deficits in psychologic and classroom performance of children with elevated dentine lead levels. *The New England Journal of Medicine, 300*, 689–695.

Needleman, H. L., Schell, A., Bellinger, D., Leviton, A., & Allred, E. N. (1990). The long-term effects of exposure to low doses of lead in childhood: An 11-year follow-up report. *The New England Journal of Medicine, 322*, 83–88.

Newson, J. & Newson, E. (1975). Intersubjectivity and the transmission of culture: On the social origins of symbolic functioning. *Bulletin of the British Psychological Society, 28*, 437–446.

Palti, H., Meijer, A., & Adler, B. (1985). Learning achievement and behavior at school of anemic and non-anemic infants. *Early Human Development, 10*, 217–223.

Peckham, C. S. & Logan, S. (1993). Screening for toxoplasmosis during pregnancy. *Archives of Disease in Childhood, 68*, 3–5.

Phillips, A. D., Voran, M., Kisker, E., Howes, C., & Whitebook, M. (1994). Child care for children in poverty: Opportunity or inequity. *Child Development, 65*, 472–492.

Piaget, J. (1952). *The origins of intelligence in children*. New York: International Universities Press.

Pollitt, E. (1994). Poverty and child development: Relevance of research in developing countries to the United States. *Child Development, 65*, 283–295.

Pollitt, E., Golub, M., Gorman, K., Grantham-McGregor, S., Levitsky, D., Schürch, B., Strupp, B., & Wachs, T. (1996). A reconceptualization of the effects of under-nutrition on children's biological, psychosocial, and behavioral development. *So-*

*cial policy report: Society for research in child development* (Vol. 10). Ann Arbor, MI: Society for Research in Child Development.

Qazi, Q. H., Sheikh, T. M., Fikrig, S., & Menikoff, H. (1988). Lack of evidence for craniofacial dysmorphism in perinatal human immunodeficiency virus infection. *Journal of Pediatrics, 112*, 7–11.

Ramey, C. T., Bryant, D. M., Wasik, B. H., Sparling, J. J., Fendt, K. H., & LaVange, L. M. (1992). Infant Health and Development Program for low birth weight premature infants: Program elements, family participation, and child intelligence. *Pediatrics, 3*, 454–465.

Richters, J. E. & Martinez, P. E. (1993). Violent communities, family choices, and children's chances: An algorithm for improving the odds. *Development and Psychopathology, 5*, 609–627.

Rogoff, B. (1990). Apprenticeship in thinking: Cognitive development in social context. New York: Oxford University Press.

Rogoff, B. (1998). Cognition as a collaborative process. In D. Kuhn & R. S. Siegler (Eds.), *Handbook of child psychology* (5th ed), vol. 2: *Cognition, perception, and language* (pp. 679–744). New York: John Wiley and Sons.

Rogoff, B., Mistry, J., Göncü, & Mosier, C. (1993). Guided participation in cultural activity by toddlers and caregivers. *Monographs of the Society for Research in Child Development, 58* (8, Serial No. 236).

Salzinger, S., Kaplan, S., Pelcovitz, D., Samit, C., & Krieger, R. (1984). Parent and teacher assessment of children's behavior in child maltreating families. *Journal of the American Academy of Child Psychiatry, 23*, 458–464.

Sameroff, A. J. (1986). Environmental context of child development. *Journal of Pediatrics, 109*, 192–200.

Samson, L. F. (1988). Perinatal viral infections and neonates. *Journal of Perinatal Neonatal Nursing, 1*, 56–65.

Schull, W. J. & Otake, M. (1986). Neurological deficit among the survivors exposed in utero to the atomic bombing of Hiroshima and Nagasaki: A reassessment and new directions. In H. Kriegel, W. Schmahl, G. B. Gerber, & F. E. Stieve (Eds.), *Radiation risks to the developing nervous system.* New York: Gustav Fischer.

Seitz, V. & Apfel, N. H. (1994). Parent-focused intervention: Diffusion effects on siblings. *Child Development, 65*, 666–676.

Sever, J. L. (1983). Maternal infections. In C. C. Brown (Ed.), *Childhood learning disabilities and prenatal risk* (31–38). New York: Johnson & Johnson.

Shaheen, S. J. (1984). Neuromaturation and behavior development: The case of childhood lead poisoning. *Developmental Psychology, 20*, 542–550.

Siegel, I. E. (1982). The relationship between parental distancing strategies and the child's cognitive behavior. In L. M. Laosa & I. E. Siegel (Eds.), *Families as learning environments for children* (47–86). New York: Plenum.

Sigman, M., McDonald, M. A., Neumann, C., & Bwibo, N. (1991). Prediction of cognitive competence in Kenyan children from toddler nutrition, family characteristics and abilities. *Journal of Child Psychology and Psychiatry, 32*, 307–320.

Simeon, D. T. & Grantham-McGregor, S. (1990). Nutritional deficiencies and children's behavior and mental development. *Nutrition Research Reviews, 3*, 1–24.

Smith, J. R., Brooks-Gunn, J., & Klebanov, P. (1997). The consequences of living in poverty for young children's cognitive and verbal ability and early school achievement. In G. J. Duncan & J. Brooks-Gunn (Eds.), *Consequences of growing up poor*. New York: Russell Sage Foundation.

Streissguth, A. P., Landesman-Dwyer, S., Martin, D. C., & Smith, D. W. (1984). Teratogenic effects of alcohol in humans and laboratory animals. *Science, 209,* 353–361.

Streissguth, A. P., Martin, D. C., Barr, H. M., Sandman, B., Kirchner, G., & Darby, B. (1984). Intrauterine alcohol and nicotine exposure: Attention and reaction time in 4-year-old children. *Developmental Psychology, 20,* 533–541.

Teberg, A. J., Walther, F. J., & Pena, I. C. (1988). Mortality, morbidity, and outcome of the small-for-gestational age infant. *Seminars in Perinatology, 12,* 84–94.

Thompson, R. A. (1997). *Early brain development and early intervention*. Unpublished manuscript.

U.S. Department of Health and Human Services. (1993). National household survey on drug abuse: Main Findings 1991. DHHS Publication No. (SMA) 93–1980. Rockville, MD: Author.

Vorhees, C. V. (1986). Principles of behavioral teratology. In E. P. Riley & C. V. Vorhees (Eds.), *Handbook of behavioral teratology* (23–48). New York: Plenum.

Vygotsky, L. S. (1933/1978). *Mind in society: The development of higher psychological processes*. Cambridge, MA: Harvard University Press.

Wasserman, G., Graziano, J. H., Factor-Litvak, P., Popovuc, D., Moriana, N., Musabegovic, A., Vrenezi, N., Capuni-Paracka, S., Lekic, V., Preteni-Redjepi, E., Hadzialjevic, S., Slavkovich, V., Kline, J., Shrove, P., and Stein, Z. (1992). Independent effects of lead exposure and iron deficiency anemia on developmental outcome at age 2 years. *Journal of Pediatrics, 121,* 695–703.

Watkins, W. E. & Pollitt, E. (1997). "Stupidity or worms": Do intestinal worms impair mental performance? *Psychological Bulletin, 121,* 171–191.

Wechsler, D. (1975). Intelligence defined and undefined: A relativistic appraisal. *American Psychologist, 30,* 135–139.

Werner, E. E. (1990). Protective factors and individual resilience. In S. J. Meisels & J. P. Shonkoff (Eds.), *Handbook of early childhood intervention*. New York: Cambridge University Press.

Westra, B. & Martin, H. P. (1981). Children of battered women. *Maternal-Child Nursing Journal, 10,* 41–55.

Wildin, S. R., Williamson, W. D., & Wilson, G. S. (1991). Children of battered women: Developmental and learning profiles. *Clinical Pediatrics, 30,* 299–304.

Winick, M. (1976). *Malnutrition and brain development*. New York: Oxford University Press.

Winick, M., Meyer, K., & Harris, R. (1975). Malnutrition and environmental enrichment by early adoption. *Science, 190,* 1173–1175.

Wodarski, J. S., Kurtz, P. D., Gaudin, J. M., & Howing, P. T. (1990). Maltreatment and the school age child: Major academic, socioemotional, and adaptive outcomes. *Social Work, 35,* 506–513.

Wolf, A. W., Jimenez, E., & Lozoff, B. (1994). No evidence of developmental ill effects of low-level lead exposure in a developing country. *Developmental and Behavioral Pediatrics, 15,* 224–231.

Wood, D., Bruner, J. S., & Ross, G. (1976). The role of tutoring in problem solving. *Journal of Child Psychology and Psychiatry, 17,* 89–100.

Zeskind, P. S. & Ramey, C. T. (1978). Fetal malnutrition: An experimental study of its consequences in two caregiving environments. *Child Development, 49,* 1155–1162.

Zeskind, P. S. & Ramey, C. T. (1981). Preventing intellectual and interactional sequelae of fetal malnutrition: A longitudinal, transactional and synergistic approach to development. *Child Development, 52,* 213–218.

# 7

# A Standard of Living Adequate for Children's Spiritual Development

## Ross A. Thompson and Brandy Randall

The obligation enunciated in Article 27 of the U.N. *Convention on the Rights of the Child* that "States Parties recognize the right of every child to a standard of living adequate for the child's . . . spiritual . . . development" poses challenges to developmental psychology and to public policy. To the former, such an obligation highlights how little systematic attention has been devoted to matters of spiritual growth by developmental researchers. Little is known even of how to conceptualize what spiritual development constitutes and the influences that guide its growth. Although there are a number of interesting theoretical perspectives to the growth of religious understanding and faith development, very little research has been oriented toward testing and elucidating these provocative viewpoints. This makes it difficult to conceptualize how spiritual awareness changes in an age-related manner or to define "adequate" spiritual development and its setting conditions.

To public policy makers, the mandate to ensure children's adequate spiritual development—like several others articulated in the U.N. *Convention*—entails a fundamental confrontation between respect for diverse worldwide sociocultural and religious traditions and the responsibilities that are potentially involved in ensuring children's universal right to adequate spiritual development. Given that alternative religious traditions embrace not only different world-views but also different portrayals of the requirements of religious observance—including, for example, different emphases on unquestioning obedience to authority, conscience-guided moral action, or right behavior guided by the pursuit of nirvana—is it possible to identify features of spiritual development that transcend specific religious traditions and cultures? Typically, developmental theorists have sought to identify universal processes of growth that are applicable regardless of cultural context, although recently sociocultural theories of development have emphasized how context-bound are many aspects of human growth (see Cole, 1992; Rogoff, 1990). Should conceptualizations of spiritual development be likewise framed in terms of broadly applicable psychosocial processes or, instead, more parochially in terms of the belief systems of each particular culture? In other words, is spiritual "adequacy" defined exclusively in the terms of a specific religious belief system, or are there broader, overarching influences that merit consideration regardless of religious values?

These are difficult questions, especially in light of our limited knowledge of the nature of spiritual development over the course of life. The purpose of this chapter is to frame some of the central developmental questions that are involved in considering what a standard of living "adequate" for spiritual development might include. We turn first to a discussion of the nature of spiritual development as it is portrayed by major theories of human growth and derivative research. Afterward, we consider more briefly, and speculatively, what that "adequate" standard of living for spiritual development might include.

## SPIRITUAL DEVELOPMENT

The concept of "spiritual development" seems initially simple and straightforward, but becomes increasingly complex as it is conceptually unpacked. The latter task requires distinguishing spiritual development from the allied (but sometimes uncorrelated) concepts of faith development and the growth of religious understanding. It involves considering the significance of spiritual development in terms of its broader correlates. Most important, unpacking the concept of "spiritual development" requires a developmental analysis in which major influences on spiritual reflection—arising from the conscious and unconscious effects of life experience, and involving concurrent growth in cognition, morality, and other developmental processes—are considered individually and in concert.

### *Spiritual* Development

The terms "spiritual development," "faith development," and "development of religious understanding" have different meanings, but are often used interchangeably by researchers and theorists from various academic fields. Our interest in spiritual development concerns the broad search for transcendental meaning that may be as simple as a young child's inquiries into how the world came into being or as complex as a theologian's metaphysical analysis. In this regard, spiritual development can be a life-long process that is related to, but distinct from, growth in intelligence, morality, ego processes, social relationships, and other facets of human development. It is, in fact, difficult to consider spiritual development independently of concurrent developmental advances that enable children to think more incisively, become more thoughtfully self-aware, engage in more deliberative moral judgment, and mature in other ways that influence spiritual reflection. One way that spiritual development is distinctive, however, is that although it entails fundamental human questions that most people encounter at some time in life, there is no necessary or inevitable process of spiritual growth paralleling maturational phases of physical, emotional, or cognitive development that all people experience. The nature of any individual's spiritual reflection, and changes in this reflective process over time, are contingent on life experience and the catalysts provided by others in the family, community, and culture. As a consequence, while some have described stages and sequences of spiritual development that become possible with the emergence of new capacities for intellectual and moral reasoning with advancing age (e.g., Fowler, 1981, 1991; Oser, 1991), most agree that there is no inevitable impetus propelling advances in spiritual reflection with increasing age. Within certain limitations, it is possible to consider individuals who are spiritual naifs and sages at almost any stage of life, based on their life experience.

Conceived in this way, spiritual development is associated with, but not the same as, "faith development" and "development of religious understanding." Faith development has been defined in various ways (Fowler's [1981, 1991] portrayal of faith development is, for instance, similar to the definition of spiritual development presented above), but is commonly described in terms of the growing sophistication of belief in a divinity. The development of religious understanding involves, in turn, an individual's progressive adherence to a propositional network of values, creeds, and practices of organized religion. Spiritual development often incorporates faith development and religious understanding, but it need not always do so. Individuals can engage in spiritual reflection outside of the teachings of organized religion, and often without reference to deity. It is important, for example, to recognize that atheist and agnostic spiritual reflection is an increasing feature of postmodern Western culture.

Viewed in this manner, it is also easy to see how spiritual development is closely tied to the mainstream beliefs and values of the culture, and also to the pluralism of beliefs that exist within society. One individual's search for life's personal meaning may be guided by traditional religious creeds, while another's may be forged from various value systems from the majority culture and/or alternative world-views. One important question concerning the U.N. *Convention* mandate is whether adequate spiritual development requires only the catalysts that are important to an individual's growth within a particular religious tradition (quite often, the mainstream belief system conveyed by parents), or whether an acquaintance with multiple belief systems is necessary for an individual's personal beliefs to be truly self-chosen and refined by exposure to alternative views.

Is spiritual development necessarily a positive influence on psychosocial growth? Although there is little good research on this issue, there has been somewhat greater attention to the controversial and richly debated topic of whether religious belief leavens society with positive values or is instead an institutionalized means of social control (''the opiate of the masses''). Religion has the potential to influence individuals in a variety of ways, of course, and it is therefore perhaps unsurprising that research has revealed a variety of consequences of religious belief. Among its positive correlates is enhanced volunteer activity (Maton & Wells, 1995), happiness (Myers, 1993), and well-being (Poloma & Pendleton, 1990). For example, Donahue and Benson (1995) found that, for adolescents, religiousness was negatively associated with delinquency, substance abuse, suicidal ideation, suicide attempts, and premature sexual involvement, and was positively associated with prosocial values and behavior. Other researchers have, on the other hand, found that religious belief is associated with enhanced prejudice and authoritarianism.

Studies such as these are helpful in appreciating that as religious beliefs become incorporated into a person's broader outlook and values, they can serve diverse purposes. But inquiring whether religious belief generally serves prosocial or antisocial purposes may be asking the wrong question. From a developmental perspective, of course, individuals vary in the maturity of their religious outlook, and this may significantly mediate the impact of religion on their attitudes and behavior. Leak and Randall (1995) differentiated between adults with a relatively immature religious outlook (based on such things as adherence to orthodoxy) and those with a relatively mature religious outlook (stemming from processes such as reflection on one's religious faith). Independent measures of authoritarianism were positively correlated with relatively immature religiosity and negatively correlated with the more mature form of religiousness. This suggests that it is not religion per se, but rather the extent to which religious values grow and mature in accord with the developing personality that helps to determine its impact on attitudes and behavior.

Religion may also be important not only because of its effects on individuals, but also on social institutions and on society at large. Churches have historically assumed quite complex roles in social beneficence and social authority; for example, many are currently involved in family support, personal counseling, community development, and remedial education programs in which volunteers are enlisted together with paraprofessionals in social service.

Taken together, the complex correlates of religion underscore that religious understanding is shaped by idiosyncratic life experience as well as maturing reflective capacities. Consequently, the impact of religion is likely to be contingent on the broader belief structures and personality processes that provide a personal context for religious understanding. Among the more important influences on religious understanding are developmental changes in reasoning, self-understanding, and moral judgment that shape a child's growing sense of self in relation to others and to ultimate concerns. We now turn to such questions of the origins of spiritual development.

## Spiritual *Development*

Spiritual development invites reflections on the transcendental and the metaphysical, on values that arise from fundamental propositions concerning human character and existence, as well as on specific religious practices and symbols. As a topic of psychological development, however, spiritual growth is fundamentally tied to questions of ultimate concern that children can conceive and articulate early in life, and ponder in more complex ways with increasing age. These questions include:

- What is the meaning or purpose of [my] life?
- Who am I? Why am I here?
- What is my future? How is that future shaped?
- What defines the differences between right and wrong? Why does egregious wrong occur in the world? What does it mean to do right? Why should I act rightly?

Spiritual development is connected to children's efforts to understand the meaning and causes of life experience. Consequently, encounters with serious injury or illness (of oneself or a close friend or relative), death, social injustice, poverty, a new birth in the family, parental divorce or remarriage, abuse, or troubled family relationships can provoke reflections associated with spiritual values and concerns. For many children, these questions are conceived and addressed within specific religious traditions conveyed by the family and community, but as noted earlier, children and adults also create their own answers outside of a given tradition, whether they are taught specific religious values or none at all.

*Constructivism.* In this light, the most appropriate orientation to the study of spiritual development is constructivism. Inspired initially by Piaget's seminal cognitive developmental studies, the constructivist orientation to conceptual development regards the growth of knowledge as an interaction between the knower and the known (see Piaget, 1952; also Flavell, 1963). Consequently, children are never viewed as passively absorbing the knowledge and belief systems they are taught, even though these beliefs may be actively socialized by parents, teachers, and other adult authorities. Instead, their internalization of religious beliefs occurs as these ideas are filtered by the child's capacities for understanding and interpreting what they are told, as well as the child's idiosyncratic needs and concerns arising from personal life experience.

In this view, therefore, the meaning to a child of a parable, didactic teaching, or other religious lesson depends significantly on the child's conceptual capabilities, as well as the child's personal questions and concerns. For example, the story of Moses speaking with God at the burning bush within the Judeo-Christian tradition is likely to mean much different things to children of different

ages. To a preschooler, the story is likely to be literally and concretely interpreted as a miracle in history or a fantastic event, provoking questions about
fire and burning (and perhaps inviting reference to fireplace devices or fire departments), where the voice came from and what it sounded like, and related
descriptive elements of the narrative. To a grade-schooler, the significance of
the story may reside more in its broader lessons concerning obedience to divine
commands, inviting parallels to authority relations they experience personally in
their encounters with parents, teachers, and others. To a young adult, the symbolic meaning of a bush that is ''burning but not consumed'' can be comprehended in terms of abstract concepts such as the holiness of the ordinary, or
perhaps reinterpreted mythically in terms of the psychological needs of the early
Hebrew community. From a constructivist orientation, therefore, the meaning
of a religious lesson is contingent in the interpretive capacities of the listener.
These interpretive capacities not only vary developmentally, but also individually among children of any particular age. To a young child who is struggling
with the inability to hear an articulate message from God, or to an adolescent
grappling with questions of personal identity or life's mission, this story may
have much different meaning than to other children of the same age for whom
these are not relevant personal concerns.

There are thus several potentially valuable perspectives afforded by a constructivist orientation to spiritual development. First, it offers a reminder that
the meaning of religious lessons is likely to be much different to child listeners
of various ages than to the adult teachers who intend to impart specific values
and ideas. Unless adults are sensitive to how religious teaching is likely to be
interpreted by young listeners, they may fail to impart the lessons they intend
and, instead, may inadvertently mislead, frighten, or demean their young audience by stories or maxims that are perceived differently by the listeners than by
the teachers. It is not only the vivid imagery of heaven or damnation that may
mislead or frighten, but also well-known stories of faith that, because they are
so familiar to adults, may have an unexpected impact when they are first heard
by young children. Within the Judeo-Christian tradition, for example, the story
of Abraham's intended sacrifice of Isaac can raise frightening questions of the
reliability of parental care, while the story of Daniel's testing of faith in the
lion's den can cause young listeners to anxiously question how they would
respond if similarly tried. Within the Islamic tradition, the gravity of obedience
to Allah in thought as well as deed can have similarly frightening implications
to young children.

Second, the constructivist perspective underscores that children forge spiritual
concepts from reflection on personal experience, deriving lessons that are often
independent of the explicit religious traditions in which they are raised. Sometimes these personal concerns are developmentally graded, such as the focus on
understanding authority relations of the preschool years, a concern with reciprocity in interpersonal (especially peer) relationships during the grade-school
years, and with identity in adolescence. But quite often the experiences prompt-

ing spiritual reflection are idiosyncratic, based on the constellation of changes and challenges with which an individual child is coping. At root, this means that spiritual issues are likely to be experienced much differently by children than doctrinal creeds provide: the God of organized religion is likely to be much different than the subjective reality of the divine experienced by children of various ages. The character of God that children thus construct from personal life experience may thus be friendly or fearful, an ally or a critic, a source of encouragement or of guilt or fear, a moral guide or an elusive spectre, a warm parent or a stern disciplinarian in ways that may vary significantly from the religious traditions within which the child is raised.

Third, the constructivist orientation emphasizes the dynamic qualities of spiritual development, particularly the likelihood of changes in religious or spiritual outlook with increasing age, conceptual competency, and growing experience. Although this seems obvious from a developmental viewpoint, it means that the religious concepts forged (and taught) in the early years of life are likely to be significantly reinterpreted, reconstructed, and reintegrated with increasing life experience in subsequent years, resulting in meaning that is much different than what it was initially. In this sense, religious and spiritual development is not the progressive acceptance of a static belief system, but rather the evolving understanding of self in relation to matters of ultimate concern.

*Constructivism in a Social Context.* Constructivist perspectives to conceptual development also emphasize the importance of shared social activity to the construction of a child's knowledge and beliefs (influenced by the revival of scholarly interest in the work of Vygotsky [1962]). In the words of Rogoff (1990), children are "apprentices in thinking" whose conceptual growth is fostered by their shared experiences with a skilled, more mature mentor. In these shared experiences, the mentor (who can be a parent, teacher, older sibling, or other more mature partner) imparts cultural skills and knowledge in the context of everyday activities in which the child is allowed to participate with the guidance of the mentor. These kinds of shared, everyday activities are familiar to most parents and teachers: In the course of meal preparation, yard work, recreational activities, gardening, and other activities the child is provided with assistance in acquiring necessary skills and performing them competently, whether the skills concern measuring and pouring, reading or counting, classification or sorting, or identifying or discriminating. In a similar manner, in most cultures children are also apprentices in the rites and rituals of religious observance, and in their guided participation with adults they learn the skills pertinent to full membership in a faith community, whether this involves mastering the vocabulary of religious practices and creeds, contributing to service activities, grasping the rituals of personal and institutional observance, or participating in religious festivals or a *hajj* (pilgrimage) to Mecca.

According to Vygotskian theory, skilled mentors support the child's acquisition of culturally relevant knowledge and skills by providing activity at the child's "zone of proximal development," which is defined as the range of skills that the child can exercise with assistance but cannot perform independently (Vygotsky, 1962, 1933/1978). As adults carefully structure their shared activity, in other words, children are challenged to new achievements that they are almost ready to master but cannot yet perform competently on their own. Shared activity at the zone of proximal development can be observed in the manner in which a parent allows a young child to balance and steer increasingly on her own while learning to ride a bike, or how a teacher gradually encourages the child to sound out more difficult words while learning to read. It may also be revealed in how a parent or teacher fosters a young child's awareness of the divine by drawing on metaphors and experiences suitable for the child's age, or discusses the death of a beloved pet with a child in a manner that is well-suited to the child's comprehension of the reality of death as well as the beliefs of their religion.

Another feature of the shared activity that contributes to conceptual development in young children is how a skilled mentor fosters the child's mastery of the cultural tools that are relevant to the growth of understanding. These tools are part of any culture, and skill in their use is essential to the growth of further knowledge. They may include the mentor's efforts to assist a child in learning to use an alphabet, slide rule, abacus, or computer. In the context of religious understanding, cultural tools may consist of a religious text or catechism, or the language of religious instruction and discourse (such as Hebrew).

The portrayal of children as ''apprentices in thinking'' emphasizes how important to conceptual growth are the structured social activities in which children participate with adults. It is important to note, however, that children still construct their own meaning from such shared experiences, and their construals may be much different from the lessons intended by their adult mentors (Rogoff, 1990). Even so, the image of children acting side-by-side with a skilled mentor in carefully guided activities that foster their conceptual growth is a heuristically powerful complement to the traditional portrayal of an isolated child who constructs meaning from personal experiences alone. Although the constructivist approach has been usefully applied to research on children's cognitive growth (see Thompson [1997] for applications to early social development), there have been no efforts to apply this viewpoint to children's spiritual development. The potential value of doing so, however, is to understand the various ways that spiritual development is a socially-constructed process in which the young child's guided participation in religious observance with a sensitive mentor interacts with the child's interpretive capacities to shape understanding of issues of religion, faith, and self.

*Psychoanalytic Theory.* Constructivism offers a new way of conceptualizing spiritual development. The typical beginning of psychological inquiry into the development of spirituality, however, is the psychoanalytic view that connects religious faith to unconscious psychological structures. In *The Future of an Illusion*, Freud (1927) portrayed religious faith as a response to human helplessness in the face of life's mysteries and the inevitability of death by invoking deities that are created from childhood prototypes of parenting figures and Oedipal issues. Humans find illusory solace, he argued, in their creation of a father-like divinity who provides protection, but who must be propitiated and feared. Many psychoanalytic thinkers have subsequently adopted the Freudian view that religions are created out of the projection and sublimation of unconscious conflict and the superimposition of wish-fulfilling fantasies. Religion, in this view, creates a network of neurotic-like beliefs that promise relief from existential anxiety through divine care but also (like other kinds of psychopathology) remain resistant to rational refutation.

A related, but much different, perspective on religious faith comes from Jungian theory (e.g., Jung, 1933, 1938, 1947). Unlike Freud, Jung did not see religion as inherently neurotic. Rather, he believed that religion helps people to stay in contact with elements of the collective unconscious that might otherwise be out of balance with the ego. Religious experience helps those who have it to live better. Jung saw the ultimate goal of life as individuation, the realization of the self, which involves the reconciliation of the conscious with the unconscious to shift the center of the personality from the ego to the self. It is a process that is characteristic not of childhood or adolescence, but of adult maturity (Fuller, 1977). Jung believed that religious symbolism was actually a description of this process (e.g., the resurrection from death to life). Jung also felt that these religious symbols or myths were universal in nature.

There is considerable value to an appreciation that religious faith arises from conscious and unconscious needs (individuals as well as institutions create the divine and represent the cosmos in their own images, for instance), but more recent neoanalytic scholars have adopted somewhat more positive portrayals of the psychological development of religious faith. Rizuto (1979, 1991), for example, enlists object relations theory to argue that a "God representation" derives from early introjected objects and constitute an important part of phenomenological experience and self understanding, often independently of explicit religious traditions. To Rizuto and other scholars within the analytic tradition (e.g., Coles, 1990), spiritual development is part of the search for meaning in a life experience that is often characterized by paradox, inconsistency, and dilemma. She argues further that the psychological impulses leading to religious faith are the same that universally also contribute to both immature and mature human capacities to fantasize and symbolize in order to address the uncertainties remaining after rational reflection has finished. In this respect, religious and spiritual experiences entail the subjective attribution of meaning to events in light of one's personal psychological realities, which themselves change over time and contribute to an evolution of the "God representation" underlying personal experience.

*Cognitive Developmental Theory.* While psychoanalytic and neoanalytic formulations trace the earliest origins of spiritual or religious experience to the initial object relations of infancy (providing a preverbal and, of course, prepropositional foundation to religious development before the advent of an explicit religious knowledge system), they are largely nondevelopmental accounts. Religious belief derives primarily from unconscious processes and, to the extent that a healthy integration of dynamic processes underlying religiosity can occur, this is largely a feature of adulthood. By contrast, researchers inspired by Piagetian theory have examined the earliest cognitive foundations for religious thought in the intuitive and imaginative thinking of preschool children. In *The Child's Conception of the World*, Piaget (1929; see also Piaget, 1962) speculated about the preoperational intellectual foundations to certain forms of religious belief. One characteristic of a preschooler's thought, for example, is artificialism: the tendency to regard physical phenomena as the products of human creation for specific, anthropocentric purposes. As Piaget argued, young children may reach a stage of "mythological artificialism" when their concern about the origins of things confronts their awareness of the limitations of human agency, at which time concepts of the creation of the world by an omnipotent deity become constructed. Closely associated with cognitive artificialism is animism: the tendency to attribute human qualities (e.g., of life, consciousness, will) to inanimate, physical events. This, too, may become incorporated into religious belief systems (e.g., an understanding of the miraculous).

Two other attributes of preoperational thought in Piaget's theory are also relevant to the spiritual development of young children. One is egocentrism: the tendency to consider events narrowly from within one's personal perspective. Because of egocentrism, for example, understandings of divine action are construed in terms of the child's most immediate needs and concerns, and prayer is experienced in terms of petitionary wish-fulfillment. Another is *heteronomous respect*, an attribute of early moral understanding by which young children regard the demands of authorities as inviolable and unquestionable (Piaget, 1935). Such a view not only underlies the young child's regard for the importance of obedience to adult authorities, as Piaget noted, but may also assume a role in early beliefs concerning the necessity of obedience to God's wishes and demands. Similarly, as children gradually begin to conceive of morality in terms of the give-and-take of reciprocal relations and advance to a new conceptual understanding that Piaget termed *autonomous morality*, it is not difficult to see how concepts of fairness and reciprocity begin to influence children's conceptions of their relations to divinity also (cf. Fowler, 1981, 1991).

These Piagetian portrayals of the characteristics of early thought have inspired a number of direct applications to religious belief (e.g., Elkind, 1970). However, the current climate of research in early cognitive development has called into question Piaget's regard for the intuitive, illogical attributes of preoperational thinking, suggesting that he may have underestimated the intellectual sophistication of preschool thought (Flavell, Miller, & Miller, 1993). Inspired partly by recent research on young children's developing "theory of mind" (e.g., Astington, 1993; Wellman, 1990), for example, cognitive developmentalists have reconsidered the presumed egocentrism of young children, instead noting the acute insight that preschoolers often exhibit into the mental processes of others. Researchers have also questioned whether related features of early thought (e.g., animism, artificialism) derive from broad, structural limitations in the child's thinking or instead derive from limited knowledge or experience with natural phenomena. While this debate is not yet resolved, it suggests that a capacity exists for greater sophistication in the religious thought of young children than was previously acknowledged within the traditional Piagetian framework. At present, however, there have been no applications of these new formulations concerning young children's reasoning capacities to questions of spiritual development.

*Other Perspectives.* Inspired both by Piagetian stage theory and his broader constructivist orientation to the growth of knowledge, a number of students of religious development have described successive stages in the growth of spiritual understanding with increasing age (see, e.g., Meadow & Kahoe, 1984; Oser, 1991; Spilka, Hood, & Gorsuch, 1985). Perhaps the most influential of these has been offered by Fowler (1981, 1991), who has sought to integrate Piaget's views of cognitive development with Eriksonian psychosocial theory (Erikson, 1963) and the moral judgment theory of Kohlberg (1969, 1970) into a series of stages of "faith development." His stages are presented in Table 7.1. They reflect the influence of several developmental processes, including the growth of intellectual reasoning skills (primarily through the lens of Piaget's theory), the importance of early attachment relationships, the search for identity in the context of the abstract thinking of adolescence, as well as adult life stages and transitions. In Fowler's view, the earliest, undifferentiated faith experience of infancy is built upon secure attachment relationships, and a preschooler's experience of faith is rooted in the young child's imaginative, intuitive conceptual qualities. In the grade-school years, by contrast, faith is channeled into conventional religious values and personal understandings of right and wrong, which subsequently become questioned in adolescence. Fowler devotes considerably more attention to adult stages of faith development than do most other theorists, arguing that advances in spirituality entail reconciling the irrational and rational features of religious experience. Like most students of this topic, Fowler has tested his theory using both a series of structured interview questions and other interview procedures with a broad range of individuals ranging in age from 6 to 90, almost exclusively from Judeo-Christian backgrounds (see Table 7.1).

One important feature of Fowler's portrayal of faith development is its multirelational quality. In other words, "faith" (broadly conceived to encompass the human search for transcendent meaning) is not only a matter of how individuals conceive of their relations with the divine, but also of how they conceive the human relationships they share with other people. Moreover, according to Fowler, spiritual development is forged not only from the conceptual and psychosocial growth processes that enable more sophisticated representations of religious experience, but also from the teaching, support, and other catalysts provided by the human community in which people live. In its most positive contributions, such a community offers children and adults the opportunity to

**Table 7.1**
**Fowler's Stages of Faith Development**

**Stage 0: Undifferentiated (Primal) Faith** (Infancy)

The earliest faith is the fund of basic trust and hope in the care of others. In an infant's attachment to caregivers, a prepropositional foundation of confidence (or uncertainty) in a caregiver's nurturance, protection, and availability provides the basis for the earliest grasp of divine care, and the confidence in one's capacity to overcome life's challenges.

**Stage 1: Intuitive-Projective Faith** (Preschool years)

Faith is magical, imaginative, intuitive, and illogical, filled with fantasy and fascinated by stories of the power and omnipotence of God and the mysteries of birth and death. These stories are internalized in terms of the concerns of children of this age—about protection from threat, the integrity of the self, the dependability of adults, sickness and health, authority and dependency, how the world functions—and thus the understandings constructed by children from religious lessons may be much different from those intended by their adult tutors.

**Stage 2: Mythic-Literal Faith** (Early school years)

Faith is captured in the stories that children hear and tell about God, and the meanings that their literal but logical interpretations of these stories provide about human relations with the divine. These relations are best understood in terms of fairness, reciprocity, and immanent justice, with God responding consistently to people in terms of human fidelity and obedience (perhaps as children experience their own relationships with parents and other authorities). God consequently becomes anthropomorphized. Participation in the symbols and observances of the religious community also fosters the initial appropriation of religious beliefs for oneself.

**Stage 3: Synthetic-Conventional Faith** (Late school years, early adolescence)

Faith is encompassed in a fairly uncritical, tacit acceptance of the conventional religious values taught by others, centered on feelings of what is right and wrong, especially in interpersonal relationships. To some extent, conformist concern with maintaining the positive regard of others shapes religious commitment. For some children, however, personal religious faith also begins to provide an important organizer of personal identity and worldview, and shapes understandings of self in the context of the wider world.

**Stage 4: Individuative-Reflective Faith** (Late adolescence, early adult years)

Faith is forged from personal reflection and experiences (sometimes entailing critical life transitions) that may cause the adolescent or adult to question prior assumptions and to reconstruct new and different beliefs and commitments that are more personally meaningful, individualized, and depend less on the guidance of authorities. At this stage, the mysteries of religious rituals and symbols become critically examined for the meanings underlying them, and may sometimes be rejected as inadequate or "demythologized."

**Stage 5: Conjunctive Faith** (Adulthood)

Faith confronts but also accepts the paradoxes and contradictions of religious life: the irrational mysteries of prayer and worship, but also the rational reflections of belief and values, for example. A capacity for dialectical understanding and recapturing the mysteries of faith are consequently both part of this stage. There is also consideration of the truths that may be found outside one's own religious traditions in various other religious and nonreligious sources, and an appreciation of how faith is shaped by one's personality, background, and (sometimes unacknowledged) needs.

**Table 7.1 (continued)**

**Stage 6: Universalizing Faith** (Adulthood)

Faith is grounded in comprehensive truths—concerning justice, love, and compassion—that may cause individuals to take unusual (sometimes radical) steps to live out their faith, such as in selfless devotion to the poor (as with Mother Teresa) or nonviolent (as with Gandhi) or even violent (as with Dietrich Bonhoeffer) resistance to political wrong. Faith is distinguished both by its lack of self-concern and its commitment to human welfare irrespective of secular or religious boundaries. Fowler argues that this level of faith development is rarely found.

*Source*: Adapted from J. W. Fowler, (1981). *Stages of faith*. New York: HarperCollins; J. W. Fowler, (1991). Stages in faith consciousness. In F. K. Oser & W. G. Scarlett (Eds.), *Religious development in childhood and adolescence: New directions for child development* (W. Damon, Editor-in-Chief) (27–45). San Francisco: Jossey-Bass.

interpret their life experiences in terms of their age-related capacities for understanding faith while also providing incentives toward further growth. This can occur in many ways, such as by providing intellectually challenging encounters with more mature members of the community that encourage children to probe inadequacies in their own thinking.

However, Fowler also focuses on the ways that religious communities can inhibit or degrade faith development, such as by narrowly conceived orthodoxies that do not permit thoughtful criticism, doubt, or exploration of alternative views, or practices that institutionalize certain kinds of religious devotion and demean alternative approaches. Fowler notes that the positive and negative relational catalysts to faith development can also occur in the home, such as when parents actively encourage children's reflective thought on spiritual issues on one hand, or so closely identify family with religious practices that defiance of parents assumes spiritual significance on the other hand. In his view that faith development is not only a matter of personal construction but also of social interaction, Fowler offers a theory that is consistent with the constructivist views of development earlier summarized.

## ADEQUATE STANDARD OF LIVING

These theoretical accounts of spiritual development, faith, and religious understanding are primarily descriptive, not explanatory, and further research is required to test and expand their formulations. Nevertheless, they provide an initial window into the conditions that foster spiritual growth in children, adolescents, and adults. Some of these conditions include:

• *Respect for the ways that spiritual reflection changes with age and growth in thinking, judgment, and personality.* This means that rather than regarding children and adolescents as immature, incomplete, or incorrect in their understanding of faith, they are instead perceived as developing persons with appropriately evolving comprehensions of spiritual issues. The ways that children interpret religious matters are accepted as suitable for their age, and this acceptance of age-appropriate beliefs is incorporated into how they are treated within the community. Moreover, even adults are regarded as developing persons in matters of faith and religious understanding, with room for further growth.

- *Opportunities to participate in religious observances that are calibrated to a child's capacities for understanding and involvement.* This means that rather than being a compulsory observer or bystander to adult observances, children and adolescents are accorded roles that are meaningful to them and are respectfully recognized by adults within the community (see Melton, 1986).

- *Opportunities for intergenerational involvement in religious activity, as well as activities that are oriented to the interests and needs of children alone.* Both are important. On one hand, intergenerational activities can be significant to spiritual development if they include the child as an "apprentice in belief" in which relevant skills, practices, and understandings are nurtured in the context of the child's guided participation in collective activity with mature partners. On the other hand, activities specifically oriented to the needs, capabilities, and interests of children are important to ensure that catalysts to faith development also occur within the child's "zone of proximal development" of spiritual understanding.

- *The growth and maintenance of relationships—particularly within the family—that inspire trust, security, and empathic human understanding.* These provide exemplars of reliable care and love that offer a foundation for faith in divine care within many belief systems.

- *Respect for individuality in spiritual understanding and its development.* This means that a "one size fits all" view of the growth of religious understanding is discouraged in favor of the view that pathways for the growth of faith are individualized based on life experience, individual personality, and how persons interpret their own spirituality. This is as true of adult spiritual development as it is of children and adolescents.

- *Human support to individuals of all ages during periods of difficulty or crisis, personal despair, or transition during which familiar beliefs may be tested and reconsidered.*

- *Acceptance of personal searching as part of the process of spiritual development.* This means a willingness by others to engage constructively with the child or adolescent in questioning and exploring more deeply the fundamental beliefs that are socialized by parents and others in the majority culture, without inspiring fear of rejection, denigration, or expulsion from the family or community. This may further mean the acceptance of doubt, critical reflection, and the exploration of alternative viewpoints as a necessary part of the process of faith development.


These describe, in many respects, the "standard of living" that is nurturant of spiritual development. Although the manner in which these conditions are incorporated into any religious community will be tailored to the particular values, expectations, and world-view of its membership, it is hard to think of any doctrinal system that is fundamentally inconsistent with these prescriptions. This is because many of these conditions are founded not only on theoretical views of spiritual development, but are, more fundamentally, respectful of the dignity and worth of people of all ages as human beings.

Who is responsible for ensuring that these conditions occur? Although there is within the United States a strong legal presumption of family responsibility as well as family autonomy in the care of offspring, for centuriès religious traditions have emphasized the local community as the context for the nurturance of faith. It is not that families are unimportant in the view of major religions, but rather that the family is not perceived as functioning independently of the support, guidance, and values of the broader local religious community in which it is embedded. Thus, adherence to the U.N. *Convention*'s mandate to ensure a standard of living adequate to children's spiritual development may require a reorientation of perspective concerning the parties that are responsible for doing so.

However, a central term in the Article 27 mandate of the U.N. *Convention* is "adequate." What is meant by a standard of living "adequate" for spiritual development? The term is undefined by the U.N. *Convention*. If, however, adequate means (consistent with a dictionary definition) "barely satisfactory or sufficient," it is arguable that a standard of living adequate for spiritual development probably encompasses circumstances in which many of the conditions described above that nurture spiritual growth are absent. Even when children and adolescents grow up in religious communities that are disrespectful of their developmental needs, intolerant of questioning or dissent, and unsupportive of individual differences in spiritual perspective, faith development often occurs. Indeed, spiritual development often occurs in conditions of physical and material deprivation. Most religious traditions divorce any direct association between physical or material sufficiency and spiritual well-being, with some arguing that material prosperity is even antithetical to holiness. Consistent with this view are many illustrations of spiritual acuity and devotion in conditions of abject poverty. Robert Coles (1990) offers an evocative example in his study of children's spiritual lives of a ten-year-old girl living in one of the Brazilian favelas who says: "I shouldn't blame Jesus! I do, though, sometimes. He's right there—that statue keeps reminding me of Him—and the next thing I know, I'm talking with Him, and I'm either upset with Him or I'm praying for Him to tell me why the world is like it is" (Coles, 1990, 91).

Jonathan Kozol (1995) provides similarly powerful illustrations of children growing up in desperate poverty in the New York City ghetto in which children (and adults) cling to a fundamental faith in divine guidance. When considering the recent death of an 8-year-old boy from a fall down an unguarded elevator shaft, Kozol asks his aunt how this can be regarded as the will of a beneficent deity. This exchange follows:

The aunt replies, " 'I have to believe God picks a person when his work on earth is done."

"At eight years old?" I ask, and then regret my question.

"You can be eight years old and still your work is done. . . . God knows when somebody has suffered long enough." (Kozol, 1995, 106)

Such illustrations of faith in the context of material despair challenge any necessary association between a nurturant human environment, material sufficiency, and spiritual development. But spirituality is nevertheless connected to the conditions of life. When children or adults encounter crushing political persecution, enduring poverty, relentless problems with health or physical well-being, or inescapable relational abuse, a spiritual price is also paid for these oppressive life experiences. In these hopeless conditions, people of all ages are prone to succumbing to spiritual despair. Hope may, in fact, be the essential minimum condition for a standard of living that is barely "adequate" for spiritual development.

In the end, however, trying to define the nature of "adequate" standard of living for spiritual development may be asking the wrong question. Children grow spiritually in conditions that nurture them physically, intellectually, psychosocially, and emotionally, and which respect their dignity and worth as members of the human community. Children more than adults seem to exemplify the possibilities for faith development even in difficult circumstances because of their characteristically boundless hope for the future. It is incumbent on the human community that seeks to nurture faith to provide them with more, however, than mere hope.

## REFERENCES

Astington, J. W. (1993). *The child's discovery of the mind.* Cambridge, MA: Harvard University Press.

Cole, M. (1992). Culture in development. In M. H. Bornstein & M. E. Lamb (Eds.), *Developmental psychology: An advanced textbook* (3rd ed.). (731–789). Hillsdale, NJ: Erlbaum.

Coles, R. (1990). *The spiritual life of children.* New York: Houghton Mifflin.

Donahue, M. H. & Benson, P. L. (1995). Religion and the well-being of adolescents. *Journal of Social Issues, 51,* 145–160.

Elkind, D. (1970). The origins of religion in the child. *Review of Religious Research, 12,* 35–42.

Erikson, E. H. (1963). *Childhood and society* (2nd ed.). New York: Norton.

Flavell, J. H. (1963). *The developmental psychology of Jean Piaget.* New York: D. Van Nostrand.

Flavell, J. H., Miller, P. H., & Miller, S. A. (1993). *Cognitive development* (3rd ed.). Englewood Cliffs, NJ: Prentice-Hall.

Fowler, J. W. (1981). *Stages of faith.* New York: HarperCollins.

Fowler, J. W. (1991). Stages in faith consciousness. In F. K. Oser & W. G. Scarlett (Eds.), *Religious development in childhood and adolescence: New directions for child development* (W. Damon, Editor-in-Chief) (27–45). San Francisco: Jossey-Bass.

Freud, S. (1927). *The future of an illusion.* London: Hogarth.

Fuller, A. R. (1977). *Psychology and religion: Eight points of view*. Washington, DC: University Press of America.

Jung, C. G. (1933). *Modern man in search of a soul*. New York: Harcourt, Brace.

Jung, C. G. (1938). *Psychology and religion*. New Haven: Yale University Press.

Jung, C. G. (1947). *Essays on contemporary events*. London: Kegan and Paul.

Kohlberg, L. (1969). Stage and sequence: The cognitive developmental approach to socialization. In D. A. Goslin (Ed.), *Handbook of socialization theory and research* (347–480). Chicago: Rand McNally.

Kohlberg, L. (1970). From is to ought: How to commit the naturalistic fallacy and get away with it in the study of moral development. In T. Mischel (Ed.), *Cognitive development and epistemology* (151–235). New York: Academic.

Kozol, J. (1995). *Amazing grace: The lives of children and the conscience of a nation*. New York: Harper Perennial.

Leak, G. K. & Randall, B. A. (1995). Clarification of the link between right-wing authoritarianism and religiousness: The role of religious maturity. *Journal for the Scientific Study of Religion, 34*, 245–252.

Maton, K. I. & Wells, E. A. (1995). Religion as a community resource for well-being: Prevention, healing, and empowerment pathways. *Journal of Social Issues, 51*, 177–193.

Meadow, M. J. & Kahoe, R. D. (1984). *Psychology of religion: Religion in individual lives*. New York: Harper & Row.

Melton, G. B. (1986). Populism, school prayer, and the courts: Confessions of an expert witness. In D. Moshman (Ed.), *Children's intellectual rights: New directions for child development* (W. Damon, Editor-in-Chief) (63–73). San Francisco: Jossey-Bass.

Myers, D. G. (1993). *The pursuit of happiness*. New York: Avon Books.

Oser, F. K. (1991). The development of religious judgment. In F. K. Oser & W. G. Scarlett (Eds.), *Religious development in childhood and adolescence: New directions for child development* (W. Damon, Editor-in-Chief) (5–25). San Francisco: Jossey-Bass.

Piaget, J. (1929). *The child's conception of the world*. London: Routledge.

Piaget, J. (1935). *The moral judgment of the child*. London: Routledge.

Piaget, J. (1952). *The origins of intelligence in children*. New York: International Universities Press.

Piaget, J. (1962). *Causal thinking and the child: A genetic and experimental approach*. New York: International Universities Press.

Poloma, M. M. & Pendleton, B. F. (1990). Religious domains and general well-being. *Social Indicators Research, 22*, 255–276.

Rizuto, A.-M. (1979). *The birth of the living god: A psychoanalytic study*. Chicago: University of Chicago Press.

Rizuto, A.-M. (1991). *Religious development: A psychoanalytic point of view*. In F. K. Oser & W. G. Scarlett (Eds.), *Religious development in childhood and adolescence: New directions for child development* (W. Damon, Editor-in-Chief) (47–60). San Francisco: Jossey-Bass.

Rogoff, B. (1990). *Apprenticeship in thinking: Cognitive development in social context*. New York: Oxford.

Spilka, B., Hood, R. W., & Gorsuch, R. L. (1985). *The psychology of religion: An empirical approach*. Englewood Cliffs, NJ: Prentice-Hall.

Thompson, R. A. (1977). Early sociopersonality development. In W. Damon (Ed.), *Handbook of child psychology* (5th ed.) (Vol. 3). *Social, emotional, and personality development* (N. Eisenberg, Vol. Ed.) (25–104). New York: Wiley.

Vygotsky, L. S. (1962). *Thought and language.* Cambridge, MA: MIT Press.

Vygotsky, L. S. (1933/1978). *Mind in society: The development of higher psychological processes.* Cambridge, MA: Harvard University Press.

Wellman, H. M. (1990). *The child's theory of mind.* Cambridge, MA: MIT Press.

## 8

# The Meaning of a Standard of Living
# Adequate for Moral and Civic Development

### Judith Torney-Purta

To create a society where everyday life, including adult and institutional practice, is based on respect for the personhood and dignity of children is, in part, a matter of a legal framework such as that established by the U.N. *Convention on the Rights of the Child*. Such a society is also a matter of an unwritten social contract within a nested set of groups and communities who practice this respect and establish a socialization and educational process designed to foster it. For such a social contract and community to exist would have ramifications for issues ranging from prevention of crime, bullying, and violence to promotion of youth opportunities to freely participate in in-school and out-of-school associations.

The creation of such a community and social contract permeating everyday life depends on several elements, each of which has been dealt with extensively in recent theory and associated empirical work in developmental psychology and educational research. One of these elements is law, but as Melton (1988) reminds us, formal codes are embedded in social practice. Taking this social practice as a starting point, the following areas will be discussed: First, the nature of the context and socialization process in which this social contract is formed and enacted, including consideration of the nature of developmental change. Second, the nature of children's views of the domains relating to rights, morality, and civic participation.

This is a somewhat artificial division into influences and outcomes of socialization, provided primarily to give structure to the discussion. Under each of these two points, a section will present a theoretical and research background from current thinking in developmental psychology, while a second section will discuss some concrete models and indicators. In a concluding section I will suggest directions for future research and consider some further implications.

## THE NATURE OF THE CONTEXT AND SOCIALIZATION PROCESS IN WHICH THE SOCIAL CONTRACT IS FORMED AND ENACTED

Although there are many changes in children that can be attributed to maturation, developmental psychologists attribute most changes in social cognition and evolving views of issues such as politics, law, and morality to *both* maturation *and* interactions with the social environment. In other words, the developmental process is not totally spontaneous, but rather is channeled through sociocultural activity. Important parts of the social environment include parents, siblings, peers, and adults in the school and neighborhood with whom the child has everyday contact. In many cases these individuals can be thought of as representing institutions (including the law, the polity, the economy). Those who are interested in providing more optimal developmental environments for children can have some impact upon maturational processes (for example, by ensuring that health services and adequate nutrition are available, especially in early life), but these parties can have a much more profound impact on social interactions. This positive impact can be maximized through developmentally enhancing aspects of the social, moral, and civic context or habitat. A number of recent theoretical advances assist in providing this developmental dimension to the study of legal socialization and psychological jurisprudence.

In particular, the theoretical basis provided by Rogoff (1995), Lave (1996), and Greeno (1994) on the role of children's participation in communities of practice, as well as the model adopted by the IEA Civic Education Project in studying political and legal socialization, provide appropriate steps toward the further definition of "children's rights to a standard of living adequate for the child's . . . moral development."

### Situated Cognition and Everyday Life Experiences in Communities

A recent set of theoretical proposals has resulted in understanding new ways in which everyday life experiences influence children. The *cognitive* point of view stresses mechanisms existing within the individual. In this view, knowledge consists of a set of conceptual structures (schemata) and strategies for reasoning and problem solving that can be assessed by asking the person to perform certain tasks, for example thinking aloud while solving a problem or responding to a Piaget-style interview. The role of the environment in development is not totally ignored, but it is assumed that as long as the child has not been deprived of opportunities for activities such as exploration, these cognitive structures will mature and can be used similarly in whatever circumstance the individual finds him or herself throughout life. As researchers with training in anthropology or in cross-cultural psychology have studied these issues, a new approach has been consolidated and fruitfully applied.

This *situative approach*, as conceptualized by Greeno (1994), looks at both internal processes (symbolic structures in the individual) and external circumstances. The external context is not a set of distinct and unrelated reinforcements, but a set of social practices and interactions with other individuals who provide an ongoing stream of collaborative constructions of meaning and responses to the individual that serve to embed activity in a situation. In this approach, sometimes called situated cognition, knowledge consists of the ability to participate in a community's practices, in using its tools of material culture and in its processes of discourse. These "communities of discourse and practice" provide a situation for children's development and ongoing use of understandings and concepts. This includes families and other institutions within the community.

In elaborating this view, Rogoff (1995) discusses three planes of analysis— apprenticeship in culturally organized activity, guided participation with social partners, and participatory appropriation by the individual. These processes operate simultaneously in the developmental process. Rogoff has chosen these phrases carefully, and explicitly avoids the term "internalization" because it implies that something static crosses a boundary between the environment and the individual rather than dynamic processes of interchange.

Pioneering work in understanding communities of practice has been conducted by Lave (1996) and her associates. She also views learning as an aspect of participation in social practice usually involving culturally derived tools. Her studies have focused especially on learning by apprenticeship in all types of societies and settings. For example, she describes Moroccan tailors' apprentices, who are not merely developing expertise in sewing but also in relating to a master (who defines expertise) and to a community in which different modes of dress hold different connotations of status. In each of these situations for cognition, learning (becoming more skilled at tailoring) relates the individual to a community that is meaningful and important to his or her social identity and to a group of other individuals. These collaborators or partners in discourse may include adults or peers, but peer-directed practices and adult-directed ones differ in many respects.

Various communities of practice have been studied. Lampert (1990) observed the ways in which mathematics classrooms became communities of discourse and practice about the subject of mathematics in which students and teachers collaborated to construct knowledge. Some educational programs have been built on this model. Cole has established and studied a series of technology-rich educational programs called The Fifth Dimension, many of them in after-school centers (Cole, 1996). I have studied how teams of adolescents participating in a computer-assisted international simulation become members of a discourse community of diplomacy, and also co-construct knowledge with teammates as they prepare to enter messages into a computer system for transmission to other teams (Torney-Purta, 1996a). At the undergraduate level, I have also developed a Children's Rights Simulation in which developmental psychology students who are unfamiliar with the U.N. *Convention on the Rights of the Child* are asked to prepare a list of children's rights that they believe should be recognized in the world community and to justify each by reference to psychological theories they have studied. They enter these rights into a networked computer system and discuss them on-line, becoming participants in a community of discourse in which children's rights and developmentally appropriate contexts are related. Many of these applications could also be related to Vygotsky's theory (1978), especially his concept of scaffolding, in which adults or more competent peers provide structure at the early phases of task participation that is gradually withdrawn as the learner becomes more skilled at a task or type of participation in a community of discourse and practice.

In the situated cognition perspective, young people move from peripheral to more central participation in a variety of overlapping communities (at the school or neighborhood level, as well as potentially at the national level). From this situated cognition point of view, socialization is not limited to adults' explicit attempts to teach or socialize the young about topics such as rights and duties. The political and moral community itself (and its everyday practices of discourse) surrounds and provides a situation or context for the developing sense of the dignity of the human person.

For young people, the peer group also plays a vital role as a community of discourse and practice (and should not be viewed simply as an obstacle to socialization or education). The reaction of peers to ideas and how peers value different ways in which the individual behaves or spends time are essential parts of the situation or context for social cognition. For example, in my research on a computer-assisted international studies project, the peer group became the point of reference for students' judgment, often replacing the adult (see Torney-Purta, 1996a). Ogbu's research on peer groups in African American youth, as they may create a context devaluing achievement, presents a concrete example of this process (Ogbu, 1993). However, one need not confine oneself to urban schools for examples of peer influence. Motivation to achieve (or not achieve) or to behave in a moral (or immoral) way or to treat individuals with dignity (or not) is at least in part constructed within the peer group in most schools.

These emphases upon everyday communities of participation and ways in which students become full and legitimate participants in them provides a framework within which a more specific model can be developed in the next section.

### The Study of Civic Education Cross-nationally and Its Model for Understanding the Context of Moral and Civic Development

Although a great deal of previous research on political and legal socialization exists, little has been conducted in the 1990s. In response to the need to better understand these processes, particularly in the light of rapid democratization across the world, IEA (the International Association for the Evaluation of Educational Achievement, headquartered in the Netherlands) is conducting a second Civic Education Study (the first having been published by Torney, Oppenheim, and Farnen, 1975). About one-third of the approximately twenty-five participating countries are in Western Europe, one-third in Central and Eastern Europe, and one-third in the Pacific Rim.

The countries have submitted text material relating to eighteen case study framing questions for an international data base. For example, three of these case study framing questions are:

- What are young people expected or likely to have learned about law and the rule of law, the constitution (written or unwritten), the courts, the national/regional legislature, elections, and other institutions of government by age 14 or 15?
- If "human rights" are a central concept, how are they defined and what do they mean, and what are young people expected to have learned about them by age 14 or 15?
- What are young people of 14 or 15 expected or likely to believe about the mass media as sources of information about politics and government?

The purpose of these case studies is to obtain a picture of what civic education and associated terms like democracy, national identity, and political participation mean in diverse countries and not to be limited to North American views. Further, the case studies and data base provides material about the ways in which curriculum, textbooks, school organization, educational standards, and teacher training are intended to promote civic education outcomes for students who are 14 to 15 years old. National Expert Panels composed of individuals from education and community groups in each country prepared extensive answers to these case study framing questions, which were then reviewed by the International Planning Committee (Torney-Purta, Schwille, & Amadeo, 1998).

The National Expert Panels in fourteen of the countries voted on which of the framing questions were of greatest importance in their countries. Considerable agreement was found, and three areas have been chosen for in-depth study by all countries in Phase 1 and for concentrated attention in the Phase 2 survey instruments. These three areas are Democracy, Governmental Institutions, and Citizenship (including human rights); National Identity; Social Cohesion and Social Diversity. Three other topics—dealing with the media, economics, and local problems (including the environment)—form an optional fourth topic.

The second phase of the project will consist of a test and survey of about two hours in length, including both cognitive and attitudinal items developed on the basis of information in the case studies. These instruments will be administered to nationally representative samples of students aged 14 or 15 in 1999, following extensive piloting of instruments (Torney-Purta, 1996b).

The theoretical model developed for organizing the information being collected shows one way of considering how the everyday life of young people in homes, with peers, and at school serves as a situated context for their thinking and action in the social, political, legal, and moral environment. In other words, it takes the perspective described in the previous section.

At the center of this IEA model is the individual student. Surrounding the process is the public discourse or discussion within the country that frames the goals and values important in the society as a whole (and, in some cases, particular to groups within the society). One of the greatest values of international documents, such as those on human rights highlighted in this volume, is that they promote public debate and discussion on values and the nature of social practice (see also Melton [1988] where the issue of the law as moral symbol is discussed).

The model for the IEA project conceptualizes the impact of this public discourse on the individual through contacts with a set of "carriers." They include family (parents, siblings, and sometimes extended family), school (teachers, intended curriculum, and participation opportunities in classrooms and broader venues), peer group (functioning through interactions both in and out of class), informal community or neighborhood, and the still broader more formal community. In addition to these face-to-face contacts there are also carriers to be found in the mass media of communication (especially television). Theories such as that of Bronfenbrenner (1988) would call most (but not all) of these carriers part of the individual's microsystem. Previous work in political socialization calls these "agents" of socialization. However, this model differs from the conceptualization of socialization agents as operating independently of each other rather than in an embedded and reciprocal fashion.

The outer octagon that circumscribes all the processes mentioned above includes what Bronfenbrenner would call the "macrosystem." In the model being described, this includes institutions, processes, and values in domains such as politics, economics, education, and religion. It also includes the country's position with respect to other countries, many of the symbols and narratives important at the national level, and the social stratification system (including ethnic and gender opportunity structures). International organizations, covenants, and declarations could also be placed here. Although this model was designed to assist in the process of conceptualizing the nature of civic education across a range of countries, in many respects a variant of this model could be used for systematizing issues relating to the establishment of the type of moral atmosphere and community of respect for children and their dignity that is envisioned in this volume. In particular, it recognizes the extent to which the child is embedded in a habitat of communities influencing the sense of social cohesion and a social contract.

In summary, recent work in developmental psychology stressing the importance of the context presented by the community and the formal and informal opportunities for apprenticeship and guided participation provided there orients both our conceptualization of the moral and civic socialization process and attempts to conduct research on it across nations.

## THE NATURE OF CHILDREN'S VIEWS OF THE DOMAINS RELATING TO THEIR RIGHTS

### Morality and Social Convention

The previous section examined the context and living situations of children and adolescents. In the next section we will examine the nature of the domain of morality and civic life as it is observed in the understanding of children and adolescents. Although the stages of moral development proposed by Lawrence Kohlberg were formative twenty years ago, there has recently been considerable debate that has shaped a somewhat more nuanced understanding of the separate domains existing in this area. Recent research by Turiel and his associates supports the proposition that "individuals have different types of social interactions, and these social interactions lead to the construction of different . . . domains of social knowledge'" (Smetana, 1995). The domain of morality is different from other forms of social knowledge in that it is obligatory, applicable to everyone in a universal sense, and does not depend upon formal agreements or laws, consensus within a group, sanctions by authorities, or institutional conventions and arrangements.

The distinction between social convention and morality is fundamental to our discussion as well. "Moral" issues are those that entail concerns with the value of life, physical or psychological harm, integrity of person, rights, or the unfair or unjust deprivation of something to which a person is entitled. These issues are very similar to those associated with human dignity in the *Convention* and other human rights declarations and documents (Melton, 1992). An action is immoral if it is wrong in an intrinsic sense, whether or not a law exists to prohibit it or an authority exists to exert sanctions. In contrast, social conventions are defined relative to law and custom, and may be relatively arbitrary. For young children, the issue of not hitting others is a moral issue. Whether one takes off one's shoes before entering the classroom is a matter of social convention. From an early age, children can make relevant distinctions between the importance and severity of transgressions against rules applying to moral issues and those applying to social conventions (Turiel, 1979).

Several years ago I used this theory to frame a study with thirty-nine children aged 9 through 13 to explore the extent to which human rights are deeply embedded belief structures that correspond to moral issues in Turiel's sense (Torney & Brice, 1979). These children were asked questions taken directly from the *Universal Declaration of Human Rights*; for example, "suppose that in another country it was decided that it was all right to put someone in prison for several years without going to court or having a trial. In that country they had no laws saying people should have a trial before being put in jail. Would that be right?" Other questions dealt with slavery, limitations on movement, torture performed to obtain evidence of criminal guilt, and not informing family members of a prisoner's whereabouts. All of the thirty-nine children believed that slavery or limitations on movement could not be justified, even if no law existed prohibiting them, although none of these respondents said they had ever heard of the *Universal Declaration of Human Rights*. At least 90 percent voiced the same opinions with respect to the other provisions of the *Declaration* dealing with basic human rights and civil and political rights. This suggests that human rights issues are moral issues connected with deeply held beliefs about human beings. Some of the young people commented spontaneously that a government that holds people in slavery, tortures them, or refuses them a trial "is not a good government" or "can't expect much respect from its people."

More recently, Helwig (1995) reported on several studies of young people's views of civil liberties using the same distinction between morality and social convention, and finding the same near unanimity about human rights as moral issues. He reported that young adolescents "conceptualized freedom of speech and religion as moral or universal rights not defined by law and applying across national and cultural boundaries. It was judged wrong for governments to place general restrictions on these rights in the United States and other countries" (Helwig, 1995, 185). He found that some of those interviewed were able to apply abstract ideas about rights to judging social events even when there was an explicit conflict with other social or moral concepts.

The data concerning American and Norwegian children reported by Melton and Limber (1992) shows the complexity of the judgments necessary when approaching the parts of this domain dealing with law and rights. I would argue that children have characteristic understandings of political and civic institutions, and that some but not all of these views are related to moral issues as this section defines them. These understandings form a domain of civic, political, and legal understanding. Here one finds institutions such as constitutions, laws and elections, and human rights (especially civil and political rights). It is a domain needing elaboration and research as a step in creating a climate of respect for children's rights.

A related way to look at these issues is to contrast the character of proximal (face-to-face) and distal (non–face-to-face) encounters that young people have. One might look at the civic domain as consisting of matters of morality and social convention and also as a domain that is distinctive because political institutions are experienced by individuals distally (through symbols or leaders). Such an orientation helps us understand one of the findings of these studies— individuals are much more likely to extend rights such as free speech to individuals or groups that they know (proximal experience) than to more distal institutions, such as "the press."

Defining a civic domain might also allow us to extend Aber's conceptualization of positive development as a series of stage-salient developmental tasks to be negotiated (Aber, 1994). He presents these stages from infancy through middle to late childhood (11 years of age), with some overlaps between ages (e.g., early school age from 6 to 9, middle to late childhood from 8 to 11). The stage-salient developmental task I propose to add would be appropriate for the

10 to 13 year old period (early adolescence), and would consist of developing a sense of connection and participatory action related to the community and to more distal political institutions.

In summary, theoretical distinctions made by Turiel (elaborated by Smetana, Helwig, and myself) between issues of morality and social convention assist in defining the moral domain and in relating it to the civic domain. They also help to understand the dimensions of a community-relevant socialization process to build a habitat adequate to children's moral and civic development.

## Monitoring in the Domain of Morality, Rights, and Civics

The first IEA Civic Education Study in ten nations, in which more than 30,000 young people were surveyed in 1971, included a number of items dealing with human rights, primarily attitudes toward civil liberties, women's rights, and equality (Torney, Oppenheim, & Farnen, 1975). More recently the Organization for Economic Co-operation and Development (OECD) has initiated a wide ranging project to formulate educational indicators (including both inputs and outcomes). During its early phase the outcome indicators were limited to cognitive tests in fields such as mathematics and science. More recently a subgroup has had quite a bit of success dealing with "Cross-Curricular Competencies" tested in nine countries in two areas: political knowledge and attitudes, and self perception/self concept (Torney-Purta, Peschar, & Waslander, 1996).

In a chapter on "affective outcomes" prepared for a volume raising issues related to the monitoring of educational standards cross-nationally, I raised a number of issues that are important when dealing with non-cognitive outcomes such as these (Torney-Purta, 1994b). One of my suggestions builds on a model for understanding moral behavior (Rest, 1983), healthy peer relations (Dodge, 1986), and solutions to social and political problems (Torney-Purta, 1994a). These three models lay out several distinct steps that the individual goes through when confronting a situation. At the first step, incoming social cues are attended to; at the second step, these cues are interpreted and integrated in memory about previous similar situations. In both of these phases the individual is interpreting the situation as presenting certain opportunities or constraints, for example as presenting a decision involving a moral issue or not. In a third phase, the individual identifies the alternative responses, and at the fourth and fifth phases, a response is chosen and enacted.

This set of steps can also be applied in the civic domain. One hopes that students, when faced with a problem in their community, will possess an image of their local government as responsive to citizen action, will understand that group action is generally more effective than individual action, and will perceive problems in their communities as amenable to cooperative solutions (the first and second steps of the model), will be able to think of several alternative ways in which they might work with others to solve these problems (step three), and finally will take civic action. One way of developing an indicator or measure

for students' ability to engage in such a process would be to design a hypo-
thetical situation in which they are asked to recognize a problem, analyze its
components, and think of alternative ways to solve it. Preferably the problem
should involve some issues of morality, as it has been defined above, and should
have ramifications within the social and political community.

This is one of the directions being taken in the student test and questionnaire
development for the second phase of the current IEA Civic Education Project,
but it has broader potential applicability in monitoring as well (Torney-Purta,
1996b).

## CONCLUSION

Psychological research on these issues has been largely confined to North
America and the Nordic countries. When one examines a data base consisting
of more diverse societies, especially those of Central and Eastern Europe, the
pervasiveness of ruptures of the community and political process become obvious. There are many difficulties in creating a climate for respect for children
in this area of the world. During the formative years of those who are currently
parents and teachers, it was the case that human rights and democracy had been
redefined by the political system. National identity and the social contract were
problematic, and groups that might form a community of political and social
practice were often disrupted. Given the rapid changes across the world and
these associated problems, a substantial program of new research is necessary
to study the social, moral, political, and legal contexts in which children develop
and the nature of their views of rights and of moral and political issues.

Speaking more generally, the developmental perspective can enrich a variety
of the aims of inquiry in the area of psychological jurisprudence. Limber and
Flekkøy (1995) describe the important tasks of clarifying concepts associated
with children's rights and developing ways of monitoring. Some sections of this
paper have attempted to lay the groundwork for these tasks.

What might be the outlines of a plan of action or intervention to provide
appropriate opportunities for moral and civic development for young people?
The concepts of apprenticeship, modeling, guided participation, scaffolding,
identifying alternatives, attending to moral issues, articulating reasons for behavior, and encouraging reflection are all important. These concepts all have
important roots in developmental psychology, which is not very often applied
to areas such as children's rights. And if these ideas are to be applied internationally we need more information about the variations that exist as well as the
common concerns and interests across countries. One thing is clear, however—
the family, formal education, and the overlapping informal communities in
which the child grows and develops must all be part of this effort.

In conclusion, let me suggest how the analysis in this paper relates to three
of the roles that Melton (1992) saw for psychological inquiry in the legal system.
First, he noted that this inquiry should ''identify those aspects of life that are

most fundamental to sense of dignity'' (387). Further research on moral and social conventional issues and on proximal and distal experiences is a first step. Second, he argued that this inquiry should ''enhance a sense of community through explication of the values of the community . . .'' (387). Research relating to the situative cognition approach, particularly on children's informal apprenticeships in communities of practice and discourse could make a considerable contribution to this aim. Facilitating proximal and distal connections so that parents become effective advocates for children in general, not just for their own children, would be of great assistance in building such a sense of community. Third, he pointed to the role of this inquiry in clarifying ''the variables affecting legal socialization, so that settings and policies can be designed in a manner that will enhance the development of democratic values'' (388). The program of research being undertaken through the IEA Civic Education Project using the model described is one way to carry forward this aim.

## NOTES

Support for released time from the Research Board of the Graduate School at the University of Maryland is gratefully acknowledged.

1. A domain is a separate conceptual system existing within an individual's cognitive structure, often with an associated affective component attached.

## REFERENCES

Aber, J. L. (1994, November). *Indicators of positive development in early childhood: Improving concepts and measures.* Paper presented at the Conference on Indicators of Children's Well-Being, Bethesda, MD.

Bronfenbrenner, U. (1988). Interacting systems in human development. In N. Bolger, C. Caspi, G. Downey, & M. Moorehouse (Eds.), *Persons in context: Developmental processes.* Cambridge: Cambridge University Press.

Cole, M. (1996). *Cultural psychology: A once and future discipline.* Cambridge, MA: Harvard University Press.

Dodge, K. (1986). A social information processing model of social competency in children. In M. Perlmutter (Ed.), *Cognitive perspectives on children's social and behavioral development* (77–126). Hillsdale, NJ: Lawrence Erlbaum Associates.

Greeno, J. (1994, August). *Situativity of learning.* Paper presented at the American Psychological Association, Los Angeles, CA.

Helwig, C. (1995). Social context in social cognition: Psychological harm and civil liberties. In M. Killen & D. Hart (Eds.), *Morality in everyday life* (166–200). Cambridge: Cambridge University Press.

Lampert, M. (1990). When the problem is not the question and the solution is not the answer. *American Educational Research Journal, 27,* 29–63.

Lave, J. (1996). Teaching, as learning, in practice. In M. Cole, Y. Engestom, & E. O. Vasquez (Eds.), *Mind, culture, and activity.* Cambridge: Cambridge University Press.

Limber, S. & Flekkøy, M. (1995). The U.N. *Convention on the Rights of the Child*: Its relevance for social scientists. *Social Policy Report: Society for Research in Child Development*. Ann Arbor, MI: SRCD.

Melton, G. (1988). The significance of law in the everyday lives of children and families. *Georgia Law Review, 22*, 851–93.

Melton, G. (1992). The law is a good thing (psychology is, too). *Law and Human Behavior, 16*, 381–398.

Melton, G. & Limber, S. (1992). What children's rights mean to children: Children's own views. In M. Freeman & P. Veerman (Eds.), *The ideologies of children's rights* (168–187). Dordrecht: Kluwer Academic Publishers.

Ogbu, J. (1993). Differences in cultural frame of reference. *International Journal of Behavioral Development, 16*, 483–506.

Rest, J. (1983). Moral development. In J. Flavell & E. Markman (Eds.), *Handbook of child psychology* (Vol. 3) (556–629). New York: Wiley.

Rogoff, B. (1995). Observing sociocultural activity on three planes: Participatory appropriation, guided participation, and apprenticeship. In J. Wertsch, P. Del Rio, & A. Alvarez (Eds.), *Sociocultural studies of mind*. Cambridge: Cambridge University Press.

Smetana, J. (1995). Morality in context: Abstractions, ambiguities, and applications. *Annals of Child Development, 10*, 83–130.

Torney, J., Oppenheim, A. N., & Farnen, R. (1975). *Civic education in ten countries: An empirical study*. New York: Halsted Press.

Torney, J. & Brice, P. (1979, August). *Children's concepts of human rights and social cognition*. Paper presented at the American Psychological Association, New York.

Torney-Purta, J. (1994a). Dimensions of adolescents' reasoning about political and historical issues: Ontological switches, developmental processes, and situated learning. In M. Carretero & J. Voss (Eds.), *Cognitive and instructional processes in history and the social sciences* (103–122). Hillsdale, NJ: Lawrence Erlbaum.

Torney-Purta, J. (1994b). The monitoring of affective outcomes. In A. Tuijnman & T. N. Postlethwaite (Eds.), *Monitoring the standards of education*. Oxford: Pergamon.

Torney-Purta, J. (1996a). Conceptual changes among adolescents using computer-networks in group-mediated international role playing. In S. Vosniadou, E. DeCorte, R. Glaser, & H. Mandl (Eds.), *International perspectives on the design of technology supported learning environments* (203–219). Hillsdale, NJ: Erlbaum.

Torney-Purta, J. (1996b). The Second IEA Civic Education Project: Development of content guidelines and items for a cross-national test and survey. *Canadian and International Education, 25*, 199–213.

Torney-Purta, J., Peschar, J., & Waslander, S. (1996, August). *Continuity in studies of political socialization cross-nationally*. Paper presented at the International Society for Behavioral Development, Quebec City, Canada.

Torney-Purta, J., Schwille, J., & Amadeo, J. (1998). *Civic education across countries: Twenty-four national case studies*. Amsterdam: IEA/Eburon.

Turiel, E. (1979). Distinct conceptual and developmental domains: Social convention and morality. In C. B. Keasey (Ed.), *Nebraska symposium on motivation* (77–116). Lincoln: University of Nebraska Press.

Vygotsky, L. S. (1978). *Mind in society: The development of higher psychological processes*. Cambridge, MA: Harvard University Press.

## 9

# The Social Development of the Child

*Malfrid Grude Flekkøy and
Natalie Hevener Kaufman*

## INTRODUCTION

The U.N. *Convention on the Rights of the Child* must be seen as a whole, and interpretation, implementation, and monitoring must be based on its guiding principles (dignity and integrity, "the best interest of the child," and "the evolving capacities" of the child). Selecting one article for analysis is useful, but no single article can be completely understood in isolation. The various parts of Article 27 must be related to other articles in the *Convention*.

The social development of a child requires that the child gradually learn the rules and norms of interaction in the culture in which she or he lives. Social development assumes that certain ties within society are of special importance. Among these are the relationship values necessary for building democracy. Therefore, sustaining positive social development includes learning democracy. Since democracy requires participation from all members of society who exercise critical and creative thinking, the participation rights are highly significant. The dignity and integrity of the child requires us to attend to the child's participation rights, which have consequences for how children are raised.

Respect for the child also means taking into consideration the competence of the child, which changes as the child grows. Competence is best considered as a continuum rather than as an either/or skill. Realization of this has led to research on "part-competencies," which revealed that children can understand and are capable of more earlier than we believed twenty years ago. In practical terms, knowledge about competence must mean that children's participation in social decision-making can begin in nursery school, while basic skills in expressing opinions and making choices start even earlier. The possibilities and opportunities for children's learning about participation are all around us. So we, as adults, need to become aware of them and encourage children to use them. The importance of participation for development of a sense of self is well documented. Less well documented, but indicated by research in several countries, is the importance of participation for combating depression and possibly suicide in young people.

## SOCIAL INTERACTION

"Wild children" brought up by animals or in isolation have demonstrated how crucial social interaction is to learning the language, norms, and social rules of society. Children must learn the "external" rules governing social interaction, and these must be internalized and merged or combined with a sense of morality, so that the individual can make socially acceptable judgements, choices, and decisions even when there are no external rules or nobody else is present to oversee the actions of the individual. Social learning has to do with cognition, reasoning, and understanding, but also with emotional experiences and maturity.

To function in a democracy children must gradually learn to take responsibility for themselves and for the groups to which they belong, based on a feeling of belonging and of identification with the group. They must be able to express opinions and to know when to compromise and when to persist. They must be able to make decisions with due consideration of other people. Consideration of others and acceptance of responsibility are not learned from one day to the next. If children are to respect and have tolerance for others, including people of different ages, genders, race, nationalities, traditions, and cultures, they must be met with that same kind of respect themselves, for their dignity and integrity as well as for their differences.

The adoption of the U.N. *Convention on the Rights of the Child* has provided a new context in which we are now looking at the basic requirements for social development.

In our view, the *Convention* has brought into focus the basic need for integrity and dignity, which is the right of every human being, which clearly includes children. But the *Convention* also forces us to look at old and new knowledge with a different perspective, emphasizing the competence of children as they grow (the evolving capacities concept) and the other rights that are important for social development, particularly the rights to self-expression and participation.

Including social development in Article 27 of the *Convention* was not indisputable. It was included in the first Polish draft. By 1982 "socially" had been dropped, as had "the best interest of the child" in this article. But by 1984 the NGO Ad Hoc Group again proposed inclusion of "social development," which was accepted and sustained during the drafting process (Kaufman & Blanco, chapter 2, this volume).

## THE SELF-EXPRESSION AND PARTICIPATION RIGHTS

Two groups of articles in the *Convention* reflect the child's rights to participate. The first focuses on the forms of participation and the conditions of participation. Articles 12, 13, 14, 15, 31, and 40 give the child the right to participate by expressing views and opinions orally, in writing, or through other media. Article 12, the most important participation article, demands that the child's opinion be respected and given due weight when decisions that affect her or his life are taken. There is no age limit attached to this requirement.

While several articles refer to the individual child's right to participate as an individual, Article 15 spells out the child's right to participate as member of a group. This is important, because in a group the child learns the power of organization and the tactics and procedures of the democratic process. The group may well be the family, but also groups of peers enable the child to deal with the adult world more efficiently. Together children can be stronger than they are individually.

Article 31 specifies participation in cultural and artistic activities, and two articles, 12 and 40, concern the child's participation in the judicial system. Other contexts, including the family or the school, are not specifically mentioned. The *Convention* concerns first and foremost the relationship of child and state. National law can be put in place to do this or the family can be persuaded, which can actually be done without reference to the *Convention*. School may be a different matter, because schools often represent the meeting of the public authority, which establishes schools and determines curriculum, and the child. Actually the child will learn the first lessons in practicing the right to influence, state opinions, and participate in decision-making in the family, whether the adults want it or not. The difference between the way the *Convention* would dictate and what parents do may lie mostly in the attitudes of the parents, particularly with regard to whether or not they respond with respect for the child's dignity and integrity.

The *Convention* does place limitations on the child's right to voice opinions. The decision to enable the child's expression should be in the best interest of the child, and it should not be inconsistent with procedural rules, infringe on other rights, or contradict national order. Expression of participation rights must be learned. Determining how the child can express opinions and share in the decision making process should be influenced by knowledge of the evolving capacities combined with the need to protect the child against decisions that may lead to consequences the child cannot handle.

The other group of participation rights focuses on the requirements of participation. Some paragraphs within one group of rights overlap with the content of the other group, so—as always—it is necessary to see the *Convention* as a whole and not consider articles isolated from the context. The responsibilities of parents concern bringing the child up in a way appropriate with his or her evolving capacities and with providing appropriate direction and guidance. The state is responsible for necessary assistance to the parents. Appropriate information is a requirement for formulating a rational and sound opinion. But what happens when the state, perhaps represented by the schools, and the parents disagree on what *is* "appropriate" information. Often they will agree. Certain information will obviously be important for the development of the child, and some will by consensus be injurious to the child's well-being. But there may be gray zones, and the school may then provide information that the parents would prefer that the child have later or not at all.

## RELATIONSHIP BETWEEN PARTICIPATION AND SOCIAL DEVELOPMENT

In order to understand what the Article 27 reference to social development actually means, it is necessary to explore the essential role of participation in the child's social development. From birth, the baby has the ability to attract adults' attention and so plays a part in determining adult behavior, participating in the planning of family life. Some would argue that this kind of impact has nothing to do with true participation. It may be easier to accept that this is at least rudimentary self-expression. We would argue that interaction with other people from birth establishes a basis for more active participation later on, and that unless we are willing to accept that self-expression and participation actually start at least at birth, it is impossible to determine exactly when the exercise of these rights begins. These rights include more than having an influence on decisions affecting the child's (everyday) life. The baby also receives and imparts information (Article 13) and has freedom of thought, conscience, and religion (Article 14). What children of this age basically need with regard to adequate information is often available within the family setting. Article 13 does not postulate that freedom of expression is limited to spoken language. Most babies obviously (often loudly) make themselves heard, even when their "opinions" or feelings may be difficult to understand.

Apart from the fact that the newborn does influence behavior, recent research has indicated that the precursors of emphatic behavior are present perhaps even before birth. Researchers of various schools have described the early interactions between the baby and the adult as more than arbitrary or random, even at birth. Some newborns a few minutes old may imitate facial expressions of emotion that they see in other people (De Casper & Fifer, 1982; De Casper & Spence, 1986). A mother's speech patterns change in response to the infant's face movements, coos or frets, hand gestures, and body movements. Studies of this "intuitive motherese" show that its physiognomic and kinesthetic patterns are universal and unlearned, as is its reception (Fernald & Simon, 1984; Fernald &

Kuhl, 1987; Grieser & Kuhl, 1988). At six weeks, a baby may show a capacity to choose and sustain preferred visual orientations, for example, mother's face. Eye contact can be controlled by either one of them, and they both act to keep control of the pattern of their engagement.

The newborn baby's influence is unplanned and unconscious. But at the age of two months the patterns have changed. This indicates that the babies have learned something during the first 8 weeks of life. Early observations of Bowlby (1969), Brazelton, Koslowski, and Main (1974), and Stern (1974, 1985) indicate that the infant as well as the adult is capable of matching the pacing and rhythms of each other's behavior and making adjustments that are self-correcting for the interaction system. Trevarthen (1977) notes, "Exchanges between two-months-olds and their mothers tend to be precisely patterned in time. The nature of patterning shows that it is a mutually generated effect, in which the intentions of both partners are essential, and both may adjust their acts to obtain better fit to those of each other" (32). Trevarthen (1992) also argues, "At birth, or soon after, being especially alert during the first 24 hours, infants appear ready to enter into an engagement of feeling with another" and describes such "engagement of feeling" in a 3-week-old baby born 12 weeks premature. He also points to observations of peer sociability (reciprocal gazing, smiling, vocalization, and sometimes reaching for the other) in children 3 months old (1992, 135).

Much of what goes on within the baby and between the baby and others is, of course, not consciously planned or performed by the baby. Yet the child is obviously aware of what is going on, as it happens. According to Stern (1985), the child's development of self between 2 and 5 months of age includes perception of the ability to influence happenings in the world and in people, combined with integration skills that give the child a sense of physical entity, continuity in time, and patterns of emotions. Gradually behavior patterns that fail to elicit pleasurable or rewarding responses fade. Also, as experience and memory span as well as cognitive capacities increase, there is reason to believe that the child's choices become more active, as inner representations of relational dynamics cause expectancies on the part of the child. The early beginnings of planning capacity and problem-solving are evident at least when the child begins to creep and crawl, in the first months of the second half year. Once they can crawl, infants are no longer totally dependent on caregivers to secure things they want. But coupled with this emerging independence, this is also a period during which many children are exposed to an increase of adult control. This is not the first experience of conflict between child and adult. Even from birth—or at least within the first weeks of life—babies who are not carried continuously will at times have been fed either earlier or later than the hunger impulses appear. A compromise may be found between satisfaction of the wishes of the parents and the need of the child. The point here is that even at this stage socialization begins and "negotiation" is necessary in decisions.

In the second half of the first year, the child, again according to Stern, will be aware that the physical aspects of interpersonal dynamics have their basis in internal conditions, for example, feelings, motives, and intentions, and that other people have their own subjective inner life. The child may now use the emotional expressions of the other person to regulate his own behavior. In the ''cliff experiment,'' whether or not the child ventured over the glass covering a visual cliff depended upon the mother's emotional expression. Also children at this stage will signal understanding of emotions expressed by the other through one modality (e.g., face or voice) using a different modality (e.g., gestures). The infant will also increasingly take the initiative to elicit play or laughter from a parent (Hubley & Trevarthen, 1979), at times recreating a ''routine'' or ''joke'' without any obvious connection in the present context.

## THE TODDLER'S SOCIAL DEVELOPMENT

Starting to walk and being able to reach things and move about more independently is important. Development of language is perhaps even more important. These new skills may very well lead to an experience of omnipotence for the child, who does not yet realize the limitations imposed by lack of skills or by the world (Erikson, 1950).

Knowing and recognizing the meaning of words, the child gradually will also understand and perhaps respond to verbal instruction, for example, the word for ''no.'' The combination of a short memory span and the immediacy of situational demand may preclude acting consistently on the instructions, particularly if the instructions themselves are inconsistent. Children will also start verbalizing their own demands and wishes, indicating that they are beginning to be able to reflect upon themselves. The act of deciding seems more important than the subject of the decision. Many power struggles between adults and toddlers can be avoided since the adult is more aware of the child's limitations than the child is and is able to modify the situation accordingly. At this age children can begin to make choices, if the situation is tailored to their understanding and comprehension. The choice between two pairs of mittens is possible even when the choice between going out or staying inside may not be.

## THE PRESCHOOL CHILD: WIDENING CIRCLES

To be able to participate in an active, conscious way with other people in a democratic, decision making process, children must be able to comprehend that others may have different, yet valid, points of view, different feelings, and different reactions than their own. Research has demonstrated that children's abilities to think about their social worlds, to understand or consider others' thoughts, intentions and feelings appear far earlier than Piaget originally led us to believe. Piaget and his co-workers concluded that perspective-taking ability develops in three sequential stages, with egocentrism dominating until the age of 6. By splitting the concept of perspective-taking into cognitive perspective-taking, affective perspective-taking, and spatial perspective-taking, differences have been demonstrated in the age-levels at which these appear and in how the different aspects develop. By simplifying and making more familiar the original Piaget spatial task (the landscape in the sandbox to be matched with photographs of the view from different angles), Borke (1971) and Flavell (1978) have demonstrated some degree of spatial perspective-taking in 3- and 4-year olds.

Different levels of cognitive role-taking skill have also been described. Selman (1976) has recorded what he calls "egocentric role taking" in children at age three years, when children can understand that others may have distinctive thoughts and feelings, but cannot yet distinguish between their own and others' perspective of the same experience. Children at this stage judge that others will view an experience in the same way they do, moving at age 6 to a stage where they can make the distinction between self-centered and other-centered viewpoints, but without the ability to differentiate their own actions or thoughts from the other's viewpoint. This stage has, however, been demonstrated in 4-year olds (Marvin, Greenberg, & Mossler, 1976) in experiments that demand less verbal proficiency and in other ways are more experientially direct and concrete for the child. In much the same way, affective perspective-taking has been demonstrated in 3-to-4-year olds (Dickstein, Lieber, & McIntyre, 1976).

The newly acquired ability for perspective-taking may be the basis for new developments in play, when peers systematically begin to adjust and combine their lines of play invention to create a single frame of play (Garvey, 1982). A 3-year-old playing alone will display rich imagination and create reproductions of dramatic episodes for the child's real-life experiences, but has little ability to share this world with a child from a different kind of home. The shared fantasies of 4-year olds has, as Trevarthen (1992) puts it, "attracted the interest of many researchers concerned with language development and with the grasp of cultural knowledge in dramatic or pretend form. However, this is a field which still waits on a theoretical synthesis, the thinking of most experts being fragmented by attempts to explain cognitive development or the acquisition of language" (129).

Five-year olds demonstrate improving skills in cooperative play, which depends on recognition of and adjustment to the separate feelings, experiences, and ideas of another person on the basis of a mutual desire to share. As Trevarthen (1992) observes, "The preschoolers then enter a new plane of symbolic awareness because they have begun to share interpretations with a person of similar level of experience and similarly observant of the culture around them" (179). It is, therefore, easier for a preschool child to "decentralize" in relation to peers than to adults, and that this field of experience is one that children cannot get if they spend all their time with adults or children who are very much younger or older. Comparing children in different cultures, Whiting and Edwards (1988) found that there were major differences in terms of how much time children spent with different categories of child companions; children's culture, developmental age, and sex strongly determined the company they kept. They note, "Nevertheless, when children of a given age are in the presence of a particular kind of company—a particular class of child companion—there are transcultural consistencies in their profile of interaction'' (268). Furthermore they found that ''similar patterns of social behavior also result from the shared physical and cognitive capacities of young children and shared dimensions of the scripts for the daily lives of young children. However, as children mature and gain new capacities based on transformation and reorganization of their cognitive skills, they acquire new motives or intentions for social behavior. . . . [which] . . . diminish the power of . . . [the similar] responses'' (269). Much of the children's behavior is aimed at establishing gender identity, practicing sex-role behavior, and acquiring knowledge on culturally important skills. Since sex roles and skills vary from culture to culture, children in different settings will grow apart, and girls and boys within the same culture will engage in more differentiated behavior. The 5- to 6-year old's perception of the roles of other people also changes. Younger children could, for instance, see an aunt as a person who could offer comfort, but when older she was perceived as a ''woman'' and, as an adult, someone to be avoided. The younger children might formerly perceive both older and younger siblings as playmates, but now may see the elder as an authority, the younger as a pest. Interestingly, in different societies an age difference of about two years seems crucial. The younger child will try to model behavior after the older child, but not if the age difference is more than two to three years. This may indicate that ''decentralizing'' is easier when the age difference is no more than three years.

Social competence is first established in relation to adults, in the feedback activities between baby and parents that start soon after birth. By age 5, the child is capable of understanding simple reasons and rules, but does not yet know how rules are made. The child is (at least sometimes) willing to modify her own wish or her ideas, her right to make decisions, in relation to the social functioning of the group.

Contact with and recognition by peers is something the children must gain. They must use language the other children understand. Unlike communication with parents, the child cannot get away with a private kind of communication. So competency at this stage is about understandable, common language communication as a well as about social relationships. Play is the important vehicle for learning how to solve the conflicts that occur in role playing. This type of learning is different from the learning children do in relation to adults, simply because peers are equals.

As development proceeds, the complexity of decision-making, responsibility and self-confidence increases, particularly as widening circles of activity lead to interactions with peers and other adults as well as parents. During the preschool years the child's ability to think about time and space as well as cause and effect also increases. Combined with the effects of gaining more experience, the child will also be able to make ''wiser'' choices and decisions.

## SOCIAL DEVELOPMENT IN THE SCHOOL AGE YEARS

During the school age years, the child certainly moves away from the family into the wider world of peers. The focus on development has been on cognitive, social, and moral development. In this connection, social and moral development are of particular interest. The theoretical models of Piaget, Kohlberg, Gilligan, and others describe stages of moral development that in many ways correspond with and are dependent upon the stages of cognitive development. Rules and morals are of particular concern and interest to children during this period, developing from an individual-based, concrete perception of rules and morals as external guides to behavior to a more abstract perception of rules and morals as principle issues, necessary for the functioning of society. This development depends upon social stimulation, "the kind that comes from social interaction and from moral decision-making, moral dialogue, and moral interaction" (Kohlberg as cited in Flekkøy & Kaufman, 1997, 101). Cognitive development alone will not lead to moral development. An absence of cognitive stimulation may, however, codetermine the ceiling of moral level. The bridge between cognitive level and moral level lies in the person's level of role-taking, that is, the person's ability to take the attitude of others, become aware of their thoughts and feelings, putting oneself in their place, and gradually being able to take the consequences of this understanding. The richer the variety of role-taking opportunities a child is exposed to, the better his/her possibilities are for moral learning. One of the clearest determinants of moral stage advance in children is the disposition of parents to allow or encourage dialogue on value issues. Other elements of the child's environment also make a difference. According to Kohlberg (1976) children growing up on an Israeli kibbutz demonstrated a higher level of moral development than, for example, children growing up in an American orphanage. The American orphanages lacked not only interaction with parents, but involved very little communication and role taking between staff adults and children and among the children themselves.

There is an increasing awareness of the importance of the learning experiences that children from the age of three to four years through their teens can only get in a peer group (Frones, 1987). In a group of equals, a child learns how a democracy functions, what the rules for making rules are (Piaget, 1955; Kohlberg, 1968), and which attitudes, skills, and behaviors are acceptable among equals. Fewer and fewer families can provide such learning opportunities at home. A younger generation with one to two members can never out-vote two parents, and the children are always smaller, younger, and with less experience than the majority. The children, of course, benefit from this situation, but to learn the rules of democracy, how equals can function together peacefully, children need other children in addition to the family.

In the peer-group, membership depends on the group as well as on the individual. The peer group, in contrast to the family, is a group where belonging is not assured simply by membership. Children, among peers, learn when they are excluded and what the conditions are for joining again. They can also voluntarily leave the group, even "forever," with the family as a retreat. The group can expel an unwanted member or let a wanted member back in, on conditions or according to implicit or explicit rules formulated by the group. Making rules for group behavior or for the group's activities teaches children how rules are made, how they can be changed, what makes a leader (which may not be entirely positive), and what kinds of behavior are acceptable to remain in the group. The child can join and leave various groups and participate in several groups simultaneously. Being a long-term or short-term member of a variety of peer groups provides diverse experiences.

In the family, the child belongs regardless of behavior. The family offers learning possibilities that a peer group cannot give: how to solve even long-standing conflicts in lasting relationships with people who care about the child regardless of what the child does, with people the child cannot get rid of (even when she or he briefly wants to do so) or who rarely seriously want to get rid of the child.

Consequently, children need to spend some, but not all, of their time with other children. They also need time together without adult control. The sometimes rough but necessary learning among children, teaching each other how groups of equals function and how to solve conflicts among equals, cannot be achieved if the groups are constantly controlled by adults. Interesting results of recent studies of "deprived" environments (Parker, Greer, & Zuckerman, 1988), aimed at identifying the strengths of these environments, was that "opportunities for play with peers and older children with minimal adult interference enhanced the development of self-reliance, self-control, cooperation, empathy and a sense of belonging" (1232).

## SOCIAL COMPETENCE

Social competence is for many children the basis for acceptance by their peers. Socially competent children have more friends and are in general happier with their relationships to other children. But social competence is not in itself sufficient; children also need to feel competent and have the social skills that are required and wish to use them. This requires motivation. The social skills include the ability to cooperate, share, help others, and follow the rules or understand the consequences of breaking them. Asking for help when needed, standing up for oneself, reacting in adequate ways to the behavior of others, being able to wait for a turn, compromise, and finally to empathize by showing concern and respect for the feelings and views of others are part of the complicated set of skills included in social competence.

Socially competent children are generally well adjusted, have fewer problems in schools and at home, can handle difficult situations better, and are more accepted by peers than less socially competent peers. A Norwegian study (Ogden, Backe-Hansen, & Kristofersen, 1994) confirmed these general principles, but also uncovered some differences, such as those between girls and boys. At age 10 both sexes were less differentiated in their own views of social competence than their parents and teachers. Children seemed to feel that if they could cooperate, they were also good at self-control and self-presentation. The girls scored higher on empathy and cooperation than the boys. Girls also had a tendency to underestimate their own abilities as compared to adult evaluation, while the boys tended to overestimate their skills. At age 14 the picture was very much the same. Again, the girls were given higher scores on empathy and cooperation, by the adults as well as by themselves, while boys and girls were considered equal in self-control and self-representation.

## RIGHTS AND SOCIAL COMPETENCE

Given the time it has taken many adults to accept the idea that children should have rights, it may be surprising to many even to think about how children themselves perceive their rights. Children have obviously had rights, although not a convention, long enough to have some ideas about what rights are and which are important to them.

As with moral development, views on competence and rights change over time, and normally one expects that acceptance of rights for the child might change as the child matures. The levels appear to move from concrete here and now—what one wants to have or do—to the somewhat more abstract—what one should be able to have or do—to abstract principles—what one must be able to have or do as a matter of principle, such as natural rights (Melton & Limber, 1992, 174). These levels correspond with the cognitive development of children, so that the idea that rights are not revocable by authority is not established until early adolescence, when the child develops more abstract thinking. Age seems to be the most powerful determinant of concepts of rights, but social class and culture also have an effect, as demonstrated in comparisons between American and Norwegian children (Melton & Limber, 177–179).

## CONCLUSION

Living conditions that are adequate for promoting a healthy social development include adults and other children. Sensitive adults who respect the dignity and integrity of the child are needed as interaction partners, consultants, models, and teachers. Adults can help by encouraging self-expression in ways that are socially acceptable, tailoring possibilities and explaining alternative options for choices, and teaching children how and when they can share democratic decision making. Adults are also needed to protect children against hazardous consequences of choices and decisions. Children also need a spectrum of different social learning situations, a continuum from solitary play (or even boredom) to the peer group (without adults) to the mixed age-group even with adults as equal members, to adult-led groups and the close-knit stability of the family, spanning generations.

Article 27 read in context with the rest of the *Convention* supports a wide range of activity necessary for the child's development. It also identifies the centrality of the family in promoting the child's social development as one dimension of the child's total developmental needs, and that such development relies on an adequate standard of living.

## NOTE

The authors wish to thank María L. Blanco for her helpful assistance with this chapter.

## REFERENCES

Borke, H. (1971). Interpersonal perception of young children: egocentrism or empathy? *Developmental Psychology, 57,* 263–269.

Bowlby, J. (1969). *Attachment and Loss: Vol. 1. Attachment.* New York: Basic Books.

Braten, S. (1992). The virtual other in infants' minds and social feelings. In A. H. Wold (Ed.) *The dialogical alternative: Towards a theory of language and mind* (77–97). Oslo: Scandinavian University Press.

Brazelton, T. B., Koslowski, B., & Main, M. (1974). The origin of reciprocity: The early mother-infant interaction. In M. Lewis, & R. Rosenblum (Eds.), *The effects of the infant on its caregiver* (49–76). New York: John Wiley.

De Casper, A. J. & Fifer, W. P. (1982). Of human bonding: Newborns prefer their mother's voices. *Science 208,* 111–118.

De Casper, A. J. & Spence, M. J. (1987). Prenatal maternal speech influences newborns' perception of speech sounds. *Annual Progress in Child Psychiatry and Child Development,* 5–25.

Dickstein, E. B., Lieber, L. E., & McIntyre, C. W. (1976). The development of cognitive, affective and perceptual role-taking skills. Unpublished paper, quoted in S. G. Moore & D. R. Cooper (Eds.), (1982) *The young child: Reviews of research* (Vol. 3). Washington, DC: National Association for the Education of Young Children.

Erikson, E. H. (1950). *Childhood and society.* New York: Norton.

Fernald, A. & Kuhl, P. K. (1987). Acoustic determinants of infant preference for mother's speech. *Infant Behaviour and Development, 10* (3), 279–293.

Field, T. (1990). *Infancy.* Cambridge, MA: Harvard University Press.

Flavell, J. H. (1978). The development of knowledge about visual perception. In N. Keashey (Ed.), *Nebraska symposium on motivation* (421–453). Lincoln: University of Nebraska Press.

Flekkøy, M. G. & Kaufman, N. H. (1997) *The participation rights of the child.* London: Jessica Kingsley Publishers.

Frones, I. (1987). On the meaning of peers. In *Canadian Seminar on Childhood Implications for Child Care Policies.* Vienna: European Centre for Social Welfare Policy and Research.

Garvey, C. (1982, December). Communication and the development of social role play. *New Directions for Child Development, 18*, 81–101.

Gilligan, C. (1982). New maps of development: New visions of maturity. *American Journal of Orthopsychiatry 52*, 2.

Grieser, D. L. & Kuhl, P. K. (1988). Maternal speech to infants in a tonal language: Support for universal prosodic features in motherese. *Developmental Psychology, 24*, 14–20.

Hubley, P. & Trevarthen, C. (1979). Sharing a task in infancy. In I. Uzgiris (Ed.), *Social interaction during infancy: New directions for child development* (Vol. 4). San Francisco: Jossey-Bass.

Kohlberg, L. (1968). The child as a moral philosopher. *Psychology Today, 2*(4), 25–30.

Kohlberg, L. (1976). Moral stages and moralization. In T. Lickona (Ed.), *Moral development and behavior* (31–53). New York: Holt, Rinehart & Winston.

Lombardi, K. L. & Lapidos, E. (1990) Therapeutic engagements with children: Integrating infant research and clinical practice. *Psychoanalytic Psychology 7*, 1.

Marvin, R. S., Greenberg, M. T., & Mossler, D. G. (1976). The early development of conceptual perspective-taking: Distinguishing among multiple perspectives. *Child Development, 47*(2), 511–514.

Melton, G. B. & Limber, S. P. (1992). What children's rights mean to children: Children's own views. In M. Freeman & P. Veerman (Eds.), *The ideologies of children's rights* (167–187). Dordrecht: Kluwver Academic Publishers.

Murray, L. & Trevarthen, C. (1985). Emotion regulation of interaction between two month olds and their mothers. In T. M. Field & N. Fox (Eds.), *Social perceptions in infants*. Greenwich, CT: Ablex.

Ogden, T., Backe-Hansen, E., & Kristofersen, L. (1994). *Barnog Unges Sociale Kompetanse*. Oslo: Prosjekt Oppvekstnettverk.

Parker, S., Greer, S., & Zuckerman, B. (1988). Double jeopardy: The impact of poverty on early child development. *Pediatric Clinics of North America, 35*(6), 1227–1240.

Piaget, J. (1952). *The origin of intelligence in children*. New York: International Universities Press.

Piaget, J. (1955). *The moral judgement of the child*. New York: International Universities Press.

Selman, R. L. (1976). Social-cognitive understanding: A guide to educational and clinical practice. In T. Lickona (Ed.), *Moral development and behavior* (299–316). New York: Holt, Rinehart & Winston.

Stern, D. (1974). The goal of structure of mother-infant play. *Journal of the American Academy of Child Psychiatry, 13*, 401–421.

Stern, D. (1985). *The interpersonal world of the infant: A view from psychoanalysis and developmental psychology*. New York: Basic Books.

Trevarthen, C. (1977). Descriptive analyses of infant communication behaviour. In H. R. Schaffer (Ed.), *Studies in mother-infant interaction: The Loch Lomond symposium* (227–270). London: Academic Press.

Trevarthen, C. (1992). An infant's motives for speaking and thinking. In A. H. Wold (Ed.), *The dialogical alternative: Towards a theory of language and mind* (99–137). Oslo: Scandinavian University Press.

Whiting, B. B. & D. Edwards (1988). *Children of different worlds*. Cambridge, MA: Harvard University Press.

# PART III

# COMMUNITY CONTEXT

# 10

# Significance of Community Wealth for Child Development: Assumptions and Issues

*Frank D. Barry*

Not surprisingly, given its focus on national governments, Article 27 contains no mention of communities or neighborhoods or any role or responsibility they may bear in providing adequate conditions of living for a child's development. In addressing only the largest and the smallest units of organization (states parties and families), Article 27 leaves any role for communities or other intermediate units to be inferred. As a basis for making such inferences, this chapter will present three key assumptions regarding the role of the community in child development; it will end with a discussion of several issues that arise with communities in relation to Article 27.

## CRITICAL ASSUMPTIONS

### Communities Are Diverse in Nature and Must Be Broadly Defined

Much time and effort has been invested in defining community. Rather than re-engaging in this process, it may be more productive to simply respect diversity in definition. The word "community" can be used to describe a small crossroads hamlet, an entire town or city, an urban neighborhood, a group with shared customs or interests (i.e., the Moslem community, the business community), or even macro units (a "community of nations"). For us, the most important context of community is the opportunity for face to face—or at least direct—personal contact and communication for children and for their families, with respect to childrearing and everything that involves.

In most instances pursuing this aspect will result in a community defined in geographic terms, but the definition may vary for different economic levels. For some families, access to frequent and easy transportation (i.e., a car or a good transit system) or to a telephone or electronic communication may extend the concept of community well beyond the core neighborhood in which they actually live. Obviously such mobility is common among those at higher income levels, but face to face geographical community is still very important to low income families who have fewer resources. Low-income people typically cannot so easily communicate with people outside their immediate area, and as a result, they have less ability to choose their friends than people with more ability to get around; to a much greater extent, their neighborhood constitutes their "world." As Garbarino puts it, "Rich people can afford a weak neighborhood better than poor people, who therefore must rely much more heavily on the social resources of their ecological niche for support, encouragement and feedback" (Garbarino, 1980, 81). The relative freedom and mobility of middle and upper class professionals, planners, and policy makers may lead them to underestimate the importance of community for child development for those with fewer resources (Barry & Garbarino, 1997).

## The Community is the Primary Environment or Habitat within which the Family Functions, and the Community Therefore Directly Affects the Quality of Parenting and Child Development within Its Boundaries

Dr. Urie Bronfenbrenner (1979) established the importance of the community for child development through his discussion of the significance of microsystems in which the child interacts directly with others (i.e., as in a family, school, or day care center)—and mesosystems, which serve as bridges between at least two of these microsystems. In short, not only these subsystems, but the linkage between them play critical roles in that child's development. Cochran et al. (1990) demonstrated the importance of networks for parenting and child development. Rosenbaum et al. (1993) found that children of low-income families who were moved from a violent inner-city housing project to a suburban community were much more likely to enter college and obtain employment than children of similar families who were moved out of the housing project, but remained in the same depressed community. And Garbarino and Kostelny (1992) discovered a strong relationship between child abuse reporting and fatalities, and perception of community effectiveness among those familiar with the community. Wilson (1987) and Schorr (1988) have linked child outcomes to neighborhood quality. Finally, numerous reports have recommended strengthening neighborhoods and communities as a means of preventing various social problems (Blyth, 1993; Carnegie Council on Adolescent Development, 1994; National Commission on Children, 1991; U.S. Advisory Board on Child Abuse and Neglect, 1993; Wynn et al., 1994).

All of these findings concern aspects of communities in which people relate directly to each other. Clearly if these communities provide a poor environment for raising children, families will have a difficult time securing the conditions of living necessary for the child's development. Community quality is therefore critical to child development.

## The Community Is the Child's Introduction to the World beyond His or Her Family and Home

While the previous assumption implies an indirect effect of the community on the child via the family, the current assumption implies a more direct impact by community, as the child grows old enough to begin functioning outside its family. Typically, the growing child's first interaction with the world outside its home takes place within his or her community—with relatives who live nearby, neighbors, storekeepers, adults and children in the neighborhood, in day care settings, schools, religious organizations, youth organizations, and so forth. As the child grows older, he or she establishes a face to face network that includes both other children and adults who serve as guides and mentors. The people in this network contribute, positively or negatively, to that child's physical, mental, spiritual, moral, and social development.

Reaching out to form new relationships is an important task of adolescence. Young people develop their identities by reaching beyond their immediate families to find a place for themselves in the broader community. The supports and opportunities they encounter will play an important role in the success of their transition from school to work and from childhood to adulthood. They need good role models, adults and other youth who can influence them positively. Boys need good male role models especially if they have grown up in a single mother household. Adolescents need to find a place outside their homes where they feel they matter—where they can belong to something (National Commission on Children, 1991).

Apprenticeships, part-time jobs, participation in family or local farms, industry, or business, as well as sports, art, drama, after school activities, and community service can serve as constructive responses to this need. If the community does not provide constructive opportunities for youth to socialize and develop, youth may create their own opportunities, but these will not necessarily be constructive. The proliferation of violent gangs in some areas illustrates what can happen in the absence of positive opportunities (Arthur, 1992).

Besides constructive opportunities and positive role models, communities play an important role in raising children and youth by establishing standards of behavior, and monitoring and intervening when behavior is unacceptable (Sampson, Raudenbush, & Earls, 1997). In an early study, Maccoby, Johnson, and Church (1958) were able to demonstrate that incidence of juvenile delinquency was related to neighborhood integration and willingness of unrelated adults to intervene. More recently, Erez (1987) found that only 17 percent of criminals interviewed in a Philadelphia cohort study had planned their crimes. Most crimes and acts of delinquency were impulsive and spontaneous; they occurred when there was "a good opportunity." Such "opportunities" would appear related to the extent of community monitoring and the likelihood that those who take advantage of them will be seen, recognized, reported, and disciplined.

In some communities, particularly among poorer areas in the United States, the underlying theme for teenagers is the lack of a significant role, the lack of integration into the economy and society. In these communities, idleness and boredom have become a predominant theme, and in some of them juvenile delinquency and even crimes are committed simply to create excitement. In fact, Erez found the "search for excitement" to be the most frequent reason for the act that led to a youth's first arrest.

In some other parts of the world, particularly in developing countries, the chief concern is the reverse—not idleness, but exploitation of children and youth through excessive labor at very low wages, which does not allow time for play, education, or other essentials of child development. And in still other settings, concern centers on street youth who have been left to fend for themselves by families unable to support them, and are largely neglected (or worse) by the community.

## ISSUES

These assumptions lead to five policy questions for discussion:

1. How should "community wealth" be defined? Do community wealth and an adequate standard of living refer to more than economic factors? If we are concerned with child development, the answer would appear to be yes. It might be useful to think of wealth as "capital"—because this allows us to incorporate the concepts of "human capital" (productive and well educated residents, as defined by Parkman in this volume) and social capital, which Putnam defines as "networks, norms and trust that facilitate coordination and cooperation" (Putnam, 1993, 4). Putnam and others believe these forms of capital are necessary for economic development. Are they necessary for child development, too?

From a child development perspective, a community should be able to provide children with time with nurturing adults, traditions, guidance, teaching, acceptance, love, caring, productive roles, mentoring, and monitoring. All of these are noneconomic "goods" that can best be provided to children and youth at family and community levels. Should these be included in a definition of wealth? At times these "soft" qualities may be inconsistent with economic wealth, as some families and communities will sacrifice some of them in order to accumulate economic and material goods. And achieving at least a basic level of wealth is important to child development, too. But it seems obvious that both forms of wealth are essential for children to develop properly, even if the trade-off between them is not always clear.

If wealth is to include more than money, how can it be measured? How would we know whether a community has it or not? More to the point, how would we know whether a community has enough of it to satisfy Article 27, paragraph 1?

One possible answer would be to infer from the outcome. If an unusually large percentage of children in a particular community grow up unable to function effectively in their country's culture, we could conclude that this community lacks wealth in some form—at least from the perspective of childrearing. Conversely, a community that produces an unusually large number of distinguished and effective adults presumably has a high degree of the community wealth we are interested in. We might also consider whether a low income community that produces a higher than predicted number of capable and effective adults would be "wealthy" even though the percentage of such adults is lower than that of a higher income community with a higher predicted rate, based on its socioeconomic status.

Perhaps it would help to ask how a child would define community wealth. We might ask for example, what things a child would look for in a community if he/she could decide where to live. And what attributes would a child miss most if they were lacking in a community? This will doubtless depend on the age and personality of the child, but it is likely that economics would be only one factor. In a survey to determine attitudes of rural students in New York state toward their home communities, Hedlund (1993) found that personal relationships and community supports were viewed as important community assets.

If Putnam (1993) can argue effectively, as he does, that human and social capital are important in the production of economic wealth, then we should have no trouble including these dimensions in the definition of community wealth, whether the term is used in an economic or child development context. Geographically defined communities produce not only economic goods, but also children—most of whom become productive workers and parents. The quality of these "locally produced" persons is arguably just as important to the community's long-term economic and social wealth as the quality of its economic products. Therefore factors contributing to effective childrearing should be considered an important dimension of community wealth, however the term is used.

2. Is there a minimum standard of community wealth, below which a community simply is not adequate, and therefore in violation of Article 27, paragraph 1? As a result of intensive observation and study, it has been possible to establish environmental standards and requirements for various forms of wildlife. Consequently we know what kinds of forest cover is needed to sustain spotted owls in the Pacific Northwest of the United States (Thomas, 1990). We know what kind of water acidity levels are required for various species of fish. Do we know with the same precision what requirements our own communities should meet to produce competent adults? Would such requirements be universal or would they vary across different countries and cultures and across time?

This question is important because our communities in many respects serve the same function for people as a forest does for spotted owls. Both the forest and human communities provide the context and habitat for raising and social-izing the young of the species. But can community adequacy be universal? What children need to function effectively in their society depends partly on the re-quirements of their culture as well as their biological and psychological needs. In India poverty is defined as having access to less than 2,100 calories per day (2,400 in rural areas) (Fonseka & Malhotra, 1994). A more wealthy country might set a higher standard for caloric intake, but presumably some biological minimum might be found. In other areas, identification of basic needs is more difficult. For example, the type and amount of education needed may vary con-siderably across both cultures and time. In the United States, relatively few jobs required a high school education before World War II, but today there are few that do not.

Would running water and electricity be considered essentials? Perhaps yes, especially in industrialized societies, but most of the world's population func-tioned successfully without either for many centuries. What about television? What about two parent families? How much difference can exist in what is considered adequate without creating destructive tensions?

In short, there would be two components to any minimum standard: first, biological requirements, which presumably would be somewhat constant across time and place and second, cultural components that vary across time and place—and even biological requirements will vary according to average physical size, climate, and lifestyle. So a universal minimum standard probably would not be useful if it went beyond biological requirements. To be useful, any stan-dard should be based on what it takes to raise a child to function effectively in his or her society as an adult—at least to the extent of being able to support a family, raise children effectively, and participate in maintaining the institutions of civilization that his or her culture enjoys. This would not subject Indians living in a rain forest to the same standard applied to wealthy suburbs in the United States or large metropolises in Latin America, but would at least ensure continuation of the prevailing culture in each.

3. To what extent is there a community responsibility for raising children, and to what extent is this the responsibility of families individually? This ques-tion gets at the substance of the popular African proverb: "It takes a whole village to raise a child." It involves at least two important issues: First, to what extent does community wealth involve a collective responsibility for raising children? For example, could "community wealth" imply a community of wealthy individual families making individual arrangements for their children's needs, or must it involve some form of community decision making, resource sharing, and collective action to support parents and to provide for children's needs?

This issue comes into full focus when children become adolescents and begin to move beyond their families and parentally established boundaries. What should be the role of the community in providing constructive roles and oppor-tunities for them? What should be the community role in monitoring and regulating their behavior? Is the ability to do this implied in the definition of community wealth?

The second issue involves monitoring of parents. To what extent does community wealth imply a community willingness to monitor or compensate for individual parental inadequacy? Would a wealthy community provide formal or informal supports to parents to minimize the conditions that result in child abuse, for example? And if child abuse still occurred, would it have an effective means of intervening to stop it? Would it at least have a means of providing compensatory care to minimize its effects? Or would it assume that in a community with a high standard of living, every family has the resources to raise its children successfully, and that it's up to each family to do so without interference from neighbors?

The answers to these questions are somewhat complex. Wealthy people may not interact much with their immediate neighbors, and therefore their neighborhoods may appear to lack social capital and cohesiveness. But, as discussed earlier, their concept of community may be less geographically oriented, and they and their children may participate heavily in networking via telephone or e-mail as well as frequent use of family automobiles. But does this relieve such people of the responsibility for paying attention to issues and needs in their immediate neighborhood? It is not clear how to weigh attachments to neighbor against income because to a certain extent one can substitute for the other. But one thing is clear—a community whose residents have a strong attachment to place and to their neighbors, and also an adequate income level, will have more community wealth than a community with one but not the other.

4. What is the role of the community in enforcing the U.N. *Convention*? This question follows from the previous question about community versus family responsibility. Given the importance of community as the context in which families function and its demonstrated effect on childrearing, does the community unit have any implied obligation or responsibility to enforce the U.N. *Convention*? This question may seem out of place because obviously communities have no international or sovereign status and they cannot participate in any U.N. ratification procedure. But communities are where the families and children are. It is hard to imagine an effective national policy being implemented without participation and involvement at the community level.

In reality, implementation and enforcement will probably not be meaningful to children except at the community level, since communities are the major context for interaction between families, children, and society. Communities are where children and families will feel the effects of government policies and actions or the lack thereof. Therefore the relationship between national government, with the power to sign and ratify the convention, and communities, with the power to affect families and children directly, is critical. Will this relationship be one of education, involvement, and empowerment or top down authoritarianism or perhaps benign neglect?

Regardless of their importance in the rearing and socialization of children, some communities may have little freedom to make decisions or changes, or to take collective action. They may be bound by traditions or beliefs that perpetuate a fatalistic or dependent mentality, or they may be controlled by a highly centralized government. Some may lack an effective decision making structure and others may lack resources. Some may be victims of national or international economic policies or economic changes that have weakened or eroded their economic base. Some of these problems may lie mainly within the community, while others lie totally beyond the community's ability for resolution. But one reality is constant regardless: Article 27 will not affect children's lives until it reaches the community level, however that occurs. Ideally it should take the form of a working partnership between national and intermediate governments and the community itself.

5. To what extent are national or provincial governments responsible for community wealth and well-being? To what extent does the U.N. *Convention* imply a government obligation to nurture and strengthen its communities and neighborhoods, since that is where its families and children are? To what extent and how should development strategies focus on communities and neighborhoods as opposed to, say, national infrastructure or defense? And to what extent will the interests and survival of neighborhoods and communities be protected in relation to large infrastructure projects? Halpern (1995) documented the manner in which urban highway construction was actually used to destroy minority communities in U.S. cities during the 1950s and 1960s. Will adherence to the principles of children's rights require governments to avert such social harms?

A major related issue involves redistribution of wealth and power. Does the government have an obligation to redistribute resources (economic wealth) to those communities that may need it most? How much obligation does a national government have to transfer resources from relatively wealthy areas with good farmland or manufacturing to poor, perhaps mountainous or desert areas where the standard of living is much less adequate? Should industries be subsidized to provide jobs in such areas as a means of strengthening these communities— and perhaps preventing or slowing migration to overpopulated urban centers? Should the government do more in these areas to finance services and improve infrastructure than it does in relatively well-off areas? Does the national government have an obligation to promote and direct economic development where living standards indicate it is most needed or where development can occur most efficiently? To what extent does economic development need to be tempered or regulated to insure that children's needs are not sacrificed in the process—to limit child labor and serious damage to the environment, for example?

## CONCLUSION

It is hard to answer all these questions. But posing them at least helps put things in perspective. For example, whether or how much a government ought to subsidize weak local economies or redistribute wealth to satisfy Article 27 is clearly debatable. But it should be much easier to agree that governments at least ought not to undertake projects or policies that seriously weaken communities. In the United States, major construction projects require environmental impact statements to assess, among other things, their impact on wildlife. Surely their impact on communities and their physical and social infrastructure is no less important.

Perhaps we can distinguish between attempting to compensate for natural environmental factors, such as climate or altitude, which are relatively hard to overcome, and the effects of man-made forces, which are a more logical domain of government. By this criteria, arguably the most important obligation of national governments with respect to communities would be to protect them from harm by toxic forces created by man, war, discrimination, ethnic harassment, as well as industrial pollution. Preventing unrestricted economic forces from undermining entire communities in the case of disinvestment in U.S. inner cities (Wilson, 1987; Halpern, 1995) would be another, more complex example of a such a toxic force. Unfortunately while these are the factors for which our species is most clearly responsible, responding to them is an area in which many governments have acted least responsibly. Obviously it is an area in which implementation of Article 27 is most urgent.

This chapter has raised more questions than answers. Hopefully others will be able to go farther than I in finding useful answers.

## REFERENCES

Arthur, R. (1992). *Gangs and schools*. Holmes Beach, FL: Learning Publications.

Barry, F. (1995). Should we have environmental standards for communities? *Human Services in the Rural Environment, 19*, 27–35.

Barry, F. & Garbarino, J. (1997). Children in the community. In R. Ammerman & H. Hersen (Eds.), *Handbook of prevention and treatment with children and adolescents*. New York: Wiley.

Bronfenbrenner, U. (1979). *The ecology of human development: Experiments by nature and design*. Cambridge, MA: Harvard University Press.

Blyth, D. (1993). *Healthy communities, healthy youth: How communities contribute to positive youth development*. Minneapolis: Search Institute.

Carnegie Council on Adolescent Development. (1994). *A matter of time: Risk and opportunity in the out of school hours*. New York: Carnegie Corporation.

Cochran, M., Lamar, M., Riley, D., Gunnarson, L., & Henderson, C. (Eds.). (1990). *Extending families: The social networks of parents and their children*. New York: Cambridge University Press.

Erez, E. (1987). Situational or planned crime and the criminal career. In M. Wolfgang, Thornberry, & R. Figlio (Eds.), *From boy to man, from delinquency to crime*. Chicago: University of Chicago Press.

Fonseka, L. & Malhotra, D. (1994). India: Urban poverty, children and participation. In C. S. Blanc (Ed.), *Urban children in distress: Global predicaments and innovative strategies*. Yverdon, Switzerland: UNICEF, Gordon & Breach Science Publishers.

Garbarino, J. (1980). *Understanding abusive families*. New York: Lexington.

Garbarino, J. & Kostelny, K. (1992). Child maltreatment as a community problem. *Child Abuse and Neglect, 16*, 455–464.

Halpern, R. (1995). *Rebuilding the inner city: A history of neighborhood initiatives to address poverty in the United States*. New York: Columbia University Press.

Hedlund, D. (1993). Listening to rural adolescents: Views on the rural community and the importance of adult interactions. *Journal of Research in Rural Education, 9*, 150–159.

Maccoby, E., Johnson, J., Church, R. (1958). Community integration and the social control of juvenile delinquency. *Journal of Social Issues, 14*, 38–51.

National Commission on Children. (1991). *Beyond rhetoric: A new agenda for children and families*. Washington, DC: National Commission on Children.

Putnam, R. (1993). The prosperous community: Social capital and economic growth. *Current* 356, 4–9.

Rosenbaum, J., Fishman, N., Brett, A., & Meaden, P. (1993). Can the Kerner Commission's housing strategy improve employment, education and social integration for low income blacks? *North Carolina Law Review, 71*, 1519–1556.

Sampson, R., Raudenbush, S., & Earls, F. (1997). Neighborhoods and violent crime: A multilevel study of collective efficacy. *Science, 277*, 918–924.

Schorr, L. B. (1988). *Within our reach: Breaking the cycle of disadvantage*. New York: Doubleday.

Thomas, J. W. (1990). *Statement of Dr. Jack Ward Thomas, Chief Research Wildlife Biologist. Forest Service, Department of Agriculture*. Report of the Interagency Scientific Committee to address the conservation of the northern spotted owl: Hearing before the Subcommittee on Public Lands, National Parks and Forests, May 23 (29–37). Washington, DC: Committee on Energy and Natural Resources, U.S. Senate.

U.S. Advisory Board on Child Abuse and Neglect. (1993). *Neighbors helping neighbors: A new national strategy for the protection of children*. Washington, DC: U.S. Department of Health and Human Services, Administration for Children and Families.

Wilson, W. J. (1987). *The truly disadvantaged: The inner city, the underclass and public policy*. Chicago: University of Chicago Press.

Wynn, J., Costello, J., Halpern, & Richman, H. (1994). *Children, families and communities: A new approach to social services*. Chicago: Chapin Hall Center at the University of Chicago.

# 11

# Community Obligations and the Categorization of Children

### *Leroy H. Pelton*

The U.N. *Convention on the Rights of the Child* obviously focuses on prescription for children as a special category of human beings. My intent here is not to denounce such an effort nor to urge hasty repeal, but to begin to consider some problematic implications of human categorization in the context of community obligations, policy, and practice.

There is no reason for people to form or maintain a community other than to benefit the individuals within it. Communities have certainly been known to serve some of their individual members at the expense of others, or to neglect as well as to exploit or oppress some of their members. In all of these arrangements, nonetheless, the community exists because the interests of at least some individuals are served. It follows that a just community is one that benefits all of its individual members, not only some, and that the first responsibility of a just community toward its individual members is nondiscrimination.

If a just community exists to benefit every individual within it, then surely it must benefit and protect those most in need. Such a community cannot allow anyone within it to go hungry, shelterless, unclothed, or without medical attention. If it did, then what would be the meaning of community or its reason for being? To benefit some, but not others? To help the wealthy, but not the poor? Such a community would not be a just community, and this proposition has been recognized universally and throughout the ages, despite the fact that it has always been, at best, imperfectly implemented.

In ancient Hebrew society, farmers left corners of their fields unharvested, enabling whosoever was in need to come by and take what was needed to sustain them. This practice was called *tsedakah*, a Hebrew word that means charity, but also justice. The farmers' response was to need without judgment. Apparently, it was assumed that those in need would take and others would not.

In feudal times, churches and monasteries helped the poor. In colonial America, the colony or township coordinated the taking in of widows and children by others in the community, and soon appointed overseers of the poor. Thus communities have always recognized their obligations to the poor among them (Morris, 1986; Trattner, 1989).

However, probably whenever communities have grown larger than face-to-face communities, suspicion has arisen, undoubtedly along with the reality, that some individuals not in need of aid were taking it anyway, and that some, although capable of doing available work, were foregoing work and, in effect, unfairly living off the work of others in the community. They were not doing their fair share for the community while taking from the common wealth. In colonial times in America, this was not yet a problem since everyone in the township knew everyone else and their circumstances personally, but as towns and cities grew and immigration became massive, the special problems inherent in communities of strangers arose.

These problems are real: The community wishes to fulfill its obligation to help the needy, but it does not want to encourage fraud and freeloading. Thus it tries to distinguish between the "deserving" and "undeserving," and takes measures to discourage would-be freeloaders. Seen in this light, and judging from the welfare problems at present in, for example, the United States, perhaps we can appreciate without contempt the efforts made by historical communities to deal with these problems. The development of poorhouses and workhouses, the stigmatizing of the poor, the efforts to judge whether applicants for assistance were truly "worthy" and to categorize their need, and the paltriness of the material assistance actually given do not necessarily reflect any cruelty and lack of generosity and human decency on the part of the community and its policymakers. Rather, they may represent earnest attempts to come to grips with real policy problems. The difficulty is that no large community has ever figured out a way to address these concerns without hurting the "worthy needy" at the same time, or without leaving some individuals—even children—to continue unfed, unhoused, or unclothed.

Yet children, it would seem, have a special claim upon any community that would aspire toward justice. They are dependent upon adults for their sustenance and development and are recognized as innocent victims of poverty, by virtue of the fact that they had no control over what families or situations they would be born into. Moreover, they have no obligations, as yet, to contribute to the community. However, being members of the community, they are entitled to its benefits. In no sense can their claims on the common wealth be regarded as fraudulent, or can they be suspected of "freeloading." The community is obliged to respond without judgment to children in its midst who are in need.

From this perspective, it would be difficult to imagine how any categorical approach to social welfare could discriminate against children. Yet consider the

American Social Security Act, which, in the tradition of the Elizabethan Poor Laws, divided the needy into categories based on group characteristics and not need alone. The result was that the program for the poor elderly, for example, provided for higher cash benefits than did the program for dependent children. Moreover, able-bodied poor men (and poor women without children) were not even included in the Act. Thus a hierarchy of benefits was formed that implicitly judged the poor elderly to be more worthy than poor children and poor non-elderly adults to be unworthy. Welfare categorization disperses those in need among different categories, thereby setting up individuals of equivalent need for differential treatment.

But why would children as a category suffer from such an approach? Historically, although needy children have been regarded as innocent without equivocation, their parents have been suspect. The predominant assumptions have been that they are lazy, ignorant, unintelligent, imprudent, impulsive, prone to gambling and drinking, irresponsible, and immoral. It would be impossible to assist their children without "rewarding" their own deviant behavior, if their children were to remain with them. We would be encouraging their parents to be freeloaders upon the community. The choice has always come down to leaving the children with suspect parents or removing them for separate treatment.

But when there came to be too many children to remove, and therefore most children of even those parents whose "worthiness" was suspect had to be dealt with while still with their parents, a compromise was reached. Benefits that would have been set higher if based solely on the worthiness of children had to be tempered by the suspect worthiness of their parents. Thus benefits would fall at some in-between value. Proof of this is that communities have always been willing to support needy children more generously in institutions or foster homes than with their own parents.

Another perennial problem with public assistance that has been posed and grappled with from time to time is the fear that such assistance would generate a "spirit of dependency." That is, if things were made too decent even for honest and earnest poor people—by giving them cash assistance in their homes rather than material assistance in poorhouses or workhouses, or by giving them too "comfortable" a level of assistance—a habit of laziness might be aided or abetted. Also, unless the level of assistance were set below the remuneration of the lowest-paying jobs available, it might provide some people with a disincentive to work.

During the current wave of attacks on welfare in the United States, reforms have been implemented that disallow public assistance benefits for an additional child born to a mother while she is on welfare, require mothers to work or receive job training on penalty of having their public assistance benefits reduced or eliminated, and place a time limit on the receipt of benefits.

These "reforms" are aimed at controlling mothers' behavior, but hurt children in a discriminatory manner. Children that are born on welfare, through no fault of their own, will be denied benefits. If mothers do not comply with job-training requirements, it is their children who will be kicked off welfare. A society that withholds welfare benefits from some needy children and not from others, on the basis of irrelevant differential circumstances, practices discrimination, and by doing so in regard to the members of one category of welfare (children) and not to those of others, it practices double discrimination.

Mindful of the criticisms that the new policies will hurt innocent children, some conservatives have advocated that children be placed in "orphanages" ("The Orphanage," 1994), and that we should encourage single women to give up their children for adoption at birth (Herrnstein & Murray, 1994, 416). Indeed, such suggestions are merely the end result of the logic inherent in current welfare reforms, but also in past policies.

The categorical approach to social welfare, then, is deeply and morally flawed. It no doubt curtails freeloading, but only at the price of violating a higher value, that of a community fulfilling its basic obligations to children and other "innocent" people. In regard to children, the categorical approach leads a community to neglect their needs to a large extent or, in lieu of that, to the extreme measures of separating children from their parents.

Of course, Piven and Cloward (1971) have powerfully argued that a major function of public welfare is to regulate the behavior of poor people, primarily by quelling potential disorder that might lead to the overthrow of the prevailing order and government, thus unseating those who are currently in power. But the fact that the categories of welfare divide up people more on the basis of their presumed worthiness than their potential for disruptiveness indicates that altruism and a desire to do justice, as much as self-interest, motivate the community to establish welfare policy, however misguided the categorical approach has proved to be.

In arguing against the categorical approach, what we are really saying is that all children are minimally worthy of some basic provision of need. But then so are all individuals. A just community must establish in policy a floor of compassion under the needs of all individuals that responds to pure need regardless of "worthiness." Indeed, even criminals are given the basic necessities of life in prison, at the community's expense. The real question then becomes at what height to set this floor of compassion. But there is no reason, therefore, to have various welfare programs for different categories of individuals in need. No individual is "worthier" of minimal subsistence level provisions than any other, if we believe in the sanctity of human life.

Certainly, there are some special differential needs of children that must be advocated for separately and addressed separately. But one category of people or need must not be pitted against another. Every individual deserves the concern, the will, and the effort of our society to afford her or him justice, equal opportunity, and a minimal level of comfort. Surely, it is best to tend to the nurturing of individuals while they are still young, but we cannot abandon others simply because they are middle-aged or older. We must not attempt to weigh and debate the relative worth of one category of human beings over another, whether they be children or adults. All are valuable, period. The 8-year-old girl must not be allowed to live in squalor, ignorance, and hopelessness, but so must not her parents, nor the 80-year-old man.

But if a community is to benefit every child within it, then each child must have equal opportunity to develop his or her talents, abilities, and potential. Access to education is necessary for this. And first, to be able to take advantage of education, his or her minimal health and safety must be assured. A child who comes to school hungry or undernourished is at a disadvantage for learning.

Fortunately, given that a society has limited resources to be redistributed, or that it would want to redistribute, there is abundant evidence in recent history that growing up in a middle-class or wealthy family is not a necessary prerequisite for future economic or career success, provided that basic supports, such as universal education, are in place.

By providing a minimal floor of compassion, a community addresses dire need while at the same time preserving a system of incentives for merit, productivity, and accomplishment. Supportive and preventive services, then, can be seen as promoting the opportunities of individuals (through, for example, education, provision of day care, and health care) to gain rewards from working hard, and can be designed with such objectives in mind. Such provisions as public health care and education are basic supports that affirm that the rationale for the existence of the community is to protect and benefit every individual within it.

But as child development expert James Garbarino suggests, "personally impoverished families clustered in socially impoverished places" produce neighborhoods and situations in which "the conditions of life conspire to compound rather than counteract the deficiencies and vulnerabilities of parents" (Garbarino, 1981, 234, 237).

Ravaged inner-city neighborhoods that are drained of resources cannot be expected to be able to fund or provide their own services. They need help from the outside and from government. We cannot justifiably categorize our communal concerns any more than we can justifiably categorize people. Wealthier and poorer neighborhoods are responsible for each other. The community exists at the national level, and not merely at a neighborhood level. The existence of a national government and a national treasury are proof of a national community, and if such a community is a just one, then these instruments that represent it are utilized to serve all of the individuals within the community, no matter where they reside.

Yet national communities, both wealthy and poor, interact with each other in order to benefit themselves. By setting up countless international transactions, they form a world community. If this world community is to be a just one, then these transactions must be aimed at benefiting all individuals, regardless of communal or any other categorization. Ultimately, a just national community must be morally concerned with the individuals of other national communities with which it interacts and from which it benefits, and must recognize the existence of a world community.

## REFERENCES

Garbarino, J. (1981). An ecological approach to child maltreatment. In L. H. Pelton (Ed.), *The social context of child abuse and neglect* (228–267). New York: Human Sciences Press.

Herrnstein, R. J. & Murray, C. (1994). *The bell curve: Intelligence and class structure in American life.* New York: The Free Press.

Morris, R. (1986). *Rethinking social welfare: Why care for the stranger?* New York: Longman.

Piven, F. F. & Cloward, R. A. (1971). *Regulating the poor: The functions of public welfare.* New York: Vintage.

"The Orphanage." (1994, December 12), *Newsweek,* 28–33.

Trattner, W. I. (1989). *From poor law to welfare state: A history of social welfare in America* (4th ed.). New York: Free Press.

## 12

# The Application of Human Capital Theory to Article 27

*Allen M. Parkman*

Article 27, paragraph 1, of the *Convention on the Rights of the Child* places a duty on states parties to recognize the right of children to a standard of living adequate for their physical, mental, spiritual, moral, and social development (LeBlanc, 1995; Van Bueren, 1995). The *Convention* links a child's standard of living to other aspects of a child's moral and social development and notes that the right to an adequate standard of living extends beyond the child's right to survival. While the states have a duty to recognize this right, the parents have the primary responsibility to secure it with states assisting the parents in the areas of nutrition, clothing, and housing and in the recovery of maintenance.

This chapter discusses the role of human capital in assisting children to obtain an adequate standard of living. Human capital consists of individuals' improved productivity that results from investments made in them (Becker, 1993; Rosen, 1989). Therefore, increases in human capital are a central component of the ability to obtain an adequate standard of living. The concept of investing in people has a very wide application as it covers not only formal schooling and on-the-job training, but also a variety of other undertakings such as preschool interactions with parents, improved healthcare, and information acquisition. The primary benefit of human capital investments is a higher income, which is a foundation for an adequate standard of living, but the gains from enhanced human capital are not exclusively monetary. Studies show that investments in human capital, especially in education, promote numerous non-income benefits such as improved health based on better nutrition and less smoking, greater social awareness reflected in a higher propensity to vote and improved birth control knowledge, and a deeper appreciation of the arts (Michael, 1972).

Clearly, education plays a major role in the acquisition of human capital. However, since education and the states' roles in it are covered by Articles 28 and 29, the other influences on human capital will be discussed here.

## THE ROLE OF THE PARENTS

Parents have a central role in their children's acquisition of human capital through their investments in their children's knowledge, skills, values, and habits. Obviously, these investments involve the parent's time as well as money. Helping with homework can be as important as paying for private education. Investments during early childhood are crucial to later development because differences among young children grow larger over time because children learn more easily when they are better prepared.

Having described human capital and the important role that parents play in its acquisition does not provide us with a clear understanding of the incentives for and abilities of parents to provide it to their children. Recognition of the role of these incentives and abilities in human capital theory provides valuable insights for states to effectively implement Article 27, paragraph 1. Children have very little control over investments in their human capital, as those decisions initially are made by their parents with society later assuming a more active role. As self-interested decisionmakers, parents' investments in their children are influenced by their constraints of time and wealth and by their preferences. Gary Becker (1991) has written at length about the links between parents and children based on the parents' welfare being linked to the welfare of their children. While increasing their children's welfare is a benefit for the parents, it has to be balanced against the costs of those decisions. For example, parents are assumed to maximize the welfare of children when no reduction in their own consumption or leisure is entailed. When costs are associated with investments in children in the form of money or reduced leisure time, the parents' incentives are reduced for them to make decisions that increase their children's welfare.

The consideration of the costs and benefits of children has a central role in determining whether adults have children and, if they have any, how they act toward them. Increased productivity within a country leads to two effects on adults' demand for children (Becker, 1991). As people become more affluent, they want more of all desirable things, including children. However, there is a countervailing force since the affluence can only be attained by employment. As the potential earnings from and opportunities for employment increase for adults, the cost of sacrificing employment opportunities to assume parental responsibilities go up. In addition, some of the newly obtainable goods and services such as recreational activities conflict with the demands of parenthood. Children are desirable, but so are gourmet meals, vacations in the Caribbean, and fancy cars. Some adults may conclude that the costs of children are too high and their attraction too low, so they will elect to go childless.

Here we are concerned with adults who have and, we assume, want children. These parents will invest in their children's human capital so long as the benefits exceed the costs from their perspective. Their investments in their children will be influenced by a number of factors. We would expect investments per child to increase when the parents have larger incomes, are better educated, anticipate a long-term relationship with the child, have fewer children, and are not being subjected to discrimination (Haveman & Wolfe, 1995).

Parents experience a financial constraint on their ability to invest in their children when the family is poor and education is privately funded. Not only do more financial resources assist in financing education, but they also can increase travel and cultural activities that also contribute to human capital. Recognizing the financial constraints on children from poor families, public financing and provision of education has become common in most countries. Therefore, these constraints on investments in children probably have declined during this century in the United States and in many other countries because incomes have risen and government subsidies to education have grown.

The educational level of the parents is important because educated parents are in a better position to appreciate, encourage, and prepare their children for formal education (Becker, 1991). Wanting an education may not be instinctive, so the support and encouragement of parents can play a central role. In addition, while less educated parents may want to invest in their children by working on their school project with them, they may not be capable of providing that assistance.

A more subtle concern is the durability of the relationship between the parents and the children. Parents should be inclined to invest more in children with whom they expect to have an ongoing relationship because they will be in a position to benefit from their children's successes and to suffer due to their failures. This influence is particularly important in less developed countries as children's accomplishments will be more apparent to parents since they are less likely to move away from their parent's location. Parents in these countries have an additional incentive to be concerned because their children can be an important source of support for their parent's later years. Many of the less developed countries do not have the public pension plans that are common in the more industrial nations. Alternatively, these links can be weaker in industrial societies in which both parents and children frequently move. The prospect of divorce also can be another important cause of reduced contact between a parent and a child. If a father anticipates that his marriage is going to be dissolved with the mother receiving custody of the children, he has a weaker incentive to invest time and money in his children. Under those circumstances, there are fewer rewards from being a good parent and fewer costs from being a poor one.

The number of children in a family has been shown to have a strong influence on the investment per child because fewer funds are available per child. In addition, the incremental value of children's accomplishments tends to decrease as the number of children increases within a family, so that a given investment in a child has a smaller return to parents. Economists observe that the additional enjoyment from commodities decreases as their number increases, and that can occur with children. If a couple has only one child, that child can be the focal point of the parents' existence. Alternatively, in a large family the parents can be less aware of and concerned about the accomplishments of each child. The human capital invested in each child and, hence, the earnings of each child would then be negatively related to number of children as found in many studies (Becker, 1993). Last, parents who are discriminated against because of their race, caste, or other permanent characteristics anticipate a lower rate of return to investments in their children's human capital and, therefore, have incentives for making smaller investments in their children.

The preferences of the parents can also be important. Different preferences among ethnic groups in the United States have significant effects on their children's human capital as some have small families and the children become well educated, while others have big families and the education of children suffers (Becker, 1993). It should come as no surprise that children from the ethnic groups with small families and large investments in human capital typically rise faster and further than do children from other groups. At the same time, with more flexible access to publicly funded education, there is evidence that the influence of family background in the United States on children's achievements is smaller than in less developed countries.

## THE ROLE OF GOVERNMENT

Governments have an important role in encouraging parental investments in children's human capital based on their influence on the forces noted above. Parents are more inclined toward investing in their children when they are more affluent, are better educated, anticipate a long-term relationship with the child, have smaller families, and are not being subjected to discrimination.

Increasing the affluence and education of its citizens should be a fundamental policy of all states. When the issue is the funding of education, the state has a central role, as noted in Articles 28 and 29 of the *Convention on the Rights of the Child*. This is especially important because of the difficulties that lower income people have in borrowing to fund education. The fundamental problem is that human capital is poor collateral for a loan. At the same time, it is important to recognize the difference between state funding and state provision of education. As already discussed, state funding of education in less developed countries and among lower income families in more developed countries is fundamental. However, there is a much weaker justification for the dominant role of public provision in education. Public education monopolies can become as interested in providing well-paying jobs for teachers and administrators as providing education. Students often benefit from education systems that provide freedom of choice among a variety of schools.

Anticipating long-term relationships with their children has a strong influence on the willingness of parents to invest in their children, and the root of these relationships lies with the stability of family relationships. While states should not discourage the geographic mobility of its citizens, it does have a central role in encouraging family stability. As well meaning as they may appear, policies such as no-fault divorce and support for never-married-parent households strongly discourage family stability to the detriment of children.

No-fault divorce discourages the long-term commitment and increased specialization by parents—both of which tend to increase investments in children—that have traditionally been the cornerstone of the family relationship (Parkman, 1992). When spouses know that a marriage can be dissolved unilaterally, they become more concerned about their narrowly defined welfare and less about the welfare of their spouse and children. Careers are emphasized over parenting (Parkman, 1998). This is particularly true because divorce is likely to reduce the interaction of at least one parent with the children. Mutual consent as a basis for divorce for couples with children encourages parents to work harder to improve the quality of their marriages including the welfare of their children (Parkman, 1993).

While financial support for single-parent households appears to solve the problems facing many poor children, it just creates other problems for those children by discouraging family formation (Kimenyi & Mbaku, 1995). Public support often provides a higher standard of living than that available from a child's father, discouraging the parents from establishing a long-term relationship. Still, all studies show that growing up in a one parent household, especially when the parent is a never-married woman, results in a lower level of human capital in the form of educational attainment (McLanahan & Sandefur, 1994). Therefore, the welfare of children can be improved by discouraging these households (Parkman, 1997).

Children generally receive larger investments in human capital in smaller families. States can influence the size of families by reducing either the supply of or the demand for children with the recognition that some forces affect both. A reduction in the supply of children can be encouraged by programs such as the broad dissemination of birth control information, while the demand can be reduced by programs such as those that increase family income, especially by improving the employment opportunities for women. Higher incomes have been shown to reduce the birthrate, as parents choose to have fewer children and invest more in each child.

Last, the state can encourage investments in human capital by discouraging forces that artificially reduce the returns to investment such as discrimination that is covered by Article 2. Therefore, reduced discrimination opens up opportunities for individuals, but also encourages parents to invest more in their children. The speed with which individuals' incomes converge compared to those of their parents is a measure of the degree of equality of opportunity in a society.

## BENEFITS EXTEND BEYOND THE INDIVIDUAL

The benefits of human capital extend beyond the primary beneficiaries by increasing the standard of living of others as there is strong evidence that there is a close link between investments in human capital and economic growth in a country (Becker, 1993). Rates of return on investments in human capital rise rather than decline as a country's stock of human capital increases at least until the stock becomes very large because investments in human capital tend to be complementary. Someone with extensive education is more productive in a society with many educated people. Rates of return on education and other human capital investments are higher in developed than in undeveloped countries.

Long periods of sustained growth result from the expansion of scientific and technical knowledge that raises the productivity of labor and other inputs in production with this knowledge embodied in people. All countries that have managed persistent growth in income have also had large increases in the human capital of their labor forces through additional education and training. In a study of the U.S. economy it was found that the increase in schooling of the average worker between 1929 and 1982 explains about one-fourth of the rise in per capita income during that period (Denison, 1985).

Compelling evidence of the link between human capital and technology comes from agriculture (Becker, 1993). Education is of little use in traditional agriculture, and therefore, farming methods and knowledge are passed on from parents to children. Farmers in countries with traditional economies are among the least educated members of the labor force. By contrast, modern farmers must deal with highly complex issues such as hybrids, breeding methods, fertilizers, complicated equipment, and intricate futures markets for commodities. Education is of great value since it helps farmers adapt more quickly to new hybrids and other new technologies. Therefore, it is no surprise that farmers are about as well educated as industrial workers in modern economies.

## CONCLUSION

Increasing the human capital per child in a state is fundamental for boosting its children's standard of living. By becoming more productive, the children will have higher income earning capacities that increase their material well-being, but they will also be more capable of making welfare enhancing decisions in other areas such as their health and appreciation of the world. Parents will normally be the primary sources of these investments in human capital. We would expect investments per child to increase when the parents have larger incomes, are better educated, anticipate a long-term relationship with the child, have fewer children, and are not being subjected to discrimination. States serve a secondary role by creating an environment that encourages parents to make these welfare enhancing decisions and by funding most education.

## REFERENCES

Becker, G. S. (1991). *A treatise on the family, Enl. Ed*. Cambridge, MA: Harvard University Press.

Becker, G. S. (1993). *Human capital (3rd ed.)*. Chicago: University of Chicago Press.

Denison, E. F. (1985). *Trends in American economic growth, 1929–1982*. Washington, DC: Brookings Institution.

Haveman, R. & Wolfe, B. (1995). The determinants of children's attainments: A review of methods and findings. *Journal of Economic Literature, 33*, 1829–1878.

Kimenyi, M. S. & Mbaku, J. M. (1995, July). Female headship, feminization of poverty and welfare. *Southern Economic Journal, 62*(1), 44–52.

LeBlanc, L. J. (1995). *The Convention on the Rights of the Child*. Lincoln: University of Nebraska Press.

McLanahan, S. & Sandefur, G. (1994). *Growing up with a single parent*. Cambridge, MA: Harvard University Press.

Michael, R. T. (1972). *The effect of education on efficiency in consumption*. New York: National Bureau of Economic Research.

Parkman, A. M. (1992). *No-fault divorce: What went wrong?* Boulder, CO: Westview Press.

Parkman, A. M. (1993). Reform of the divorce provisions of the marriage contract. *BYU Journal of Public Law, 8*(1), 91–106.

Parkman, A. M. (1997). The government's role in the support of children. *BYU Journal of Public Law, 11*(1), 55–74.

Parkman, A. M. (1998). Why are married women working so hard? *International Review of Law and Economics, 18*(1), 41–49.

Rosen, S. (1989). Human capital. In J. Eatwell, M. Milgate, & P. Newman (Eds.), *The new palgrave: Social economics* (136–155). New York: W. W. Norton.

Van Bueren, G. (1995). *The international law on the rights of the child*. Dordrecht: Martinus Nijhoff.

## PART IV

# IMPLEMENTING ARTICLE 27 IN VARIOUS CONTEXTS

## 13

# A Cross-cultural Examination of Article 27 of the U.N. *Convention on the Rights of the Child*

*Virginia Murphy-Berman*

Article 27 of the *Convention on the Rights of the Child* states that children have a right to a standard of living that is adequate for their physical, mental, spiritual, moral, and social development. The purpose of this chapter is to examine Article 27 from a cross-cultural perspective.

## THE MEANING OF CULTURE

Culture has been defined in various ways. For instance, it has been identified as being a shared way of looking at the world, a common way of construing or bringing meaning to events, and/or a property of the physical structure or environment in which individuals live (Berry et al., 1992). Culture can also be conceptualized as the shared constraints that impose limits on the behavioral repertoire available to members of various social-cultural groups (Poortinga, 1992). Elements of all of the above will be used when the term culture is referred to in the following discussion. The analysis will suggest that culture may serve to filter the way the child's basic rights articulated in Article 27 are interpreted and construed. These differences in construal could occur at many levels, including how the term ''adequate standard of living'' is operationalized, how the child's development is believed to best be enhanced, and how maturity in cognitive, moral, and physical spheres is identified and defined.

### Definition of Adequate Standards of Survival and Child-rearing Goals

Article 27 states that children should be provided a standard of living that is ''adequate'' for their development in multiple dimensions. Clearly, different notions of what would qualify as "adequate" would be expected to exist across cultures, dependent in part on the level of resources available in the society. Thus, for instance, what may be considered barely minimal living conditions in the richer Western countries may be seen as well above average conditions in some of the poorer developing nations of the world.

Beyond altering perceptions of what are considered necessary standards for basic existence, level of resource availability may also influence the emphasis that is placed on certain types of child-rearing goals. For instance, in poor agrarian societies in which infant and child mortality is quite high, guaranteeing basic child survival and protection may be seen as more important than facilitating growth and enhancement (LeVine, 1988). Thus, satisfaction of some needs for children may necessarily take sequential priority over fulfillment of others.

## The Value of Children

Differing role expectations for children may also affect the way in which the term "adequate standard of living" is construed across cultures. In many societies, for instance, children may be required and expected to contribute substantially to their own and their family's well-being, while in other wealthier countries such an economic role for children may be less valued and necessary (Monroe, Monroe, & Shimmin, 1984). This difference in the connection of children to resources may affect the way parents and children see their obligations to each other and may influence the extent to which different family members feel responsible for their own and other's well-being. Kagitcibasi (1992) suggests that as societies gain wealth and child work is less needed, the focus tends to change from the consideration of material value of the child for the family to an emphasis on the needs of the child within the family. In the transition, she asserts, societies shift from a parent-family centered outlook to a more child-centered one.

Role expectations for children and parents may also become increasingly less reciprocal as the level of resources in the society increases. For example, in a survey of what parents expect from their children at different points in their lives, Kagitcibasi (1990) reported that in many Western societies parents do not anticipate that their children will or should take care of them in their old age, while in many non-Western societies, taking care of elderly parents is seen as an obligation of older children, in part as a kind of payback for the parents' earlier care of them. Thus, the way childhood is defined, the role of children in society and their expected obligations to their parents over the life cycle, and the responsibility of children for securing resources may all show considerable cultural variability.

## Processes Thought to Facilitate Development

Further, cultural differences exist in the notions of what processes facilitate maturity and development in moral, cognitive, and spiritual spheres. Some cultures, particularly those in the West, promote growth through self-discovery and independent striving, while others, particularly those in non-Western areas, believe that development is best enhanced through adherence to duty and by fulfillment of obligations to the family and society.

One way to examine these dimensions is to assess cultural differences in so-called individualist versus collectivist orientations. The concept of "individualism/collectivism" has been defined in multiple ways (see Kim, 1994; Triandis, 1990). A description by Kim (1994) serves to capture the main features of the differences in these orientations.

According to Kim, individualism is a philosophy that assumes that individuals are rational and able to use reason to make personal choices. As part of this philosophy, he states, traditional, ascribed roles and communal social orders are rejected and emphasis is placed on the individual's right to choose freely and define his or her own goals. In individualistic cultures, laws, rules, and regulations are institutionalized to protect individual rights; people within the culture are encouraged to value privacy and freedom of choice.

Individuals in so-called collectivist cultures, in contrast to this, are more bound by certain roles and status positions. Further, in such cultures individuals are encouraged to put other people's and the group's interest before their own and are rewarded for fulfilling carefully prescribed duties and obligations. Collectivist institutions could also be described as more paternalistic in nature, and social harmony tends to be emphasized more than self-fulfillment and independence (Kim, 1994).

The way the self is construed may be vastly different in cultures that ascribe to these different types of values. Markus and Kitayama (1991), for instance, assert that in independent or individualist Western cultures, the so-called identity nightmare is not to have one's own uniqueness recognized. Thus, individuals in such cultures are constantly challenged to "find" themselves by clearly articulating their separateness from others. By contrast, in more interdependent cultures, the identity nightmare would stem from not feeling sufficiently connected with one's group. Here the challenge would be to learn to attend well not to one's own needs but to the concerns of others, and to fit in harmoniously with one's environment.

Miller (1994) echoes these themes. She suggests that cultures can be divided into those holding that development occurs mainly through adherence to prescribed roles and obligations versus those promoting growth and development through the exercise of individual personal choice. In the latter (mostly individualistic Western cultures) duties and obligations can be seen as potential impediments that can stand in the way of self-growth and development. In the former (mostly less individualistic non-Western cultures) it is only through recognizing and doing one's duty that one can achieve one's full humanity. These orientations are significantly different and would be expected to have a major impact on how spiritual, moral, and cognitive growth is perceived to best be facilitated.

**Structures that Facilitate Development**

Differences may additionally be apparent in the beliefs about what types of structures facilitate positive development. These differences may occur at many levels.

First, the distribution of power among individuals within the family and within the society varies across cultures. In some cultures very hierarchical arrangements are emphasized that promote a high degree of power inequality among individuals. In these cultures, a great deal of discrepancy exists in terms of the power and status ascribed to different family members such as husbands and wives, parents and children, and older and younger siblings. In other cultures, more egalitarian relationships among individuals are held to be the ideal. Hofstede (1983) refers to this notion of how power is allocated among individuals within society as "power distance." Cultures with high power distance tolerate and support considerable inequality in power distribution, while cultures with low power distance adhere to norms that stress more even distribution of power across all the members of the society.

A second dimension on which families vary across cultures is the degree to which roles within families are viewed as open and evolving versus more fixed and circumscribed. In the more fixed-role societies, the duties of a father or son or wife or daughter are very clearly delineated and considerable consensus exists within the society as to what obligations should go along with each of these roles. In cultures that promote less fixed-role structures, considerable variation and latitude is permitted both in terms of how various family roles are understood and in terms of the duties and obligations thought to accompany each.

In addition, what is considered to be an ideal family unit also differs across cultures. In some cultures, for instance, family arrangements in which individuals live together in large extended family networks are valued, while in others smaller nuclear or even single-parent units are seen as equally viable and even the preferred way to promote the healthy development of the child (Bond, 1992).

Thus, the child's experience of being *in* the family is likely to be very different in different cultural contexts. What may be considered "good" for the child and necessary for optimal development in one culture may be considered quite aberrant in another. The way the child sees his or her role in connection to the family and the larger society also would be expected to be quite culturally variant. All of this might be expected to impact how individuals from different cultures might construe the appropriateness of different types of family policies proposed to facilitate the achievement of the outcomes for children outlined in Article 27 of the *Convention*.

**The Meaning of Maturity**

Beyond differences in conceptions of the structures through which optimal outcomes for children are best achieved, varying notions also exist across cultures about what constitutes positive development in different spheres. As suggested, the experience of being in a family at any one point in time varies considerably across cultures. The experience of being in a family across time also varies. These across time differences relate, in part, when interdependence is valued by a culture (Triandis, 1990; Markus & Kitayama, 1991; Kim, 1994). In cultures that value interdependence, cooperation, compliance, nonassertiveness, and strong loyalties to one's group and family are stressed. These traits are felt to enhance the child's ability to maintain connectedness to the family throughout the life cycle, as they shift from care receiver in childhood to caregiver in adulthood and back to care receiver in old age.

In cultures that stress an independent orientation, on the other hand, child autonomy and self-sufficiency are more valued. It is expected that the child will at some point become quite independent of the family environment in which he/she was raised. Thus, attributes such as independence and assertiveness, which would enable him or her to make this separation successfully, are rewarded.

Different notions of maturity are also reinforced by variations in expectations for the type of job role the child will likely (or ideally) move into upon reaching adulthood. In many countries in the West, work roles that stress independence and self-sufficiency are idealized. By contrast, jobs that emphasize group loyalty and belonging and that offer security for obedience and persistence may be more valued in other cultures. These different work expectations would clearly affect how different types of socialization practices are viewed and how different types of personality traits are evaluated (Kohn, 1969).

## Implications for Policy Formulation

The above discussion suggests that wide variations exist in how children's rights to an "adequate" standard of living might be construed across cultures. These include differences in how the term "adequate" is operationalized, differences in conceptions of what processes best promote positive development in different spheres, and differences in how "positive development" is defined.

Beyond these types of definitional variations, basic differences may also exist across cultures in how the very notion of "children's rights" is understood. In some cultures, protection of one's rights may be perceived as being central to the achievement of human dignity and worth and to be a key principle around which other cultural values are organized. In other cultures, human worth and dignity may not be as directly linked to notions of rights. Miller (1992) suggests that cultures, in fact, can be divided into those that are rights-based versus those that are more egalitarian or duty-based.

An important issue for decisionmakers is how to appropriately represent and balance these various types of orientations in the formulation of workable and effective international policy and programs. Clearly different cultures pose different challenges for policy development and implementation. In the more individualist Western cultures where the rights of the individual are strenuously affirmed, the challenge may be to place less stress on independence, autonomy, and achievement so that important family, community, and societal support systems and the fulfillment of culturally valued obligations are not undermined (e.g., see Bellah et al., 1985). In less individualistic cultures, the challenge may be how to sufficiently stress duty and strong family and group loyalties without suppressing the development of individual autonomy and rights expression (Kagitcibasi, 1987). Another challenge in less individualistic cultures may be how to define community sufficiently inclusively and broadly so that it goes beyond particular in-group concerns.

Each culture must meet these challenges in ways that are compatible with important societal norms and values, but also in ways that facilitate the growth and development of children. This is indeed a tall order, but one that must be met if a document like the *Convention on the Rights of the Child* is to have maximal positive impact on the lives of children throughout the world.

## REFERENCES

Bellah, R. N., Madsen, R., Sullivan, W. M., Swidler, A., & Tipton, S. M. (1985). *Habits of the heart: Individualism and commitment in American life*. Berkeley: University of California Press.

Berry, J. W., Poortinga, Y. H., Seagall, M. H., & Dasen, P. R. (1992). *Cross-cultural psychology: Research and applications*. Cambridge: Cambridge University Press.

Bond, M. H. (1988). *The cross-cultural challenge to social psychology*. Newbury Park, CA: Sage.

Bond, M. H. (1992). The process of enhancing cross-cultural competence in Hong Kong organizations. *International Journal of Intercultural Relations, 16*, 395–442.

Dasen, P. R. (1984). The cross-cultural study of intelligence and Piaget and the Baoule. *International Journal of Psychology, 19*, 407–434.

Hofstede, G. (1983). Dimensions of national cultures in fifty countries and three regions. In J. Deregowski, S. Dzuirawiec, & R. Annis (Eds.), *Explications in cross-cultural psychology*. Lisse, Holland: Swets and Zeitlinger.

Kagitcibasi, C. (1987). Individual and group loyalties: Are they compatible? In. C. Kagitcibasi (Ed.), *Growth and progress in cross-cultural psychology*. Lisse, Holland: Swets and Zeitlinger.

Kagitcibasi, C. (1990). Family and socialization in cross-cultural perspective: A model of change. In J. Berman (Ed.), *Cross-cultural perspectives: Nebraska Symposium on Motivation*. Lincoln: Nebraska University Press.

Kagitcibasi, C. (1992) Linking the indigenous and universalistic orientations. In S. Iwawaki, Y. Kashima, & K. Leung (Eds.), *Innovations in cross-cultural psychology*. Lisse, Holland: Swets & Zeitlinger.

Kim, U. (1994). Individualism and collectivism: Conceptual clarification and elaboration. In U. Kim, H. Triandis, C. Kagitcibasi, S. Choi, & G. Yoon (Eds.)., *Individualism and collectivism: Theory, method and application*. London: Sage Publications.

Kohn, M. K. (1969). *Class and conformity: A study in values*. New York: Dorsey Press.

LeVine, R. A. (1988). Human parental care: Universal goals, cultural strategies, individual behavior. *New Directions in Child Development, 40*, 37–50.

Markus, H. & Kitayama, S. (1991). Culture and the self: Implications for cognition, emotion and motivation. *Psychological Review, 98*, 224–253.

Miller, D. (1992). Distributive justice: What the people think. *Ethics, 102*, 555–593.

Miller, J. (1994). Cultural diversity in the morality of caring: Individuality oriented versus duty-based interpersonal moral codes. *Cross-cultural Research, 28*, 3–39.

Monroe, R. L., Monroe, R. H., & Shimmin, H. (1984). Children's work in four cultures: Determinants and consequences. *American Anthropologist, 86*, 342–348.

Poortinga, Y. H. (1992). Towards a conceptualization of culture for psychology. In S. Iwawaki, Y. Kashima, & K. Leung (Eds.), *Innovations in cross-cultural psychology*. Lisse, Holland: Swets & Zeitlinger.

Triandis, H. (1990). Theoretical concepts that are applicable to the analysis of ethnocentrism. In R. Brislin (Ed.), *Applied cross-psychology*. Newbury Park, CA: Sage.

## 14

# Entitlement to "Adequacy": Application of Article 27 to U.S. Law

### Robin Kimbrough

The role of the U.S. federal government in providing assistance to needy children and their families has been a frequent and often hotly debated topic among policy makers, child advocates, and the general public. Although Congress has provided some level of federal entitlement to assistance since the mid-1930s, many American children remain vulnerable and at risk of entering adulthood without the skills and motivation necessary to fully participate.

In the United States, more than 14 million American children (one in five) live in families with incomes less than the official federal poverty line (Children's Defense Fund [CDF], 1992). The United States has one of the highest child poverty rates among Western industrial democracies, with a rate of children in poverty that is more than twice that of adults. A 1995 study, funded by the National Science Foundation, ranked the United States sixteenth of eighteen industrialized western nations in the poverty level among children. The only nations within the study group faring worse than the United States were Ireland and Israel.

Not only are more children growing up in poverty, but these children fall even farther below the poverty line than they did in the 1970s (CDF, 1992). In 1991 more than 6 million children, or about 45 percent of poor children, lived in families with incomes below *half* the poverty level.

The declining economic condition of children is further illustrated by the increasing numbers of children and their families who are characterized as "working poor," that is, not officially below the poverty line, but not making an income sufficient to live. In 1991, nearly two of every three poor families with children contained at least one worker (Weill, 1990).

At a time when a growing number of children are spending their childhoods in poverty, Congress has recently passed, and President Clinton signed, land-mark legislation radically transforming the primary entitlement program provid-ing cash assistance to poor children and families. For the first time in more than sixty years, needy children and their families are not "entitled" to economic assistance. Families who do receive cash benefits will face a limit of two years at any given time and a lifetime limit of five years.

While the United States is significantly retrenching its assistance to children, almost every other nation has ratified and is implementing the provisions that comprise the U.N. *Convention on the Rights of the Child*. This chapter examines Article 27 of the *Convention*, which provides economic rights to children, and its possible impact on U.S. law should the United States ever ratify the *Con-vention*.

## THE MEANING OF ARTICLE 27

Article 27 of the *Convention* recognizes the right of every child to a standard of living adequate for the child's physical, mental, spiritual, moral, and social development. Article 27 further delineates responsibility between the child's parents and the states parties for ensuring that the right accorded by Article 27 is realized.

Because the *Convention* is written as a constitutive document, the language is intentionally inexplicit and amenable to interpretation (Cohen, 1993). As such, the greatest challenge in implementing Article 27 lies in figuring out exactly what it means.

### The Scope of Article 27

The language of Article 27 is distinctive for its linkage of the child's standard of living to the various domains—physical, mental, spiritual, moral, and social—of the child's development. In the narrowest sense, Article 27 establishes a standard that is purely economic. Paragraph 3 of Article 27 creates little doubt that the drafters intended that the child's material needs be met. The language specifically vests states parties with the responsibility of providing "material assistance and support programmes, particularly with regard to nutrition, cloth-ing, and housing." Moreover, in a rather unusual provision for an international treaty, paragraph 4 addresses the recovery of child support as a means of further ensuring that children of divorce and children of single parents have access to an adequate standard of living.

By linking the child's standard of living to development, however, the drafters of the *Convention* have created a "right" that far exceeds the basic elements necessary for a child's survival. The language of paragraph 2, which charges the parent(s) or others responsible for the child with the primary responsibility for securing the *"conditions of living necessary for the child's development"* (emphasis added), further supports an expansive interpretation.

Viewing a child's right to an adequate standard of living in the context of development is unprecedented and remarkable (Van Bueren, 1995). As Melton (1995) has noted, the *Convention* provides guidance about not only *what* must be provided but also *how* it must be provided. Thus, providing economic assistance solely is not sufficient. Rather, the assistance must enable the child's development, or in the words of the *Convention*, fully prepare the child to "live an individual life in society" (preamble).

Although the drafters established in Article 27 a "right to a standard of living" that is unprecedented, they also specified that the right need only be *adequate*. The ordinary meaning of "adequate" is good enough, but not remarkable; enough for what is required or needed. However, linking the child's standard of living to the child's development suggests that "adequate" must be more than minimal, and certainly this interpretation is supported throughout the language of the *Convention* in its emphasis on the well-being of the child and the ability of the child to achieve personhood.

The right to an adequate standard of living, however, is not unconditional. Although the language of Article 27, paragraph 1 is broad, subsequent paragraphs contain conditional language limiting the responsibilities of parent(s) and states parties. Article 27, paragraph 2 places with parents the *primary* responsibility of securing the conditions of living necessary for the child's development, but only "within their abilities and financial capacities." Presumably, states parties have a duty to help parents obtain the conditions of living that are necessary for the child's development in addition to providing concrete material assistance (Article 27, paragraph 3). This responsibility, too, carries conditions. The duty of the states parties is a secondary duty to take "appropriate measures within their means" to help parents and others responsible for the child implement the child's right to an adequate standard of living (Van Bueren, 1995).

States parties have a more direct responsibility for ensuring the economic provisions of Article 27, which requires states parties to provide material assistance and support programs in cases of need, particularly with regard to nutrition, clothing, and housing. While this duty, too, is conditioned on the ability of the states parties to do so, the *Travaux Preparatories* clearly document the drafters resistance to weakening the "right" bestowed by Article 27, paragraph 1.[1] Other provisions of the *Convention* similarly reinforce the responsibilities of governments in meeting the obligations established by Article 27 and in doing so at the maximum level possible. Article 6 requires states parties to "ensure to the *maximum extent possible* the survival and development of the child." Likewise, Article 4 obligates states parties to implement the provisions of the *Convention* "to the maximum extent of their available resources."

So, what does this mean? It means that with respect to the basic elements of survival—for example, clothing, housing, and nutrition—states parties have a clear duty to provide material assistance that is more than minimum. The level of material assistance provided must be sufficient to foster the child's development. However, the duty is not unfettered. While there are no guiding principles as to how the limiting language would be interpreted, it is reasonable to conclude that the adequacy of a nation's assistance would be viewed in the context of the nation's wealth.

It also means that governments have an obligation to help parents in their efforts to provide an environment that actively supports the development of the child. Thus, economic programs, alone, will not satisfy the spirit of the Article. Rather, states parties need to provide leadership and support that will enable the relationships in the child's life to be successful. This might include efforts aimed at ensuring the safety of children, both in the home and on the streets.

## The Nature of the Right Created by Article 27

A second issue that arises in interpreting Article 27 is the nature of the right created by the drafters. The very fact that children are accorded rights by the *Convention* is a subject of great debate, and often unease, within the United States. Historically, American children have been viewed as having no rights independent of their parents. It is only within the last thirty years that children's rights have begun to take shape. For example, various Supreme Court decisions have acknowledged that under certain conditions children have rights to procedural due process, freedom of speech, privacy, access to information, and freedom from unreasonable searches and seizures.

For equal protection purposes, the U.S. courts historically have drawn a distinction between rights that are viewed as "fundamental rights"—that is, any right *explicitly or implicitly* guaranteed by the Constitution—and "nonfundamental" rights—that is, those that are not so guaranteed even though they may have the utmost economic or social importance. The right to education, for example, was determined by the Supreme Court in *San Antonio Independent School District* v. *Rodriguez* (1973)[2] to be a nonfundamental right for equal protection purposes, because it is neither explicitly nor implicitly guaranteed by the Constitution. Similarly, the Court has held that classifications made by state welfare agencies for the purpose of placing an absolute limit on the amount of welfare assistance that can be received are subject only to the traditional reasonableness test as long as no "fundamental right" is affected (*Dandridge* v. *Williams*, 1970).

Although the rights to education, welfare, housing, and many other legislatively created benefits usually thought of as entitlements are not fundamental, the Constitution places some limits on the abrogation of the right (Melton & Sullivan, 1993). The Fourteenth Amendment protects against the deprivation of "life, liberty or property without due process of law." Exactly what constitutes a "liberty" or "property" interest subject to due process has not been precisely defined by the Court although the decisions of the Court provide some guidance.

The Court has found the existence of a constitutionally protected property interest in continued welfare benefits where the applicant meets the statutory criteria (*Goldberg* v. *Kelly*, 1970) and in a state guarantee of public education (*Goss* v. *Lopez*, 1975). Since the Constitution does not create property interests, however, the claim must be to an *existing interest* already derived from state or federal law (*Board of Regents* v. *Roth*, 1972), not to a mere abstract need or desire for or unilateral expectation of the benefit.

Even where a property interest is found to exist in a benefit, the notice required to terminate the benefit may be minimal. For example, in *Goss* v. *Lopez* (1975), a student suspended from school was entitled only to "oral or written notice of the charges" and an opportunity to present his or her side of the story if the student denied the charges (581).

The fact that the rights encompassed in the *Convention* are part of a treaty will not necessarily elevate them beyond a mere entitlement. Under the Supremacy Clause of the Constitution (Art. VI, section 2), a treaty is the "supreme law of the land" along with the Constitution and any Acts of Congress made pursuant to the Constitution. However, the doctrine of self-executing treaties complicates the application of treaties to U.S. law. A treaty will not be considered the "supreme law of the land" unless it is self-executing. A treaty is viewed as being "self-executing" when rights and liabilities are created without the necessity of further domestic legislative action. A treaty is not "self-executing" (and therefore not part of the "supreme law of the land") where the treaty expressly or by implication requires Congress to pass additional legislation in order to be implemented. In the case of a treaty that is not self-executing, when additional implementing legislation is enacted, it is the legislation, and not the treaty, that would create domestic law.

The *Convention* is generally regarded as having two classes of rights for the purposes of self-execution, one class that is self-executing and one that is not self-executing (American Bar Association [ABA], 1993). The *recognized* rights, including the right to a standard of living established by Article 27, are considered to be part of the class that is not self-executing. The recognized rights generally are resource intensive—that is, they require the appropriation and commitment of resources—so states parties are provided with more latitude in implementation. Article 4 of the *Convention* further supports the conclusion that Article 27 is not self-executing by stating: "States Parties shall undertake all appropriate legislative, administrative, and other measures for the implementation of the rights *recognized in this Convention*" (emphasis added).

In summary, the economic and social rights encompassed in the *Convention* are equivalent to an entitlement. Thus, while they will be accorded a level of protection, the fact that additional legislation action is necessary for implementation means that they are subject to political whim and dependent on continued public support for their existence. The recent dismantling of the Aid to Families with Dependent Children (AFDC) program in favor of welfare reform is a case in point of what can happen to an entitlement. While the AFDC program was in dire need of change, pressure on Congress from almost every segment of society to transfer greater authority for structuring welfare programs to the states has resulted in a radically transformed welfare program and a possible reduction in benefits for children.

## THE ADEQUACY OF U.S. POLICY

A basic step in enabling children to participate fully is ensuring that their families have access to adequate income. As the National Commission on Children noted in their 1991 report, poverty and economic instability place children at risk of malnutrition, substandard housing, crime-ridden neighborhoods, poor health, academic failure, high stress, and low social support.

Given the number of children who already are spending their childhood in poverty, the recent enactment of welfare reform poses an even more serious threat to the healthy development and well-being of children. To fully understand the context in which welfare reform was passed, and the possible climate should the *Convention* be ratified, it is helpful to review briefly the history of social spending in the United States.

### Leading up to Welfare Reform

The American welfare state consists of a vast array of programs that currently distribute about $1 trillion directly in social benefits. Billions more are allocated indirectly through subsidies for health, housing, day care, and pensions (including to the middle and upper classes) that are largely excluded from the conventional audit of welfare spending (Gilbert, 1995). Despite this, the actual level of expenditure on cash assistance programs for the *nonelderly* is a fraction of the federal budget (Ellwood & Summers, 1986).

Historically, the United States began federal social welfare programs in the 1930s, devoting about 10 percent of the GNP to the program until the 1960s, when the proportion of social welfare spending almost doubled, to 19 percent of the GNP. Most of the benefits were for poor people and social insurance for the elderly. In the 1970s, federal expenditures for human service programs that were not earmarked for the poor increased significantly (Gilbert, 1995). These programs included a variety of indirect social transfers for housing, health, retirement, and education as well as welfare programs, such as daycare, community mental health, and services for the elderly that were available to an increasingly middle-class population.

By 1975, welfare spending had leveled off. This was followed by a retrenchment in spending, particularly on programs for the poor, beginning in the early 1980s. By this time, the perception that social welfare programs had failed was fairly widespread. Critics of social welfare spending argued that the government's attempt to help had only interfered with private initiative and personal responsibility, that government programs had become the problem rather than the solution, and that social protection would be better left to private enterprise, charity, and voluntarism (Ford Foundation, 1989). They argued that despite record expenditures, poverty had gotten worse instead of better, and that the welfare system had caused the work ethic of the lowest income groups to collapse and family breakup and illegitimacy to soar (Christian Coalition, 1995). Over the last few years, the acceptance of welfare benefits had come to be equated with irresponsibility and lifelong dependency.

It is within this climate that Congress passed and President Bill Clinton signed into law the Personal Responsibility and Work Opportunity Reconciliation Act of 1996. This law replaces the principal social program, Aid to Families with Dependent Children (AFDC), which has provided assistance to poor children and their families for more than 60 years.

## Implementation of Welfare Reform

Enactment of the 1996 welfare reform law culminates a series of efforts, the most significant of which was the Family Support Act of 1988, to link welfare benefits with work in an attempt to encourage and prepare recipients for entry into the labor force.

Characterized as a "tough on work" law, the 1996 welfare reform law is intended to increase the flexibility of states in operating a program designed to:

1. provide assistance to needy families so that children may be cared for in their homes or in the homes of relatives;
2. end the dependency of needy parents on government benefits by promoting job preparation, work, and marriage;
3. prevent and reduce the incidence of out-of-wedlock pregnancies and establish annual numerical goals for preventing and reducing the incidence of these pregnancies; and
4. encourage the formation and maintenance of two-parent families.

The act, which encompasses the principal forms of assistance to poor children and their families, specifically ends the entitlement of individuals or families to assistance although it does not prohibit states from establishing an entitlement as a matter of state law. It contains the following key provisions:

*Income Assistance.* The primary component of the Personal Responsibility and Work Opportunity Reconciliation Act is the Temporary Assistance to Needy Families (TANF) program. TANF converts the former Aid to Families with Dependent Children (AFDC) program, emergency assistance, and work programs, such as the Job Opportunities and Basic Skills Training Program (JOBS) for AFDC families into a single block grant with essentially fixed funding. The level of block grant funding provided to states for income and work programs is based on what was spent by the state in 1994 without regard for changes in level of need (Super et al. 1996). Eligible participants have no guarantee of assistance based on need if the state block grant becomes depleted during the fiscal year. Each family is limited to five years total participation in the program during their lifetime. Legal immigrants are denied participation.

*Work Programs.* Efforts to link income support to work were initiated by Congress in 1988 with the enactment of the Family Support Act in 1994. The new welfare reform law requires individuals receiving aid to participate in work activities within two years of starting the program or face termination of assistance. Although the work requirements of the new law are much more stringent than in the past, funding for work programs was not increased under the new law.

*Child Care.* With more stringent work requirements, the new law attempts to increase the availability of child care for families receiving assistance under TANF. The new law eliminates three child care funding programs and replaces them with a single child care block grant—the Child Care and Development Block Grant. The new law also permits states to transfer up to 30 percent of their federal TANF block grant funds to the Child Care and Development Block Grant and the Title XX Social Services Block Grant (Super et al., 1996). The new law eliminates the federal entitlement to child care help for families on welfare who need child care to participate in work or training and for families who need transitional help as they move from welfare to work.

*Nutrition.* For a number of years, the food stamp program has been the principal source of assistance for food. The food stamp program has provided a non-cash supplement to both working and non-working poor. However, food stamps have often not reached a significant number of people eligible. Studies of the impacts of child poverty have indicated that 1 in 8 children in the United States under the age of 12 suffers from hunger each month (ABA, 1993). Under the new welfare reform law, food stamps are cut by $23 billion over 6 years (not including cuts to legal immigrants). According to the Center for Budget and Policy Priorities (Super et al., 1996), the poorest of the poor—those with incomes below half of the poverty line—will be the hardest hit by the reductions in food stamp assistance.

In addition to the food stamp program, more than 14.5 million children annually are served free or reduced-price school lunches, a benefit that was barely touched by the new law. Slightly more than 7 million women and children receive maternal and child health care through the Women, Infants, and Children (WIC) program.

The Child and Adult Care Food Program (CACFP), which served more than 126 million meals (80 percent of which were served to children whose family income was below 130 percent of poverty) in child care centers and family day care homes during 1995, was cut significantly by the new law. The bulk of these reductions are to family day care providers who do not operate centers in low-income geographic areas and to centers that are not operated by low-income providers.

*Supplemental Security Income (SSI) for Disabled Children.* The principal change to SSI is that the new welfare reform law restricts the types of disabilities that will enable a child to qualify for SSI. Thus, the Congressional Budget Office estimates that by 2002, about 315,000 or 22 percent of low-income children who would have previously qualified for SSI will be denied. Among the children most likely to lose benefits are those suffering from multiple impairments (Super et al., 1996).

*Child Support.* In 1984 and again in 1988, Congress acted to step up efforts to enforce child support obligations. The changes encompassed in these laws require states to expedite the process of obtaining and enforcing support orders; permit the establishment of paternity at least up to a child's eighteenth birthday; establish and apply uniform guidelines governing the amount of child support awards; establish systems to withhold part of absent parents' paychecks; recover past-due support from absent parents' tax refunds; cooperate on interstate cases; and obtain support for medical, as well as cash, needs (Weill, 1990).

The new welfare reform law contains comprehensive child support enforcement provisions. Under welfare reform, each state must operate a child support enforcement program designed to: track delinquent parents across state lines; streamline the system for establishing paternity and penalize those persons who do not cooperate in establishing paternity; provide uniformity in rules, procedures, and forms for interstate child support cases; establish central registries of child support orders, centralized collection and disbursement units, and expedited state procedures for child support enforcement; and implement strict child support enforcement (Greenberg & Savner, 1996). The child support provision also includes grants to help states establish programs to support and facilitate noncustodial parents' visitation with their children.

The passage of welfare reform has prompted child advocates to warn that the law poses serious dangers to poor children and families. According to estimates by the Congressional Budget Office, the law includes cuts of nearly $55 billion to low-income programs over the next six years with the majority of these reductions coming from the food stamp program, the SSI program and assistance to legal immigrants. As a result, it is expected that an even greater number of families will be pushed into poverty, that larger numbers of families who are already poor will get poorer, and that most of the children who would be pushed below the poverty line live in families with a working parent.[3]

While the reductions in food stamps, aid to legal immigrants, and SSI are significant (these were the provisions singled out by President Clinton as the most seriously flawed), many child advocates argue that the real danger in the new law is the abolition of the AFDC program for needy children (Bane, 1997; Super et al., 1996; Ellwood, 1996). According to Bane (1997), the "real dangers from the TANF part of the law come both from the work and time-limit requirements—which states will have many opportunities either to use constructively or to avoid—and from the enormous flexibility the states have to spend money, set eligibility requirements, and provide assistance, or not, as they wish" (48).

Another equally important issue is the fact that the new welfare law effectively undermines many years of case law establishing due process protections for recipients (Bane, 1997). By eliminating the entitlement to benefits or services, the likelihood that recipients will be able to claim due process protections and to litigate denials or terminations of assistance is sharply reduced, if not eliminated altogether. Since the new law allows states to reduce the availability of funds under TANF and since there is no longer any entitlement to funds, the argument is that the law opens the possibility that families could meet all the eligibility requirements, but that they will not receive funds because the state has exhausted its block grant funds for the year. Because of this, some child advocates argue that, like housing assistance now, cash and employment assistance could become subject to waiting lists or other forms of rationing (Bane, 1997; Super et al., 1996). These advocates fear that, unless states commit state funds to assure that all eligible families receive aid, substantial numbers of poor children whose parents are unable to find a job could be denied assistance, especially during economic downturns (Super et al., 1996).

### Other Programs to Help Children

While the benefits provided under the new welfare law are the principal benefits available to poor children and their families, the federal government does provide some additional forms of assistance, including a credit against income taxes and housing assistance.

*Earned Income Credit (EIC).* The EIC is a federal credit designed to offset Social Security taxes and supplement wages for poor families with children. While more than 11 million families were eligible for the EIC in 1988, the EIC is not sufficient to lift families out of poverty. EIC also is not as helpful for larger families since the credit does not increase as family size increases.

*Housing.* Families with children are the fastest growing segment of the homeless population (40 percent in the United States). Nearly 70,000 children, aged 16 and younger, are homeless on any given night, sleeping in shelters, churches, abandoned buildings and cars, and various other settings. More than 185,000 children are "precariously housed." While housing is a critical need for many families, federal housing assistance dropped by 80 percent from 1980 to 1989. Some additional assistance has been added in the last couple of years. For example, the Department of Housing and Urban Development has initiated a $32 million dollar initiative to provide housing assistance to families for whom the lack of adequate housing is a primary factor in the separation or imminent separation of children from their families. While the program is a step in the right direction, it will only support approximately 1,600 families.

In addition to the material supports provided to needy children and their families, the federal government provides funding for a number of programs, such as family preservation and support services, which are aimed at maintaining and strengthening families and protecting children. Nonetheless, the number of troubled families is growing, so much so that the child welfare system in most states is overwhelmed. This crisis prompted the U.S. Advisory Board on Child

Abuse and Neglect (1993) to declare a "national emergency" in child protection.

## Conformance of U.S. Policy with Article 27

Since welfare reform was passed recently, it is not yet known whether the dire consequences for children and families predicted by child advocates will come to pass or whether the law will result in motivating families who are dependent on welfare assistance to become more self-sufficient, as is hoped by Congress.

At a minimum, however, the new law appears to be contrary to the intent of the *Convention* and specifically Article 27. By signing the *Convention*, the United States has obligated itself not to act contrary to the intent of the *Convention* while the domestic process of ratification is underway. The abdication of federal responsibility for needy children by eliminating the entitlement to cash assistance and reducing access to many other benefits and services, such as food stamps, is inconsistent with Article 27, paragraph 3, which specifically directs states parties to provide material assistance and support programs, particularly with regard to nutrition, clothing, and housing. Although Article 27, paragraph 3 limits the obligation to that which is "in accordance with national conditions and within the means of States Parties," Article 4 clearly requires governments to implement the provisions of the *Convention* "to the maximum extent of their available resources." While these provisions establish a threshold that is aspirational, compliance likely will be viewed in the context of the overall wealth of the nation providing the assistance.

It is arguable that the minimalist position taken by the United States is more consonant with a "rights" orientation—that is, that people should be provided the minimal amount of assistance necessary to be able to pull themselves up out of poverty—than the more expansive position of other welfare states. Even if one accepts a minimalist approach, the new welfare law will not meet the standard. For many families, the benefits provided by the new welfare reform law will not enable them to become productive within the two year time limit. Some families simply will not be prepared within the two years to benefit from the work requirements. While some will need more extensive education and training, others have problems that are more intransigent, such as drug and alcohol addictions and mental health disorders.

The problem is further exacerbated by the fact that advancing the work goal will inevitably necessitate an expansion of system resources. In a climate where resource expansion is increasingly difficult, it is conceivable that work opportunities will not be developed at levels that really sustain families. Families will not be helped significantly if the jobs created are minimum wage, part time, and with no benefits.

While the majority of the provisions that comprise the new welfare law are inconsistent with the intent of Article 27, the improvement in child support collection is an exception. The child support provision appears to be consistent with paragraph 4 of Article 27, and is one of the few provisions of the new law that might help children. Enforcing child support obligations will not eliminate poverty for all poor children, but it will help reduce poverty for a number of children.

In summary, although the United States provides a number of programs aimed at helping needy children, U.S. support falls far short of what appears to be contemplated by the *Convention* (Weill, 1990). While U.S. efforts are insufficient, if the United States ratified the treaty, the United States would not be obligated to meet these standards immediately. Article 4 establishes the idea of a progressive achievement of rights within the context of available resources. As such, provisions like Article 27 would impose on the United States obligations of conduct, not of result (ABA, 1993). There would be, for example, no international legal duty to assure that all American children actually have an adequate standard of living, but rather that the United States is continually striving toward that end.

## IMPACT OF THE *CONVENTION* ON U.S. POLICIES AND PROGRAMS

Commentators have had mixed reactions as to whether ratification of the *Convention* would benefit American children particularly given that many of the *Convention*'s provisions are aspirational. Some have argued that ratification would not represent much of an improvement (Clark, 1992). Most have insisted that ratification will significantly help children (Law, 1994; Levesque, 1994; Melton, 1993; Calciano, 1992). Given the recent action of Congress in passing the Personal Responsibility and Work Opportunity Act, it seems more likely that ratification would benefit children, at least with respect to the implementation of Article 27.

One way in which ratification might help is by providing guidance for the implementation of government actions and programs. In adopting the *Convention*, the U.N. General Assembly conceived of a document that would function as a standard-setting instrument in the field of human rights by contributing to the protection of children's rights and the assurance of their well-being. In a climate supportive of welfare reform, ratification of the *Convention* could be instrumental in ensuring that children's material needs are met.

As was stated earlier, the new welfare reform law provides states with considerable flexibility to reduce the scope of their programs. As Bane (1997) suggests, "all the political and financial incentives are for states to cut assistance, to impose time limits shorter than five years, to meet the work requirements without spending any money, to shift responsibilities to local governments and private contractors, and to use the block grant funds for more politically popular programs . . . Politics at the state level are not likely to support spending on the very poor, given the freedom and incentives to use the funds more broadly" (49).

Although it is unlikely that the *Convention*, if ratified, would directly affect state laws at least with respect to economic rights, it still could be helpful in establishing norms or guideposts that would encourage states to meet minimum standards for such issues as welfare. As was stated previously, if the *Convention* were ratified, it, along with the Constitution and laws made pursuant to the Constitution, would be the "supreme law of the land" as long as the provisions of the *Convention* do not conflict with the provisions of the Constitution. Thus, ratification of the treaty could affect state and federal law. The Supreme Court has held that a treaty always prevails over a state law regardless of whether the law was enacted before or subsequent to the treaty (*Hauenstein* v. *Lynham*, 1880; *Missouri* v. *Holland*, 1920). However, where a conflict exists between a treaty and federal law, they are of equal weight so the most recent provision will prevail (*Whitney* v. *Robertson*, 1888; *Reid* v. *Covert*, 1957). Nonetheless, the impact of the treaty would be tempered by a determination as to whether it is self-executing. Given that the *Convention* is generally viewed as having some provisions that might be self-executing and others (e.g., the social and economic rights) that likely would not be deemed to be self-executing, state and federal law would not be directly affected by the non self-executing provisions without action by Congress to implement the rights embodied in the *Convention*.

Even if the *Convention* is not fully self-executing, its ratification could still have a tremendous impact on children and families. In addition to establishing legislative guideposts for state and federal law (Melton, 1993), the nation could still be held accountable to the other parties to the treaty under the "law of nations" (see *Clark* v. *Allen*, 1947). As early as 1900, the U.S. Supreme Court held that "customary international law" is "part of our law" (The Paquete Habana, 1900). Customary international law consists of international norms of behavior that have developed over time and have become international customs. When international documents reflect norms that have become customary, U.S. courts can use the documents to develop federal common law, however, the courts have been reluctant to do so (Levesque, 1994).

Even with the limited use of customary international law, the federal and state judiciary could refer to internationally recognized standards as a mechanism for interpreting the protections provided by domestic constitutions, statutes, and other laws. The distinction between international law that is guiding and customary international law is that the former is only persuasive, rather than binding, authority. The argument for using a treaty such as the *Convention* to guide the U.S. courts is that the United States should not lag behind the rest of the world in the protection of children (Calciano, 1992).

A case from California illustrates this principle as it relates to economic rights. In *Boehm* v. *Superior Court* (1986), the California court of appeals referred to Article 25 of the Universal Declaration of Human Rights in defining a minimum standard of living and in denying one county's reduction of public assistance grants.

Another way in which ratification of the *Convention* might help children is by providing the impetus to refocus the dialogue on welfare reform from a discussion of the worthiness of parents to a discussion of the needs of children. When AFDC was originally conceived, it was viewed as a short-term, protective measure for widowed mothers and their children who were deserving. However, the debate about welfare has shifted over the years from one of need to a critique of behavior. The losers in this debate are the tremendous numbers of children for whom poverty can be a life-threatening reality.

By conferring rights on children, the drafters of the *Convention* clearly intended to offer children greater protections than the minimalist approach that characterizes U.S. policy currently. As the ABA (1993) noted, "creating a duty to legislate is as old as the treaty-making power the Founding Fathers inserted in the Constitution. But creating a duty to legislate on behalf of children is new and, in light of the current condition of many American children, long overdue" (104). If the *Convention* were ratified, it is likely that the pressure already being felt from some professionals and members of the public, including child advocacy groups, would intensify with a focus on creating and enriching the programs and services for children that are contemplated by the convention. This, combined with a legal duty to make progress in realizing the rights bestowed by the *Convention*, could strengthen the commitment of policy makers to ensuring the healthy and full development of our most vulnerable and least powerful group—children.

Moreover, the fact that the *Convention* affords rights to children could prompt the courts to consider the protections of the *Convention* in litigation affecting children's rights. However, this does not necessarily mean that children can enforce their rights in a private cause of action. While section 1983 provides a cause of action for the "deprivation of any rights, privileges, or immunities secured by the Constitution and laws" of the United States, in *Suter* v. *Artist M.* (1992), the Court determined that section 1983 was not available to enforce a violation of the Adoption Assistance and Child Welfare Act of 1980. In determining that the Act did not create enforceable rights, the Court stated that the term "reasonable efforts" imposed only a "rather generalized duty on the State, to be enforced not by private individuals, but by the Secretary [of Social Services]" (1370).

The ability of children to enforce their rights under the *Convention* is further governed by the doctrine of self-execution. If, for example, the *Convention* were found to be self-executing and the United States failed to undertake any of the duties bestowed by the treaty, children in the United States (or their representatives) would automatically have a legal claim against the government. However, where a treaty is not self-executing, the judicial remedy available to a child aggrieved by the failure of the United States to carry out a duty would, as in the *Suter* case, depend on the terms of the implementing legislation, if any, enacted by Congress (ABA, 1993). So, even though ratification of the *Convention* might influence the provision of economic rights by the United States, ratification will not allow a child to walk into court and demand these rights.

Finally, assuming ratification of the *Convention*, the U.S. federal courts would have the responsibility of construing the language of the *Convention*. As Melton notes, "American courts are used to interpreting 'constitutional' language of the sort that permeates the Convention, and they could lead in giving meaning to the Convention in developed countries" (1993). Moreover, ratification of the *Convention* would communicate a message that the U.S. government is more willing to be held to international norms with regard to children (Calciano, 1992). Thus, it is likely that the U.S. courts would be more likely to consider the rights established by the *Convention* in their decision-making.

## CONCLUSION

The *Convention* seems to envision a society that actively supports children and, by necessity, their families. Although the United States is one of the wealthiest nations on earth, current U.S. practice falls far short of the standard articulated in Article 27, paragraph 1. Moreover, the trend toward retrenchment in social benefits is clearly inconsistent with the vision established by the *Convention*.

Even if the Article is read narrowly to focus predominantly on economic benefits, American children are at risk. At a *minimum*, "adequacy," in the context of a purely economic standard, would mean bringing children to the federal poverty line, which is the level of income that the government has determined a family needs to survive. Although this would benefit a significant number of U.S. children, few would disagree that meeting the federal poverty line is hardly adequate if a child is to thrive developmentally. Children who grow up in families where the minimal supports (e.g., adequate housing, nutrition, employment that pays a liveable wage, and access to health care) are virtually nonexistent are severely disadvantaged in their development. These children are at a much higher risk of developmental, educational, and health problems. Ensuring that children lead productive, healthy lives will require a much more significant commitment, and one that is not as susceptible to the politics of Congress. Ratification of the *Convention* would be a step in the right direction in establishing a framework for protecting and supporting children.

## NOTES

1. In response to an amendment by the U.S. delegate to introduce the phrase "in accordance with national conditions" in paragraph one of Article 27, several delegations objected on the basis that such a phrase would "weaken the basic principle contained in the introductory paragraph." As a compromise, the representative of the United Kingdom

suggested that the U.S. delegate's amendment be incorporated into paragraph 3 dealing with the implementation of the child's right to an adequate standard of living.

2. In *San Antonio Independent School District* v. *Rodriguez* (1973), the issue was whether the Texas school finance system violated the equal protection clause of the Fourteenth amendment.

Plaintiffs argued that the reliance on property taxes to fund the school system resulted in gross disparities between wealthy and poor counties in per pupil expenditures. The Court determined that since education is not a fundamental right, a statute regulating education is judged only by the traditional test of reasonableness, a "compelling" state interest is not necessary to sustain the classifications made in the statute.

3. An Urban Institute study in July 1996 of the welfare reform bill passed by the House of Representatives (the final bill is very similar to the House version) estimated that 1.1 million children—and 2.6 million people overall—would become impoverished as a result of the proposal.

## REFERENCES

American Bar Association (ABA). (1993). *Report of the ABA Working Group on the United Nations Convention on the Rights of the Child*. Washington, DC: American Bar Association.

Bane, M. J. (1997, January-February). Welfare as we might know it. *The American Prospect, 30*, 47–53.

*Board of Regents v Roth*, 408 US 564 (1972).

*Boehm v Superior Court*, 178 Cal. App. 3d 494 (1986).

Calciano, E. M. (1992). United Nations Convention on the Rights of the Child: Will it help children in the United States? *Hastings International & Comparative Law Review, 15*, 515–534.

Children's Defense Fund (CDF). (1992). *America's children falling behind: The United States and the* Convention on the Rights of the Child. Washington, DC: Author.

Christian Coalition. (1995). Contract with the American family: A bold plan by Christian Coalition to strengthen the family and restore common-sense values. Nashville: Moorings.

Clark, H. H. (1992). Children and the constitution. *University of Illinois Law Review, 1–41*.

*Clark v Allen*, 331 US 503 (1947).

Cohen, C. P. (1993). The developing jurisprudence of the rights of the child. *St. Thomas Law Review, 6*, 1–96.

*Dandridge v Williams*, 397 US 471 (1970).

Ellwood, D. T. (1996, May-June). Welfare reform as I knew it: When bad things happen to good policies. *The American Prospect, 26* 22–29.

Ellwood, D. T. & Summers, L. H. (1986). Poverty in America: Is welfare the answer or the problem? In S. H. Danziger & D. H. Weinberg (Eds.), *Fighting poverty: What works and what doesn't* (84–86). Cambridge, MA: Harvard University Press.

Ford Foundation Project on Social Welfare and the American Future. (1989). *The common good: Social welfare and the American future*. New York: Ford Foundation.

Gilbert, N. (1995). *Welfare justice: Restoring social equity*. New Haven: Yale University Press.

*Goldberg v Kelly*, 397 US 254 (1970).

*Goss v Lopez*, 419 US 565 (1975).

Greenberg, M. (1996, February). *Welfare reform in an uncertain environment*. Paper presented at "Planning a State/Local Welfare Strategy After the 104th Congress," Washington, DC, organized by the Carnegie Corporation-Funded Project Confronting the New Politics of Child and Family Policies in the United States.

Greenberg, M. & Savner, S. (1996). *A brief summary of key provisions of the temporary assistance for needy families block grant of H. R. 3734*. Washington, DC: Center for Law and Social Policy.

*Hauenstein v Lynham*, 100 US 483 (1880).

Law, K. A. (1994). Hope for the future: Overcoming jurisdictional concerns to achieve United States ratification of the *Convention on the Rights of the Child. Fordham Law Review, 62*, 1851–1876.

Levesque, R. J. R. (1994). International children's rights grow up: Implications for American jurisprudence and domestic policy. *California Western International Law Journal, 24*, 193–240.

Melton, G. B. (1993). Is there a place for children in the new world order? *Notre Dame Journal of Law, Ethics & Public Policy, 7*, 491–529.

Melton, G. B. (1995). The right to a family environment for "Children Living in Exceptionally Difficult Conditions." *Law & Policy, 17*, 345–351.

Melton, G. B. & Sullivan, M. (1993). The concept of entitlement and its incompatibility with American legal culture. In M. A. Jensen & S. G. Goffin (Eds.), *Vision of entitlement: The care & education of America's children* (47–58). Albany: State University of New York Press.

*Missouri v Holland*, 252 US 416 (1920).

National Commission on Children. (1991). *Beyond rhetoric: A new American agenda for children and families*. Washington, DC: National Commission on Children.

The Paquete Habana, 175 US 677 (1900).

*Reid v Covert*, 354 US 1 (1957).

*San Antonio Independent School District v Rodriguez*, 411 US 1 (1973).

Super, D. A., Parrott, S., Steinmetz, S., & Mann, C. (1996). *The new welfare law*. Washington, DC: Center on Budget and Policy Priorities.

*Suter v Artist M.*, 112 S. Ct. 1360 (1992).

U.S. Advisory Board on Child Abuse and Neglect. (1993). *Neighbors helping neighbors: A new national strategy for the protection of children*. Washington, DC: Department of Health and Human Services.

Van Bueren, G. (1995). *The international law on the rights of the child* (317–318). Dordrecht, Netherlands: Martinus Nijhoff.

Weill, J. (1990). Assuring an adequate standard of living for the child. In C. P. Cohen & H. Davidson (Eds.), *Children's rights in America: U.N.* Convention on the Rights of the Child *compared with United States Law*. Washington, DC: American Bar Association.

*Whitney v Robertson*, 124 US 190 (1888).

## 15

# The Application of Article 27 in the Czech Republic: Implications for Countries in Transition

*Jiří Kovařík*

I address the matter of how Article 27 is applied in the Czech Republic and its implications for countries in transition only in a rather unsatisfactory way, from the perspective that Article 27 is applied (1) unintentionally, (2) unsystematically, and (3) in an unreflected way. For in the Czech Republic, there has been no intentional, systematic, or organized effort to apply it at all. Nevertheless, the application is going on. I believe it is due to the implicit "respect for children as persons and respect for their dignity" that is part of our tradition and history, part of *an unwritten social contract*, as Judith Torney-Purta says in chapter 8 of this volume.

The evidence of that is obvious, as the existence of many social institutions and activities prove. However, it has never been reflected upon by Czechs from the point of view of the U.N. *Convention on the Rights of the Child.* What I can do now is just drafting and sketching how I think Article 27 could be applied and monitored.

## BRIEF CHRONOLOGY OF KEY TRANSITIONAL EVENTS

First, let us start with a brief outline of the socioeconomic and political context. I cannot speak for the other Central and Eastern European countries—nevertheless, I have to say that the situation of the Czech Republic has been specific and the starting conditions of transformation were favourable.

The causes underlying the relatively successful transition in the Czech Republic (compared with other post-Socialist countries) can be ascribed to favourable starting conditions such as a stable economy, low indebtedness, and the government's ability to preserve economic stability and raise positive expectations in the nation. Polls indicate popular expectations that the transition will be successful and will benefit the whole society, especially "our children." Also, the cooperating behavior and performance of the majority of the population should be taken into account. This may be the meaning of Vaclav Klaus' statement that "uniqueness of our transformation process is the coincidence of political and economic factors." Another lucky coincidence seems to be the combination of the two personalities at the head of the state—President Vaclav Havel and Prime Minister Vaclav Klaus.

The factors underlying the changes started by the "Velvet Revolution" have been the departure from the one-party totalitarian rule, from the centrally planned socialist economy, and from the stratified society. The former strata included (1) the protagonists of the regime with their clans and servile protégés, (2) the grey mass zone of ordinary people (gradually less and less silent) who aptly and pragmatically adapted themselves to the political situation, and (3) the dissidents, parallel culture groups, and underground church. This departure has been simultaneously the movement toward the political pluralism, parliamentary democracy, market economy, and a society stratified by the results of one's own efforts, abilities, and performances.

The first steps of reform, guided by the principles of building a democratic society, that is, political pluralism, legally consistent state, constitutional guarantees of human rights, freedom and responsibility, and rehabilitation of private property, took place in the framework of the Czech and Slovak Federal Republic. The year 1990 was the time of *preparing economic reforms*. The goal was to transition to a market economy without social turmoil, with rapid and massive privatization, price deregulation and liberalization, internal currency convertibility and foreign trade liberalization, and restrictive monetary and fiscal policy.

The year 1991 was the time of *liberalization and stabilization of the economy.* It was considered the crucial year of the reform. Its main goal was to avoid starting an inflation spiral, and the way to do it was through restrictive monetary and fiscal policy accompanied by restrictive wage regulation and price liberalization (with subsidies to fuel, heating, rents). Thus, the "shock therapy" of the economy and society was moderated.

In 1992 the reforms continued. The salient feature seemed to be the privatization that was becoming the engine of the economy. Small-scale privatization took place primarily through public auctions and restitution. The new social class of entrepreneurs and private business persons started to emerge. Large-scale privatization was implemented by both standard (auctions, joint ventures with foreign companies, tenders, outright sales) and nonstandard (voucher/coupon privatization) methods. The state budget was balanced.

The elections occurred in 1992, too. However, their results in the Czech Republic and the Slovak Republic were different and reflected their attitudes to the reforms. While in the Czech Republic, the right-oriented, proreform coalition[1] was formed with Vaclav Klaus (ODS) as the prime minister. The Slovaks preferred Slovak autonomy to the political and economic reforms. The velvet revolution was followed by the velvet divorce.

In 1993 the Czech Republic emerged on the geopolitical map of Europe. The Czech budget had been projected as a budget of an autonomous state. Reallocations between the Czech and Slovak Republics through the federal budget were over. Both expenditures and incomes increased. A balanced budget was the main goal of that year, and the expenditure control was the instrument to implement it. A new tax system, based on the VAT, was imposed. The economy was controlled by the prices, and the wages became (more or less) the price of work. The inflation was kept under control and the unemployment rate was very low (3–4%). The stratification of society became more and more influenced by the wage differentiation. The consent to the economic policy of the government was expressed mostly by the highly educated and professional strata of the society. Elderly people and citizens with a lower education showed less satisfaction.

The years 1994 and 1995 have sometimes been characterized as the years starting the revival of economy, sometimes as the end of nonstandard economic depression.

## IMPLICATIONS OF THE TRANSITION FOR CHILDREN AND THEIR FAMILIES

The general political and socioeconomic environment developing through the changes mentioned above influences the current situation of children and their families. However, the fifty-year history of the relations between the family and society, state and family, and state and children has to be taken into account.

In the first period of the totalitarian communist regime, both family and private property were conceived as remnants of the "old bourgeois regime." Private ownership and property were abolished, often nationalized by force, with almost immediate and destructive impact on the social and economic structure. The communist attack on family had several different forms. Some families were bluntly split; some of their members were executed or sentenced to many years' imprisonment. Many farmers were robbed of their land and property. The network of "house confidants" and "street committees" invaded the privacy of many families and decisions about children and/or parents (schools, jobs, etc.) often depended on their references. Child care and education were collectivized; foster care was abolished. The system of children's homes (separated by age groups from 0 to 1 year, 1 to 3, 3 to 6, 6 to 10 years and up) was introduced as well as the week-long nursery system (for those up to 3 years) and kindergartens (3 to 6 years). This kind of child day care was to enable women's emancipation, which in reality meant finding and getting a cheap labor force for the state industry.

However, very soon the state realized there was no substitute for the family as the vital source of future labor force; so they proclaimed family *a basic unit of society*. The ambiguous relationship between state and family deepened. Deprived of their private property, families became very apt at adjusting to new conditions. Theoretically, socialist property is supposed to be the property of everyone. However, in practice it also means it is the property of no one—there is neither individual responsibility nor concern for taking care of this property and for renewing the resources. In fact, the socialist property was "owned" by those "more equal ones" who had the right to handle it—without having almost any legally anchored and controlled responsibilities. Instead of the traditional capitalist market system, a specific socialist market developed based on the exchange of social connections and possibilities of access to the rights of disposal. Developing new adaptation patterns and mechanisms as well as protection of family interests, the family realized the disadvantages of an isolated nuclear family and tried to form networks, often based on the kinship principle. From a family's point of view, the state was represented primarily by "other" families whose interests were often antagonistic to the interests of their own family and kinship networks. In the end, this kind of "family loyalty" became opposed strongly to loyalty to higher social entities and traditional moral norms. A folk slogan, "who does not rob [the state, i.e., the others], robs his own family," describes rather realistically the adaptation consequences of the family economy on the concept of socialist property, as well as the functionalistic ideology and practice of many families (Mozny, 1991). Nevertheless, there were limitations to social connections. Sources and common property cannot be endlessly exploited and dirty connections cannot be put into any bank to be used under different circumstances. So, the need arose to transfer this uncertain social capital into economic capital. Here, of course, the concept of socialist property intervened. This is said to be one of the reasons for the minimal reluctance of many opportunists collaborating with the communist regime to change the political and economic order: They hoped they would be able to keep and legalize their socioeconomic positions.

Within the framework of limited options and ways of self-realization, marriage and family often seemed to young people to be both a place protected partially from state interference and a way to become independent of one's family of origin. Both these beliefs proved to be illusions. Too many important life starts are accumulated within a short period of time: professional career, marital life, and parenthood. Early parenthood closes some life possibilities for parents. The feeling of loss of some individual goals and opportunities may cause ambivalent feelings on the part of parents toward the child. It may also be one of the hidden reasons why children are no longer a divorce barrier.

Besides the still-prevailing type of family, that is, two biological parents and two children, a large variety of different family forms and types exists, some of them stable, some of them unstable and transitory. The child appears to be the most stable element and the mother-child dyad the most stable relationship in the family. However, despite the increasing divorce rate and the growing number of one-parent families (mostly headed by divorced mothers) more than 80 percent of children live with both biological parents. Marriage and family are still highly valued, but the scale of options and chances is now much larger than before 1990. However, the lack of time for parents and children to be together has still remained an issue of high importance. Thus, it might easily happen that the parents and family manage to supply basic biological needs of their children, but often fail to create a milieu where meaningful intergenerational experience and social support exchange take place. Psychological subdeprivation in families seems to be a problem (Matejcek, 1987; Kovařík, 1994; Kovařík & Kukla, 1996).

Czech society is supposed to be *pedocentric*—child-centered. However, the child is often, paradoxically, both at the center and on the periphery—both in the family and in the society. This is evident, for example, in the distribution of child space and time in the family and in the state approach to family (child) allowances. These allowances, when compared with other social allowances and benefits, were not indexed for more than five years. Since November 1993 the child allowance system and philosophy has changed. Instead of allowance increase by the number of children, now the age of the child is the key variable. The total child allowances per family have become means-tested benefits.

The social policy system is currently undergoing a deep transformation. The proposed system rests upon three basic pillars: social insurance, state social support, and social assistance. With regard to *social insurance*, citizens consciously plan and provide for future social events by their own contributions as well as those from their employers. *State social support* embraces a wide scale of benefits supporting primarily families with children, the aim being that for a social event receiving the society's support (such as the birth of a child), families would be able to meet their needs on a socially acceptable level. Within the new system, other situations, such as a child's protracted illness, a parent with long-term health problems, solo parenthood, a child entering tertiary education, high housing costs, commuting to school, are acknowledged. It is expected that through state social support, about 2.6 percent of the GDP will be transferred.

*Social assistance* is extended to citizens who find themselves in material or social indigence, that is, primarily to people who, for valid reasons, are unable to meet their basic living needs themselves. The task for social departments is not only to provide these people with the minimum income, but also try to extract them from the unfavorable social situations so that they can again provide for their needs themselves.

The main feature of the new benefit system is the effort, where possible, to tighten entitlements and establish means-testing. With the aim of making social policy substantially less expensive, the following measures are occurring: (1) with regard to social assistance, making the means-test more rigorous; (2) with regard to child and other family benefits, introducing the income test and establishing a limit at which point benefits will be withdrawn.

The foundation for all caps is the official poverty line (subsistence income or subsistence minimum) multiplied by a coefficient established by the government.

For example, the coefficient 1.8 is now proposed by the government for family allowances, meaning that all families on a higher income—about one-third of them—will lose their entitlement.

Poverty, so it seems, continues to be more of the "old" (families with more children) than the "new" (induced by unemployment) type. The percentage of households declaring incomes below the official subsistence income poverty fell from 4.5 percent to 2.9 percent (households), and rose from 2.7 percent to 3.5 percent (persons) and from 2.1 percent to 6.0 percent (children) over the 1988–1992 period. This somewhat contradictory result is due to the narrower definition of the subsistence minimum (which did not entirely follow the rising costs of living) for households and a more generous calibration of children's benefits.

If we were to apply the updated definition of the subsistence income (introduced in March 1993), the figures would be much higher: 7 percent for the number of households, 8 percent for persons, and 13 percent for children. We can, therefore, expect a marked (although certainly not so high) increase in the population living under the official subsistence line.

Unemployment and its consequences for family life have thus far not been a subject of special research, the reason being that the unemployment rate in the Czech Republic is very low, having stayed below 4 percent since February 1992. And only 10 percent of the unemployed are unemployed more than one year.

Envisaging the immediate future the most serious problem is housing. The withdrawal of state support for the new construction of apartments and the rent control caused a sharp decline in the supply of new apartments. Prices for new houses and apartments have made them inaccessible for young couples, even with the newly introduced construction saving schemes and planned mortgage loans.

The government's "social" approach to the already housed population is not extended to those "newcomers" who will be expected to spend about ten times more for an apartment than previously. This situation poses a grave threat to the continuity of families and generations.

The burdens imposed by the housing situation, the economic changes, and the increasingly faster pace of everyday life, with its increased stress and distress levels, lead to highly unfavorable indicators of population reproduction: fewer marriages and more divorces, fewer births and a drop below the simple reproduction line. All in all, the tendencies and programs characteristic of social protection pose no great challenge to these trends and offer little support of family life, manifesting instead the liberal doctrine of individual responsibility for oneself and one's family.

## INDICATIONS OF CHILD WELL-BEING IN THE CONTEXT OF DEPRIVATION

Let me show how some of the traditional indicators can be applied here. It is obvious that using statistical and demographic indicators such as income per capita and the population density of housing, children, and their families are disadvantaged groups. In 1980 the average living area of two-parent households with children represented only 70 percent of the average living area of childless couples. Population density in households with children is higher by 18 percent than the total average density, while the population density in childless households is 13 percent lower. Families with four or more children have almost double crowding (population density) in the home. Comparison with childless households offers a still more alarming picture; the overcrowding index for households with children is at 159%. With regard to housing, gypsy children are marginalized among the marginalized.

Now, let me focus on some additional criteria, some quality indicators that may be useful in the assessment process concerning the implementation of Article 27. Let me outline briefly the way of their discovery, recognition, and definition by the Prague school of Child Psychology and Psychological Deprivation (Langmeier & Matejcek, 1974).

In the fifties, under the communist rule, the ideology including the concept of new socialist man, that is, collectivist man, was introduced. The system of children's homes, week nurseries, and kindergartens began. The findings and results of psychological and pediatric follow-ups of children institutionalized in children's homes reveals a picture of psychological deprivation in its "embryonic state."

The problem of deprivation is not only a psychological one, it is sociologically relevant, too. Bowlby's work on maternal deprivation (1951, 1969, 1973) and the work of his critics and followers resulted in, among other things, partial theories of sensory, perceptual, emotional, parental, social, and cultural deprivation. These theories seem to be too fragmentary and often miss the target of attempting to solve the problems of deprivation disorders.

Such an attempt to solve the weak points of those partial theories has been made by professors Langmeier and Matejcek. They attacked the problem of psychological deprivation on a much broader front. They adopted a more comparative social approach than was usual in deprivation studies, and have derived models of child deprivation. They conducted content analyses of books on child-rearing written during the last hundred and twenty years and contrasted these models with the deprivation models in contemporary societies. On the ground of long-term clinical observations and experience they have developed the multilevel theory of psychological deprivation based upon a hierarchical concept of vital psychological needs.

As their student and later colleague, especially with professor Matejcek, and after rethinking the concept of *psychological needs*, I have tried to make some of the underlying ideas more explicit. The needs are not primarily understood as a certain lack, deficiency, or undesirable surplus of energy of the organism that is to be brought to the desired state of balance with a normal steady state (homeostasis). Rather, they (the needs) represent patterns of incorporating into the world—how and by what means a person enters and encounters the milieu, the environment, the world.

*Psychological deprivation* is the condition produced by life situations in which the subject is not given an opportunity to satisfy some of his/her vital psychological needs sufficiently and for a long enough period, so that the actualization and development of these needs are obstructed and distorted.

The vital psychological needs are, according to Langmeier and Matejcek (1974), as follows:

1. The need for a certain level of external stimulation—that is, for a certain amount, complexity, and variability of stimuli in general, or of stimuli in certain modalities. This is obviously necessary for the development and maintenance of an adequate level of attentiveness and activity, which is a necessary condition for the child's active relation to the surrounding world. The deprivation at this level is essentially lack of stimulation, and therapy is reactivation.

2. The need for sensory-cognitive structuring, that is, for meaningful sequences or order of stimuli, as a necessary condition for the child's effective learning. We can also call it the need for a meaningful world. Deprivation is considered lack of cognitive structure, and therapy as relearning.

3. The need for objects permitting specific affective attachment, i.e. for stable classes of stimuli that concentrate the child's individual activities. This is a prerequisite for the development of feelings of security—the need for a specific object to which he/she relates in a close, stable attachment. Initially, this object is usually mother (or mother figure). Deprivation is here regarded as lack of specific attachment, and therapy as reattachment.

4. The need for a sense of primary personal value and for stimuli that promote growth of personal identity and self-fulfillment. The child (and not only the child) needs appreciation, recognition of his/her worth, confirmation of his/her autonomous conduct, and approval of his/her assumed social roles. This again is clearly a precondition for effective personality integration. Deprivation is considered as lack of personal-social identity, and therapy as resocialization.

5. The need for an open future or the need for life prospect. This seems to be a specifically human need. A human being needs to have in front of him/her an open possibility that life, work, and self will continue. An open future stimulates *hope*, a closed future evokes *despair*—and deprivation on this level can be comprehended as lack of sense of life, and the therapy then consists in finding it.

Clinical observation of children treated in institutions has also led to the differentiation of types of deprived child personality:

1. The type *"relatively well adapted"*: The effects of deprivation are not immediately visible, but under stress they can influence the child's behavior.

2. The *socially hypoactive or inhibitory type*: Children who react toward sensory and emotionally impoverished environments only passively or apathetically and are oriented more toward things and objects than toward persons.

3. The *socially hyperactive or overactive type*: Deprived children with diffused and flit-

tering social activity and without the ability to form deeper emotional ties and attachments.

4. The *socially provocative type*: Children trying to force the adults' attention and interest by provocation. It holds for them that "if they cannot be caressed, then they want to be (at least) slapped." In the children's group they are almost unbearable, but if they are alone with an adult, they undergo a sudden change. They want to have the educator just to themselves.

5. The type of *substitution satisfaction*: Children who compensate for the lack of emotional stimuli by hyperactivity in other areas of behaviour, such as masturbation, excessive eating, aggressiveness, and so forth.

It has already been said that the psychological and pediatric findings and follow-ups of children brought up in children's homes rendered a picture of deprivation, especially of psychological deprivation in its "embryonic state" and in its making and progress. However, many of the results underlying these findings and theory could not be published, and the research activity and follow-up studies could not be conducted. However, another natural experimental situation emerged. It has been possible to follow and assess the impacts of new family-like environments (in foster care and especially in SOS Children's Villages) on the development of deprived personalities in children and to observe psychological deprivation in the state of remedy. That is why I am going to focus mainly on some findings concerning the children brought up in children's homes and in the care of foster-mothers in SOS Villages.

The sample of children from children's homes was set up in 1965. During the years 1966–1971, sixty children 12–15 years old were admitted to Thomayer's Hospital in Prague for a several weeks-long diagnostic stay. Some partial follow-up studies were conducted in 1973, 1974, 1982, 1987, and 1996.

Some of the most striking consequences of psychological deprivation are often language retardation, social behavior retardation and/or disturbances, and emotional flatness and superficiality (Langmeier & Matejcek, 1974) as well as distortion of temporal experience, known as "temporal anthropological disproportion" (Kovarik, 1973). In spite of actual loss of contacts between biological parents and children and no parental interest in their children, 34 percent of children (12–15 years old) love best their parents and develop an idealization of their families. Later this idealization decreases and is often substituted by anger, hate or indifference, and apathy to their parents. In the interview quite a lot of children said they are satisfied with their life situations. However, this satisfaction seems to be rather a resignation than a content and happiness. Their emotional life is superficial and undifferentiated; their past—the conscious part of it—is almost missing, unclear, and/or unmapped. Their future prospects are dim and without any concrete pattern.

Follow-ups of children in foster care in SOS Children's Village (Kotek, 1973; Kovarik, 1973) have elucidated some fragments of the process whereby deprivational consequences and disturbances are remedied. The developmental and intellectual level of the children, which at the beginning was very often 20 points below the average, rose during two years stay in SOS village almost to the average level. The world of the children, as shown for instance in their paintings, is structured now in comparison with the worlds portrayed by children in an institution. The drawings of children in children's homes showed mostly a "dead" house, often enclosed by a fence, without any persons. The only sign of the contact with the outside world was often just the TV aerial or an empty room, overcrowded with uniform furniture (mostly beds and wardrobes). Drawings of the children in SOS Children's Villages change after time, sometimes after months or years. The originally "dead" house now becomes a space of security and a center of family activities. The "house" is in a way *imago mundi* (Eliade, 1959; Bollnow, 1963) and a human community is now in the center of the picture.

Language development points to the fact that the child's world after adjustment to SOS living is now becoming more meaningful. Their whole situation is now basically different; it is personally accepting. And this, of course, conditions the child's total mood and thus the general readiness to experience. Time is now experienced and lived through in a quite different manner. The children who lived most of their childhood in institutions of Infants' Homes and Children's Homes have usually been unable to map their past and to envisage their future. The lack of personally important events and the frequent uniformity of the institutional environment have resulted in an almost empty past and rather dim, "foggy," obscure future. The children lived mostly in a narrow presence cut off from their past as well as their future. The lack of really significant others made the structure of social space and time muddled, confused, and not clearly arranged. The most important significant other has been a collective—a group of mates that, because of that child's rather frequent institutional changes, has not been constant and stable. Instead of an individual, personal identity, only a group or collective identity has been attained. In the new milieu of substitute family, based on the *psychosocial parenthood*, all these things have changed.

Let me emphasize that from the child's point of view, parenthood is established neither biologically nor legally but psychosocially. The parents, for the child, are those who accept him/her and who behave as mother or father. The social space is now clearly structured and oriented according to the new and really significant others, primarily the maternal person. Chances to participate in interpersonally significant and meaningful activities that enable the children, often for the first time in their lives, to experience the whole of a meaningful activity: the whole of the beginning, the course, and the ending. For example, when preserving, sterilizing, and bottling plums the children discover the future and its meaning. A careful and sensitive elucidation of the causes of the child's social orphanhood and the child's past helps the children (particularly the older ones) to incorporate this lost dimension into the history of their lives. They then can look for and find their new personal identity, where an open future has its significant meaning.

In the process of looking for and trying to develop more appropriate indicators of child well-being, I believe that the concept of multilevel psychological deprivation may be a source of inspiration. I think that the theory of psychological deprivation, derived from practice, research, and clinical experience, structures basic psychological needs in a way that reminds us of Thomas's four wishes, that is, desires for *experience, security, response, and recognition* as mentioned by Jens Qvortrup in his chapter. This theory also has important social and political as well as practical implications, especially if it can help us to grasp and understand the structure of the human being in the world and, following the common ontology, the structure of the child's being in the world.

## NOTE

1. ODS—Civic Democratic Party; ODA—Civic Democratic Alliance; KDU-CSL—Christian and Democratic Union plus Czech People's Party; KDS—Christian Democratic Party.

## REFERENCES

Alan, J. (1989). *Etapy zivota ocima socioloqa* [Life phases from a sociologist's point of view]. Praha: Panorama.

Bollnow, O. F. (1963). *Mensch und Raum*. Stuttgart: W. Kohlkammer Verlag.

Bowlby, J. (1951). *Maternal care and mental health*. Geneva: World Health Organization.

Bowlby, J. (1969). *Attachment and loss: Vol. I. Attachment*. New York: Basic Books.

Bowlby, J. (1973). *Attachment and loss: Vol. 2. Separation*. New York: Basic Books.

David, H. P., Dytrych, Z., Matejcek, Z., & Schuller, V. (1988). Born unwanted: Developmental effects of denied abortion, Avicenum. Prague: Czechoslovak Medical Press.

Dunovsky, J. (1973). *Hodnoceni somatickeho stavu a vYvoje deti v Detske vesnicce* [Assessment of physical state of children in SOS Children Village], studijni materialy Odborneho strediska SPDV, Praha.

Dunovsky, J., Bubleova, V., Cermakova I., & Karabelova H. (1990). *Psychosocialni vyvoj osob ktere byly od narozeni vychovavany mimo rodinu v detsk Ych domovech* [Psychosocial development of children living from early childhood in Children's Homes], zprava vyzkumu HPK 07–03–11, Praha.

Dytrych, Z., Matejcek, Z., & Schuller, V. (1975). *Nechtene deti* [Unwanted children]. VUPs, *ZpravY c. 34, A B*, Praha.

Eliade, M. (1959). *The sacred and the profane*. New York: Harcourt, Brace and World, Inc.

Kotek, M. (1973). *Psycholouicke poznatkv z prvni detstke vesnicky* [Psychological findings in the first Children's Village]. FFUK, Praha

Kovarik, J. (1973). *Prispevek k srovnavaci studii iednotlivych typu nahradni rodinne pece* [A contribution to comparative study of different types of substitute family care-Dissertation] Disert. prace, FFUK, Praha.

Kovarik, J. (1992). *Detstvi a ohrozene deti [Children at risk]*. Zprava VOPSV, Praha.

Kovarik, J. (1994). The space and time of children at the interface of psychology and sociology. In J. Qvortrup et al. (Eds.), *Childhood matters*. Vienna: Avebury.

Kovarik, J. & Kukla, L. (1996). Deti v CR 1996-*sitaucni analyza*, CV pro UNICEF [*State of children in Czech Republic*]. Praha: UNICEF.

Langmeier, J. & Matejcek, Z. (1974). *Psychicka denrivace v detstvi [Psychological deprivation in childhood]*. Praha: Avicenum.

Matejcek, Z. (1987). Begriff der psychischen subdeprivation. *Sozialpadiatrie in Praxis und Klinik, 9*, 9.

Matejcek, Z., Bubleova, V., & Kovarik, J. (1995). Pozdni nasledky psychicke deprivace a subdeprivace I. cast: Deti z detsk§ch domovu ve sv§ch ctyriceti letech [Late consequences of psychological deprivation and subdeprivation I.: Children from Children's Homes in their forties], *Ceskoslovenska psychologie, 6*.

Matejcek, Z., Kovarik J., & Bubleova, V. (1996). Pozdni nasledky psychicke deprivace a subdeprivace II. cast: Deti z nahradni rodinne pece [Late consequences of psychological deprivation and subdeprivation II.: Children from substitute family care], *Ceskoslovenska psychologie, 1*.

Mozny, I. (1991). *Proc tak snadno . . . (nektere rodinne duvody sametove revoluce* [Why so easy. . . . Some family causes of velvet revolution]. Praha: SLON.

Qvortrup, J. (1999). The meaning of child's standard of living. In A. B. Andrews & N. H. Kaufman (Eds.), *Implementing the U.N. Convention on the Rights of the Child.* Westport, CT: Praeger.

Torney-Purta, J. (1999). The meaning of a standard of living adequate for moral and civic development. In A. B. Andrews & N. H. Kaufman (Eds.), *Implementing the U.N. Convention on the Rights of the Child*. Westport, CT: Praeger.

## 16

# Twenty-Six Steps to Article 27: The Example of African American Children in South Carolina

*Barbara Morrison-Rodriguez*

## INTRODUCTION

The U.N. *Convention on the Rights of the Child*, Article 27, contains provisions that, if actualized for all of the world's children, would constitute the most significant revolutionary event in the history of humankind. These provisions, outlined in detail elsewhere in this book, would assure that every child has a decent standard of living necessary to promote all aspects of their development, and that parents, with state support as needed, assure that an adequate standard of living is provided for their children.

At the writing of this chapter, the United States has not ratified the *Convention*. Nevertheless, the provisions of Article 27 provide a set of goals by which to fashion family support and child welfare policy and services at the national and state levels in the United States.

This paper will use the principles of Article 27 as guidelines in (1) assessing the status of one subset of children in the United States and (2) suggesting what would need to change to move toward actualizing Article 27 for these children and their families. Data will be presented on the status of African American[1] children in South Carolina. Article 27 is especially relevant to these children because of the their ancestors' special history as slaves in one of the richest nations in the world and the enduring legacy of racism and discrimination under which they continue to live. The Preamble of the *Convention* recognizes that "in all countries of the world there are children living in exceptionally difficult conditions, and that such children need special consideration." It is the premise of this chapter that many African American children in the United States are children who need special consideration in order for their right to healthy development to be actualized.

## THE STATUS OF AFRICAN AMERICAN CHILDREN IN SOUTH CAROLINA: THE REALITY

African Americans are the largest racial minority group in South Carolina. After the end of legalized slavery there was a very brief period of relative freedom for blacks, followed by several decades of legalized racial segregation in all social institutions. Although the civil rights movement of the 1960s dismantled the legal framework for racial segregation, much of American society remains solidly segregated along racial lines. Further, the cumulative effects of racial discrimination and opportunity denied from slavery to the present have relegated far too many African American children and their parents to second-class citizenship in the richest country in the world.

The following is a descriptive overview of African American children in South Carolina with frequent comparisons to their white counterparts and particular attention to the domains of well-being referenced in the language of Article 27. It should be noted, as a relatively poor state, South Carolina is home to many poor white, Hispanic, and Native American children who are equally disadvantaged. Thus, the actualization of Article 27 would have far-reaching consequences for many of the state's poorest children.

### Economic Status of African American Children

*Child Poverty Rates.* Poverty remains an enduring aspect of the lives of too many children in the United States and in the state of South Carolina. In 1996, 21 percent of America's children lived below the poverty line, but 41 percent of African American children were poor. South Carolina's profile of child poverty mirrors that of the nation as a whole (Children's Defense Fund [CDF], 1997).

Racial disparities in child poverty are significant, particularly for South Carolina as compared to the nation as a whole. Nationally, 16 percent of white children are poor compared to 41 percent of African American children, while in South Carolina 9.5 percent of white children are poor compared to 40 percent of African American children (CDF, 1997).

Family composition is a factor in poverty rates for children. Predictably, the poverty rates for single-parent, female-headed households are the highest. Among African Americans, 56 percent of female-headed families were poor, compared to 28 percent of such families among whites in South Carolina (U.S. Census, 1990). African American children are more likely to be born into and reared in families headed by single women. On average, wages for black women are among the lowest in the country. This coupled with higher rates of father absence contributes to poverty among African American children.

There are several other reasons for the high child poverty rates. Among these are the failure of wages of the working poor to keep pace with inflation; high unemployment rates among African American males, many of whom are fathers; lack of child support from absent parents; and the decline in real dollar value of government assistance for poor families.

*Per Capita Income by Race.* The earnings potential of African American parents determines the extent of poverty among their children and their capacity to provide for the financial and material security of their families as mandated by Article 27. An examination of data on per capita income by race in South Carolina for three decades shows that African Americans still make less than half the income of whites. In 1989, the average annual income of African Americans was $6,800 compared to $14,115 for whites (U.S. Census, 1990). African American women have the lowest wage and income structures in the state. Many of them are single heads of household.

## Family Structure and Parental Competence

In order for African American families to meet their responsibilities as delineated in Article 27, they must possess the necessary family arrangements, parenting skills, and resources to foster the maximum development of their children. The research is clear that two-parent intact families are the most successful at providing for the needs of their children in the United States. There are several disturbing trends among African Americans that if continued unchecked do not bode well for meeting the needs of children.

*Declining Marriage Rates.* In 1890, just fifteen short years after the end of slavery, 80 percent of African American families were two-parent intact families (Billingsley, 1992). Slave narratives tell of long lines of newly freed slaves wishing to be legally married—a status denied them as slaves. One hundred years later in 1990, the percentage of African American married couples had dropped to 39 percent nationally.

Over the past three decades in South Carolina, there has been a marked drop in marriage rates for all age groups except persons over 55 for both genders and all racial groups. However, the decline in marriage rates is most pronounced for persons with lower incomes, especially young adults and African Americans. This decline in marriage is related to several factors. The precarious employment status of young African American males is a likely factor. Economic and employment instability makes many of them unattractive marriage partners (Wilson, 1996). Too many young black males, unanchored by marriage or committed relationships, conceive children out of wedlock. Others of these young men are delaying marriage until they complete their education and/or develop stable careers and financial stability. In addition to economic barriers, there has been greater acceptance of cohabitation and childbearing outside of marriage in the United States generally, and this value shift is shared by some segments of the

African American community. More black children are born out-of-wedlock with serious consequences for their development.

*Births to Unmarried Mothers.* In 1970, 15 percent of all babies born in South Carolina were born to unmarried mothers. By 1994 that had increased to 30 percent. The racial disparities in this regard are alarming. In 1994, 13.2 percent of white babies were born to unmarried mothers, compared to 57.8 percent of African Americans (South Carolina Department of Health and Environmental Control [SC DHEC], 1994). Nationally, only 39 percent of African American children live with both parents. African American children are four times as likely to be born to unmarried mothers, thus significantly increasing their chances of being born into and reared in poverty. When the mother is unmarried and head of household, especially if she is young, the chances of her family being poor are substantially increased. Children in father-absent families are five times more likely to be poor and ten times more likely to be extremely poor (Annie E. Casey Foundation, 1995). Further, throughout history, access to property rights has been an incentive to "legitimize" children in middle and higher income groups. A child without paternity loses access to property (inheritance rights) through male lines.

*Divorce.* Out of wedlock birth is only one reason for father absence. Divorce is another factor. The United States has the highest divorce rates in the world. Divorce is somewhat less of a factor for African American children since marriage rates are lower for African Americans. In 1994 in South Carolina, 13,129 children were involved in divorces (73 percent were white and 27 percent were African American (SC DHEC, 1994). Most of these children live with their mothers after divorce, and their economic standard of living declines.

*Out of Home Placements.* One sad indicator of the failure of parents to adequately rear their own children is the placement of a child out of the home. In South Carolina and across the nation, African American children are significantly over represented in the child welfare system. According to data from the South Carolina Department of Social Services, 64 percent of the 5,121 children in foster care in 1995 were African American. There are 9.3 per 1,000 African American children in foster care compared to 3.2 per 1,000 white children. Some analysts believe that child welfare workers spend too much time investigating reports and not enough time helping families and marshaling support for fragile families from extended kin, neighbors, and employers (Courtney & Collins, 1994; Welles, 1985; Zellman, 1992).

## Consequences of Family Structure for Child Well-Being and Development

The instability of many African American families has serious consequences for the well-being and development of African American children in South Carolina and nationally. The most apparent of these consequences is increased risk of father absence and poverty. Being poor and without a father has significant implications for the physical, mental, social, and moral development of these children. A few key indicators reveal the impact.

### Health Status Indicators

*Poor Infant Health. Infant mortality* is an internationally used indicator of the health of both child-bearing women and the children they produce. Infant mortality, the death of babies before their first birthday, is the result of poor fetal development during pregnancy, an impoverished living environment, unmet health needs, and inadequate health care. The U.S. infant mortality rate ranks eighteenth among industrialized countries. Only Portugal does worse (CDF, 1997). In 1994, African American babies in South Carolina died during the first year of life (13.8 per 1,000) at twice the rate of white infants (6.6 per 1,000). Although infant mortality rates in the United States have declined for the past three decades, significant racial disparities still exist.

*Low birth weight* (defined as weighing less than 2,500 grams [5.5 pounds] at birth) is associated with reduced survival of infants and higher rates of child disabilities among low birth weight infants. National data for 1994 indicate that the rate of low birth weight births rose for whites, remained constant for Hispanics, and declined for African American babies. In South Carolina for that same year, African American mothers (13.1 percent) were still twice as likely as white mothers (6.5 percent) to have a low birth weight baby. Although the rates are declining for African Americans nationally, the rate of low birth weight among African Americans is worse than seventy-three countries, including many in the Third World and the former Communist Eastern Bloc nations (CDF, 1994).

*Access to Prenatal Care.* Adequate prenatal care is essential to the reduction of infant deaths and childhood disability. Nationally from 1991 to 1994, early prenatal care rates increased each year for fourteen of fifteen racial and ethnic groups tracked by the U.S. census resulting in better prenatal outcomes, especially for African Americans (CDF, 1997). The picture is not so optimistic for South Carolina. In 1994, 37.6 percent of African American pregnant women received no prenatal care in the first trimester (a rate 2.3 times higher than for white women). Although access to prenatal care has improved since 1970, the gap between the races in access to our use of prenatal care has remained consistent for twenty-five years.

*Health Insurance Coverage.* Access to prenatal care, postnatal care, and primary pediatric care for children is related to their health insurance status and that of their parents. In 1994 and 1995, 10 million children in the United States (1 in 7) had no health insurance. Seventy percent of these children are white, and 60 percent live in two-parent families (CDF, 1997). Many of these children have working parents who either work insufficient hours to qualify for private health insurance or make too much money to qualify for public health insurance for the poor (Medicaid). Further, more employers are cutting back on the provision of health insurance either through reductions or elimination of benefits or increased hiring of contract and part-time labor without provision of benefits such as health insurance. The percentage of children without health insurance varies considerably by state from a low of 6.7 percent in Minnesota to a high of 17.1 percent in Florida. Between 1993 and 1995, 14.6 percent of South Carolina's children lacked health insurance, ranking the state at thirty-eight out of fifty-two states (CDF, 1997).

*Childhood Deaths.* The death of a child is a significant tragedy that often reflects the failure of the adult world to provide healthy living conditions and medical care. Between 1992 and 1994 there were 269 officially recorded deaths of children between the ages of 1 and 14 in South Carolina. Of these, 52 percent were African American, a rate that far exceeds their 38 percent representation of the state's children in this age group. These deaths were due to inadequate adult supervision and protection from accidents, poor health resulting from serious medical conditions, and cases of severe child maltreatment. According to the 1993 official report of the South Carolina State Child Fatalities Review Committee, there were fifty-eight child deaths due to severe child maltreatment, and 66 percent of these were African American children. Poverty and its related stressors—poor parenting skills, poor anger management, abuse of alcohol, and drugs—are known risk factors for child maltreatment. In addition, 20 percent of the fatalities were caused by the actions of the mother's boyfriend—a significant risk factor for children in single female-headed households.

*Environmental Toxic Exposure.* African American children in South Carolina are significantly more likely to live in areas where they are exposed to environmental toxins, reflecting a regional pattern in the southeastern United States. In 1986, the General Accounting Office (GAO, the investigative arm of the United States Congress) studied the location of hazardous-waste landfills in the Southeast. The GAO found that 75 percent of such landfills were located in areas with largely black populations, and 26 percent of these residents were below the federal poverty line (United Church of Christ Commission on Racial Justice, 1987). Race consistently proved to be the most significant factor in determining where commercial hazardous waste sites are located. Nixon (1996) summarizes the findings of fifteen studies conducted in South Carolina on toxic wastes. Regardless of the unit of analysis (census tracts, zip codes, towns, or neighborhoods), the findings show a consistent pattern: Race was stronger than any other factor, including income, in predicting where a toxic waste site would be located. Exposure to toxic wastes are proven to be related to significant health problems in children, including cancer, as well neurological damage, mental retardation, and developmental delays. Through its actions and policies, South Carolina's government and industries indicate that the well-being of African American children is less important than that of white children and children in middle-class and affluent communities.

## Social Development Indicators

*School Performance and Educational Attainment.* School performance and educational attainment are frequently used indicators of the social development of children and are essential for successful development in our high technology economy. The Children's Defense Fund (1997) reports that nearly twenty years of progress in narrowing the academic achievement gap that separates low-income and minority students from others has stopped. Between 1970 and 1988 black, Hispanic, and Native American students made striking progress. Between 1988 and 1990 that progress stopped. Between 1990 and 1995 no progress was made in increasing the number of young people completing high school (86 percent nationally). Family income (and related parental educational and occupational attainment) is related to the rate of high school drop out, regardless of race. Among African Americans, 23 percent of low-income children did not complete high school compared to 3.9 percent of high-income African American families (CDF, 1997).

Educational underachievement begins very early in life for African American children. The South Carolina Department of Education (1995) reports that among African American children:

- 40 percent in the first grade were assessed "not ready" for the first grade
- 42 percent to 49 percent are in the bottom quarter of all students nationally on standardized norm reference tests
- 43 percent to 49 percent taking basic skills tests in the 8th grade do not meet minimum standards
- 55 percent do not pass the high school exit exam on the first try

African American students, especially boys, are twice as likely to be retained in grades 1–3 and are likely to be placed in remedial and special education classes. According to some scholars (Boutte, 1993; Pigford, 1990; Thompson & Thompson, 1993) these placements are too often the result of teacher and administrator attitudes that foster lower academic expectations for African American children and place undue attention on controlling behavior (especially boys) as opposed to fostering critical thinking, problem solving, creativity, and self-expression. Some schools may be active accomplices in thwarting the educational and social development of African American children.

The most comprehensive analysis of these concerns was the 1989 study by the University of South Carolina Education Policy Center regarding state remedial and compensatory programs. It found these programs have low status as indicated by the location of the programs, the quality of the teachers, and the attitudes of teachers, students, and administrators. Most principals did not know why they were using certain remedial models, programs lacked coordination with regular classrooms, and they emphasized assignment of students to fill out work sheets emphasizing low-level basic skills with a minimum of direct teacher interaction. Annually $300 million is spent on remedial and special education classes. It is essential that the content and quality of these programs be monitored to ensure high quality standards and to ensure that they are not being used to track and warehouse poor minority students in their most critical developmental years (Morrison & Holmes, 1996).

*Anti-Social Behavior.* Another indicator of social development is the extent to which children and youth behave as a reflection of their adherence to major norms and moral values regarding appropriate personal and social behavior. Deviations from social norms are most likely to occur when young people have some degree of independence from parental control and are more influenced by peer pressure. There may also be subcultural deviations from the norms of the dominant culture that may foster behaviors considered to be antisocial.

Examples of unhealthy and life-threatening risk behaviors among adolescents are clearly evident in terms of use and abuse of alcohol and illicit drugs, early premarital sexual activity, teen pregnancy, suicide, homicide and other forms of violence, and criminal activity. Data on youth in South Carolina reveal that African American youth are much more at risk on some of these indicators, but not all compared to their white counterparts.

*Alcohol abuse* data indicate that alcohol binge drinking (five or more drinks consecutively) are highest among white males (30 percent) as compared to white females (14.7 percent), African American males (11.5 percent) and African American females (2.8 percent) (SC Department of Alcohol and Other Drug Services [SC DAODS], 1992–93; Morrison & Holmes, 1996).

*Drug use* is much higher for white high school students (19% for males and 15% for females) as compared to African American high school students (8.4% for males and 3% for females).

*Early and premarital sexual activity* data indicate that the majority of high school students in South Carolina have initiated sexual activity. The most sexually active group are African American males (86.6 percent), compared to 72.7 percent of African American females, 58.1 percent of white males, and 53.9 percent of white females. Sixty-two percent of African American males reported initiating sexual activity by age 13. Such early sexual activity not only increases the risk of teen pregnancy, but increases the risk for sexually transmitted diseases, including AIDS/HIV, which have high incidence and prevalence rates among black youth (University of South Carolina School of Public Health, 1995).

*Homicide and suicide* rates among youth are relatively small in South Carolina. The strong religious orientation of many Southern cultures may be a protective factor in this regard. However, racial patterns are detectable. In 1994 there were fifty-four reported youth homicides among youth 10 to 19 years of age. Of these, 71 percent were among African Americans youth. White youth are more likely to commit suicide.

*Criminal activity and incarceration* rates are also related to race. While African American youth represent slightly less than 40 percent of South Carolina's youth population, they account for more than 75 percent of arrests for violent crimes. African American males comprise half of all arrests and 76 percent of all arrests for violent crimes (Williams, 1996). In fiscal year 1994–95, there were 1,071 adolescents admitted to Department of Juvenile Justice facilities. Of these, 62 percent were African American males, and 7 percent were African American females. One third of the admissions were children under 14 years of age, and among these 64 percent were African American (Williams, 1996). Eighty-six percent of youths detained in the state juvenile justice system are from households with incomes less than $20,000 (Williams, 1996). The relationship of race and poverty to crime and incarceration is complex. Being poor is likely to promote criminal activity when legitimate means of acquiring money and good are unavailable or where subcultural value systems support criminal activity. It is also true that individuals who are poor and nonwhite are much more likely to be arrested for crimes and incarcerated, especially among youth. The result is that too many African American young men spend their development years behind bars with devastating consequences for their present and future lives.

As the foregoing indicators reveal, African American children in the United States and in South Carolina are significantly more likely to have their health, education, and social and moral development compromised by the combined effects of poverty and racism. It appears that South Carolina, like other states and the federal government, considers large numbers of African American children expendable. In spite of political rhetoric to the contrary, the United States is not a child-centered and child-oriented society. Our policies and actions dispute the validity of such claims. If the provisions of Article 27 were to be taken seriously, it would be a radical change from past practices, which is likely to happen only if there is a preceding shift in values, will, and commitment to the well-being of all children in America, especially those who have inherited the legacy of poverty and racial discrimination. What evidence is there that such a shift is likely to happen?

What follows is a brief analysis of prevailing social welfare policy that will have a significant impact on the well-being of poor children in the United States, including African American children in South Carolina. Of special interest is the "welfare reform" movement in the United States.

## THE ROLE OF GOVERNMENT POLICY

Article 27 states that governments should assist needy parents in meeting the needs of their children if they are unable to do so within their own means and abilities. The U.S. government has used various strategies over time to provide such assistance with mixed results. How to provide assistance to needy children and their families has been a subject of intense debate in the United States, culminating for the present in major social welfare policy changes known as "welfare reform." A brief examination of this policy shift and its potential consequences for realizing the goals of Article 27 follow.

### Negative Consequences of Social Policy: Aid to Families with Dependent Children

Of the social programs developed to assist poor families, the most notable and the most controversial was the Aid to Families with Dependent Children (AFDC) enacted in 1935 and commonly referred to as "welfare." Essentially an income assistance program, with eligibility tied to eligibility to medical insurance known as Medicaid and nutritional assistance through the Food Stamp Program, AFDC operated under federal guidelines and with federal financial assistance, but with much discretion by states in their actual cash assistance levels. Before implementation of the Family Support Act of 1988, which required states to provide assistance to families needing assistance because of unemployment, about half the states (including South Carolina) denied AFDC to families when adult breadwinners (usually fathers) were living in the household even if they were unemployed. One result of this policy is that some biological fathers failed to form families or left their families in order for the women and children to receive cash assistance under AFDC. Thus some unknown degree of father absence and related poverty is a consequence of misguided social policy aimed at ostensibly assisting poor families.

Although the majority of individuals receiving AFDC nationally are white, a disproportionate number of African Americans are "on welfare." In 1994, there were 13.97 million people on AFDC nationally and 60 percent of all poor children received AFDC. Of these, 37.4 percent were white, 36.4 percent were African American (African American represent 12 percent of the U.S. population), 19.9 percent were Hispanic, 1.3 percent were Native American, and 2.9 percent were Asian American. In 1996, the *maximum* monthly AFDC benefit for a family of three in South Carolina was $200. This in combination with food stamps would bring a family up to 47 percent of the federal poverty line adjusted for family size. In spite of the meagerness of this assistance, critics of welfare felt that too many people were unduly benefiting from this system. Further, it was believed that the system created multigenerational dependence on government assistance. Statistics indicate that 70 percent of mothers and children on AFDC leave the program within one or two years usually because of marriage or remarriage. However, 58 percent of those leaving returned to AFDC within two years usually because of divorce or separation (CDF, 1997).

Supporters felt that many families were helped, but benefits were too low to lift families out of poverty. Some felt that policies were especially unfair to intact working poor families. The politically conservative felt that the program absorbed too many public dollars and encouraged dependency on government cash assistance. Almost all Americans agreed that changes in the welfare system were needed, but there was much debate about what those changes should be.

## Welfare Reform: Implications for Poor and African American Children

The AFDC program was ended and replaced by new legislation known as the Personal Responsibility and Work Opportunity Reconciliation Act (P.L. 104–193) enacted in August 1996 and commonly referred to as "welfare reform." The new law ends the individual entitlement to federally supported cash assistance to needy families with children and provides for terminating benefits to families for failing to comply with program rules (principally around searching for and securing employment) or after a certain time period. A major concern is that states can choose to cut off or reduce benefits to children as well as the parent, if the parent does not comply with work or child support requirements.

The new law replaces AFDC with block grants to states under Temporary Assistance to Needy Families (TANF). It also has specific mandates to states to maximize payment and collection of child support obligations, a goal very consistent with Article 27. The Children's Defense Fund (1997), a major advocacy organization for children, has outlined its concerns, shared by many others, that poor children and their families will be harmed by the new welfare provisions because:

- TANF drops the guarantee of financial assistance in times of need.

- States must require parents to work within two years of receiving cash assistance and states can shorten this time limit. There is concern that many poor parents lack the education and skill to garner and maintain employment, especially when they reside in areas with high unemployment rates and limited opportunities for work.

- States must impose a five-year lifetime limit on TANF, making the lifetime limit shorter.

- TANF gives wide discretion to states in how to use block grant dollars, and almost all national standards are gone. South Carolina has set its lifetime limit at two years out of sixty consecutive months.

- Under the new law, Congress will cut $27 billion over six years from the food stamp program and $7 billion from the children's portion of Supplemental Security Income (SSI) for children with disabilities. It is expected that 250,000 to 315,000 children with disabilities in the United States will no longer be eligible for income assistance under SSI.

- Benefits are cut for most *legal* immigrants already in the United States and most of those who enter the United States in the future.

The enhanced focus on child support enforcement is seen as a positive aspect of the new law, but could possibly serve to further alienate some fathers from their children. Parental noncompliance with child support enforcement efforts might also jeopardize benefits for children.

This is a special concern for African American children given the significantly higher rates of unemployment among black males, especially young black males, many of whom are fathers.

At the time of the 1990 census, 21 percent African American males ages 35 to 44 and 36 percent of African American males ages 20 to 24 years in South Carolina were not employed (U.S. Census, 1990). In 1994, only 20 percent of child support cases were paid nationally. The collection rate in South Carolina is 26 percent. Fathers need to work to provide for their families and to pay child support when they are living apart from their children. The penalties for not paying child support can be severe in South Carolina. Fathers can be incarcerated for not complying with support orders.

## FROM CURRENT REALITY TO THE VISION OF CHILD RIGHTS

The new welfare law is the framework within which the U.S. federal government and the various states will act to ostensibly improve the lives of America's poorest children and their families. This chapter will end with recommendations for government, business and industry, communities and their social institutions, and families that are considered essential if Article 27 is to be actualized in the United States.

Because the United States has a capitalist economy, the participation of the private sector is essential to winning the war on poverty and ensuring the rights of children through wage structures and workplace policies for working parents. Although all American children would benefit from these recommendations, African American children in particular stand to gain if these actions could be realized. In the richest country in the world, implementation of these strategies is essentially a matter of will.

## TWENTY-SIX STEPS TO ACTUALIZATION OF ARTICLE 27

### Governments (Federal, State and/or Local) Must:

1. Ratify the U.N. *Convention on the Rights of the Child.*

2. Use social policy to correct historical discrepancies based on race and ethnicity that impair the ability of many parents to provide for their families. At the present time, the U.S. federal government and many state governments are dismantling legal frameworks to advance the social and economic position of racial and ethnic minority groups and legal immigrants.

3. Invest in job creation, job preparation, job placement, and microenterprise for parents leaving welfare for work and for working poor parents who wish to upgrade their skills and work opportunities.

4. Develop and implement approaches to build assets among poor families including home ownership and microenterprise.

5. Ensure that innocent children do not bear the burden of their parents' unwillingness or inability to comply with welfare reform program requirements (or within time limits). Children are entitled to society's support as a matter of their individual rights. There must continue to be a safety net for all children to insure them adequate education, housing, nutrition, and health care.

6. Create tax incentives and a regulatory framework for the development and provision of quality child care that assists working parents and lays the foundation for physical and mental development of infants and children.

7. Vigorously enforce child support rules by also assisting non-custodial parents to upgrade their skills and find work to meet child support obligations.

8. Create and adopt a workable system of national health insurance. At a minimum, ensure that children do not lose public health insurance coverage as a result of welfare reform.

9. Eliminate serious inequities in the system of public education, which gives inadequate resources and less skilled teachers to schools in poor and rural districts, many of which have predominantly African American student bodies.

10. Improve or abolish ineffective remedial and compensatory programs that set the lowest level of expectation for children, assign the least skilled teachers to the neediest children, and serve to label, track, and warehouse children, especially African American boys.

11. Provide extensive opportunities for market-relevant vocational education and skills development through technical preparation and apprenticeship programs for students not interested in college education.

## Business and Industry Must:

12. Develop work sites in economically depressed areas where local residents can access work close to their homes and families and be trained to undertake well-paying jobs, especially through technical training and apprenticeship programs. Such businesses and industries should be monitored for environmental health effects on residents.

13. Respond better to the needs of working parents through payment of just and fair wages (especially to women and racial minorities), through flexible or part-time work schedules, and through the provision of quality child care.

14. Not renege on their commitment to provide benefits to their employees, particularly adequate health insurance including benefits for dependent children.

15. Cooperate with government in efforts to collect child support from their employees.

## Communities and Their Social Institutions Must:

16. Play a more active role in the moral guidance of families and children with special attention to addressing the moral dilemmas of the modern age, including controversial subjects such as sexual promiscuity, teen pregnancy, substance abuse, and interpersonal and intrafamilial violence.

17. Work in tandem with families to teach moral values to children and youth and help young people make a healthy transition into adult responsibilities.

18. Work aggressively to take control of their communities and cooperate with law enforcement authorities to rid their neighborhoods of unhealthy, exploitative, and dangerous elements such as drug trafficking, adult and child prostitution, and liquor stores on every corner.

19. Create safe places and ample opportunities for residents to interact and get to know one another as a way to reduce fear and promote mutual assistance, especially around the care and protection of children.

## Families, Especially African American Families, Must:

20. Transmit across generations values that promote strong commitment and thoughtfulness on all aspects of family formation, from marriage to conception to family life.

21. Conceive children only when both parents are ready personally and financially to provide a permanent and loving home. Each child has a right to be a wanted child.

22. Give their children a strong moral foundation consistent with their religious values and beliefs.

23. Teach and model responsible sexual behavior for their children.

24. Teach and model racial tolerance and understanding and appreciation for the rich and wonderful diversity that is the American legacy.

25. Promote their own economic self-sufficiency and model initiative and mastery for their children. Parents must strive to complete their own education, upgrade their skills, and take advantage of all opportunities for gainful employment.

26. Create mutual support networks to assist each other with child rearing and to manage crises that threaten family stability and child safety.

## CONCLUSION

The situation of many African American children is dire. Black children in states like South Carolina still struggle to overcome the residuals of their slave past and enduring systematic racial discrimination. To the extent that their parents are poorly educated, unemployed, and exploited, these children suffer. It is, therefore, impossible to address the well-being of these children without attention to the needs of their parents.

Many child advocates are concerned that some of the provisions of the new welfare reform law will further exacerbate the problems of poor children and their parents. There is the risk that parental failure or inability to comply with work requirements or other mandates attached to assistance will result in children ultimately paying the price in a further reduced standard of living. And while strengthened child support enforcement measures are needed, they may exacerbate the problem of father absence by further estranging men from their children, particularly if the emphasis on maternal work preparation and employment is not matched by equal attention to the employment needs of fathers.

Article 27 places the major responsibility for the welfare of children on their parents as it should be. But many of these parents, especially those who are young, undereducated, marginally skilled, and unmarried will need the assistance of all sectors of society to meet their parental obligations. There will always be children whose parents are unable to meet their obligations for a variety of reasons. A safety net must be in place for these children. The provisions of Article 27 provide a framework for assuring the well-being of children regardless of their particular circumstances. For African American children, ratification of the *Convention* and a serious effort by the United States to meet the provision of Article 27 will ensure them a better future and a chance to make the most of their individual endowments in a caring and humane society. They will benefit in ways that their ancestors could not. America will benefit most from the contributions of African American children whose potential is yet to be fully realized.

## NOTE

1. The terms "African American" and "black" will be used interchangeably in this chapter. When using direct quotes or statistical citations from other works, the term used in the source document will be used.

## REFERENCES

The Annie E. Casey Foundation (1997). *Kids Count data book: State profiles of child well-being.* Baltimore, MD: Author.

Billingsley, A. (1992). *Climbing Jacob's ladder: The enduring legacy of African-American families.* New York: Simon and Schuster.

Boutte, G. (1993). Do disparities in passing rates of black and white children on state-mandated tests indicate differences in education? In *The state of black South Carolina 1992–93: An action agenda for the future* (1–25). Columbia, SC: Columbia Urban League.

Children's Defense Fund (CDF). (1994). *Wasting America's future: The Children's Defense Fund report on the costs of child poverty.* Boston: Beacon Press.

Children's Defense Fund (CDF). (1997). *The state of America's children: Yearbook 1997.* Washington, DC: Author.

Courtney, M. E. & Collins, R. C. (1994). New challenges and opportunities in child welfare outcomes and information technologies. In P. A. Curtis (Ed.), *A research agenda for child welfare* (359–378). New York: Child Welfare League of America.

Morrison, B. J. & Holmes, A. B. (1996). African-American children in South Carolina: A call to action. In *The state of black South Carolina 1995–96: An action agenda for the future* (1–47). Columbia, SC: Columbia Urban League.

Nixon, R. (1996). Environmental racism in South Carolina: Reviewing the evidence. In

*The state of black South Carolina 1995–96: An action agenda for the Future* (101–123). Columbia, SC: Columbia Urban League, Inc.

Pigford, A. (1990). The high school exit examination: An educational dilemma for black students in South Carolina. In *The state of black South Carolina 1990: An action agenda for the future* (1–22). Columbia, SC: Columbia Urban League.

South Carolina Department of Alcohol and Other Drug Services. (1992–93). State agency data files. Columbia: SCDAODS.

South Carolina Department of Education. (1995). Minority student representation among special education programs in South Carolina schools.

South Carolina Department of Health and Environmental Control (SC DHEC). (1994). Report of Vital Statistics for the State of South Carolina.

Thompson, T. & Thompson, J. (1993). The status of the black male in the South Carolina educational system. In *The state of black South Carolina 1992–93: An action agenda for the future* (26–45). Columbia, SC: Columbia Urban League.

United Church of Christ Commission on Racial Justice. (1987). *Toxic waste and race in the United States: A national report on the racial and socio-economic characteristics of communities with hazardous waste sites.* New York: Author.

United States Bureau of the Census. (1990). *Statistical abstract of the United States 1990.* Washington, DC: U.S. Government Printing Office.

University of South Carolina School of Public Health. (1995). *The 1995 South Carolina youth risk behavior survey report: 11th and 12th graders.* Columbia, S.C.: University of South Carolina.

Welles, S. J. (1985). *Decision making in child protective services intake and investigations: Final report.* Washington, DC: American Bar Association.

Williams, M. (1996). The incarceration of African-American juveniles. In *The state of black South Carolina 1995–96: An action agenda for the future* (48–74). Columbia, SC: Columbia Urban League.

Wilson, W. J. (1996). *When work disappears: The world of the new urban poor.* New York: Alfred A. Knopf.

Zellman, G. L. (1992). The impact of case characteristics on child abuse reporting decisions. *Child Abuse and Neglect, 16,* 57–74.

# 17

# Confronting the Implementation Challenge

*Arlene Bowers Andrews and*
*Natalie Hevener Kaufman*

Communities and nations that aim to promote holistic child development can look to the U.N. *Convention on the Rights of the Child* as an instrument of moral and, where ratified, legal authority. With the almost universal ratification of the treaty and numerous references to it in resolutions and declarations of the United Nations and other international organizations, it may be argued that the treaty is now customary international law and is binding on all states. The *Convention* embodies a vision of what childhood could be like if families and communities provided an adequate standard of living during the early years of life. The convergence of world opinion regarding the significance of this vision signifies a new commitment to remedy the current reality of destitution, gross inequities, and developmental threats in children's lives. Bridging the gap between the vision and reality will require unprecedented global political and social action.

The *Convention* emerged as a consensus statement from the world's governments and calls for action by states parties and nongovernmental organizations. In an increasingly democratized world, implementation will require mass action that includes private citizens and nongovernmental organizations, particularly in countries such as the United States where the market economy and the voluntary (nonprofit, civic, and religious) sectors exert powerful influence on social conditions and quality of life. As one step toward mobilizing broad awareness and support for implementation, the *Convention* calls for states parties to make the principles and provisions of the *Convention* widely known to adults and children alike.

Assuring an adequate standard of living for all children within a community or governmental unit can be facilitated by a basic three-phase action model: planning/organizing, action, and assessing impact.

## PLANNING AND ORGANIZING

Per Miljeteig, director of Childwatch International, observes that monitoring children's rights is the business of everyone concerned with children (1996, 57). The work of organizing action toward monitoring the right to an adequate standard of living begins with the emergence of leadership. Who is "concerned with children" in a particular geographic area? Is the concern manifest in the will to initiate and follow action toward a goal no less ambitious than the assurance of an adequate standard of living for holistic development for each child in the region?

In some areas, leadership has been assumed by the national government. In others, leaders are emerging from the bottom up, through neighborhood organizations, local governments, and professional associations. In far too many countries, little or nothing is happening to pursue implementation of children's rights. Around the world, advocacy groups must be convened in local communities, governmental regions, and international arenas.

An international example is the 1990 World Summit on Children held at the U.N. offices in New York (North American Congress on Latin America [NACLA], 1994). The summit produced a set of urgent social goals targeted at reducing maternal and infant mortality, child malnutrition, and major childhood diseases and increasing availability of primary school education, safe water, sanitation, and family planning resources. An agreement has been signed by 159 nations committing each to adapt the goals to its own circumstances and draw up a national action plan to achieve the goals. The consensus at the summit was essentially that "infrastructure and communications capacity in most developing nations have now reached the point at which it is physically and financially possible to bring the basic benefits of scientific progress to virtually every community" (NACLA, 38), as demonstrated by the recent global increase in immunization and oral rehydration therapy. The means are available; the will and resources must be promoted.

The case of South Africa illustrates how decades of grassroots organizing around children's rights led to the current national government assuming leadership for implementation of the rights. Rose September, in her succinct chronology of the struggle for children's rights in South Africa, notes that the plight of children culminated in the Soweto uprising beginning on June 16, 1976, which is now commemorated as the Day of the African Child throughout Africa (September, 1996). The call for children's rights permeated the struggle against apartheid. A series of post-apartheid consensus-seeking processes throughout the country has led to an ambitious agenda for child development in the South African National Plan of Action for Children (SANPAC), which embodies principles of the *Convention* and the World Summit on Children. A National Children's Rights Committee measures and monitors attainment of the rights.

The South African experience demonstrates how the work of planning involves establishing visions, mission, goals, strategies, and action agendas with clearly designated responsibilities for implementation. South Africa's formation of a new pro-human rights government coincided with the adoption of the U.N. *Convention on the Rights of the Child*, which gave to South Africa the opportunity to ground its policy and action planning for children in a human rights framework. In other areas, mobilization efforts must contend with resistance to organizing around the child's right to develop because individuals, organizations, and governments are already busy in a vast, uncoordinated effort to help children and their families, though without benefit of clear vision and organizing principles. The *Convention* offers an opportunity for collective action to more efficiently and effectively promote child development, if only people will take the time, shift their focuses, commit resources, and work together.

Disagreement about appropriate strategies and locus of responsibility also breeds resistance to organizing and planning for the attainment of the child's right to develop. Policy and program planning debates often center on the relative roles of government and the family. Article 27 requires that parent(s) and others responsible for the child secure living conditions necessary for the child's development, within their abilities and financial capabilities and with state assistance. Some governments (e.g., Norway, Germany) have enacted policies to directly ensure financial and material child support. Others, such as the United States, operate residual programs for crisis relief only, expecting the family to secure adequate routine supports from the market. Regardless of how the debate is settled in a particular area, a plan can be developed and results monitored to ascertain whether the child does in fact acquire adequate living conditions.

Planning and organizing gets people talking and leads to decisions about proposed action. Action plans are generally of two types: those that require policy action by elected or administrative officials, and those that involve social action through nongovernmental entities such as the media, business, religious organizations, the nonprofit sector, and voluntary action. The entire society must be mobilized, to some extent, if the child's rights are to be secured.

## ACTION

A child's living conditions are influenced—positively and negatively—by the composition, actions, and resources of the child's family, social networks, and broader environment. Thus, strategic actions to improve conditions and promote positive development must focus not only on the child but also on social, economic, political, and physical aspects of the environment.

As the papers in this volume suggest, securing conditions necessary for a child's physical, mental, spiritual, moral, and social development requires that the entire society be acting in the interests of children. The child requires:

- adequate and appropriate water, nutrition, shelter, clothing, hygiene, exercise, protection, health care, and preventive health education;
- cognitive stimulation and education, life skills development, affirmation of competence, opportunities for creativity and productivity;
- spiritual guidance, opportunities for reflection;
- sensitive responses to concerns about universal questions of life and death;
- discipline, respect, guidance regarding the relation of self to others and prosocial behavior;
- affection, esteem, secure relationships over time, and guidance regarding civic and community responsibility.

Somehow, the family and others responsible for the child must invest time, personal skills and energy, and economic resources into creating and maintaining these conditions. These caregivers must themselves be healthy and relatively well developed in order to support the child's development. The society can, through political and social action, enable the capacity of caregivers to adequately fulfill their responsibilities. In most developed countries, public laws and government funds make available such resources as minimum family income, food, safe and affordable housing, health care, early childhood developmental support (e.g., home visitors, child care, parental leave from work), and education.

Tools are being developed and disseminated to facilitate monitoring implementation of the rights of the child throughout the world (Edwards & Gosling, 1995; Ennew & Miljeteig, 1996). The method of implementation and expanding expertise of the Committee on the Rights of the Child are discussed in chapter 2. In addition to the states parties that are required, by their ratification, to submit regular reports to the Committee and the United Nations (particularly UNICEF), other public and private organizations are engaged in discussions of the implementation of the *Convention*. Childwatch International, for example, has established a network of research institutions as well as a variety of child advocates to begin to produce the kind of research that would be necessary to a serious implementation of the *Convention*.

Efforts have also been launched to identify a set of indicators that could be used to measure and monitor the status of children. Regular annual publication of the *State of the World's Children* (UNICEF) is valuable and useful in displaying the results as well as deficiencies of national and global efforts to improve the conditions of children. As the international community moves forward in consensus about rights reflected in the *Convention*, assessing the well-being of children across time and space, within and beyond national boundaries, becomes both possible and desirable. This effort will be informed by the global experience of country-specific statutes, policies, and reporting on national efforts to realize children's rights and nongovernmental organizations' programs on behalf of children. International health indicators are one area of acknowledged success. Another effort is that of an international group of scholars who have been working on developing indicators of the child's well-being beyond survival. And UNICEF held a conference in February 1998 to address the task of developing indicators of child well-being that would be used in association with the *Convention*'s implementation. Clearly the implementation of the *Convention* will require simultaneous energetic efforts at the local, national, regional, and global level if the child's rights, including the right to an adequate standard of living, are even to begin to be realized.

In an action planning model, this phase involves managing and monitoring the effort, quality, and outcomes of the plan. Managing and monitoring the effort involves determining what kind of action is taken, resources expended, and numbers and types of people reached. Quality management and monitoring checks the degree to which the action conforms to standards such as ethical behavior, humanitarian values, cultural competence, and appropriateness for the need. Outcome monitoring routinely reports on the effect of the action, including its intended results as well as unintended effects, and forms a basis for continuous reform of the action to improve results.

Thus, for example, if a community or government seeks to assure that each child receives adequate nutrition, it will enact a plan based on effort to assure universal food distribution (by caregiver means or subsidy) to every child in any caregiving environment. Monitoring the action would assess program quality, such as whether the food provides a balanced nutritional diet that varies by age of the child and cultural food expectations of the family, and program outcomes, such as actual intake of the food by the persons for whom it is intended.

Any parent can attest to the fact that rearing healthy children is hard work, though rewardingly productive. Article 27 establishes a collective commitment to support parents and others in this work. As communities and governments strengthen their commitment through planning and action, the enormous responsibility that parents have borne for centuries becomes more publicly acknowledged.

## IMPACT

Rights monitoring and social and political action can determine whether a child lives in conditions adequate for development. The impact of those conditions can only be monitored by assessing the child's actual standard of living as well as the child's well-being and developmental status. Such information would indicate whether each child is in good physical and mental health, behaving in a moral and responsible way, aware of spirituality, and socially connected.

Using the example above, monitoring impact of an action plan to assure adequate nutrition would have two focuses. The first would assess the actual nutritional standard of living relative to what is deemed adequate according to national, cultural, and community standards. Comparing children's diets relative to the standard would be an impact measure. Second, monitoring impact would require measuring children's physical development according to expected patterns of height, weight, bone mass, activity levels, motor and cognitive performance, and other factors associated with nutritional intake. Fundamentally, impact of the standard of living is the status of the child.

## CONCLUSION

The *Convention on the Rights of the Child* establishes a set of globally defined children's rights. Interpretation and implementation of these rights lies with the national state governments and other governmental and nongovernmental organizations of the world. Article 27 lays out both a goal and a strategy for one particular right, one that is fundamental to the implementation of all of the others. The *Convention* focus on the dignity of the child, the central role of the family environment, and the need for international cooperation are all reflected in the provisions of Article 27. The research presented in this volume establishes a foundation for interpreting Article 27, and highlights the necessity for interrelated strategies if Article 27 is to be implemented effectively.

Clearly, continuing energetic and informed child advocacy at the neighborhood, municipal, national, regional, and global levels will be necessary. The combined wisdom, abstract and concrete, reflected here can inform monitoring of the child's well-being, the identification of policies and projects that are advancing the child's status, and the design and adaptation of culturally competent programs. Such serious implementation of the entire *Convention* will, we hope, help all of us to move toward a world in which all our children reach the high levels of physical, mental, spiritual, moral, and social development that will enable them to thrive and dream.

## REFERENCES

Edwards, M. & Gosling, D. (1995). *Tool kits for monitoring and evaluation*. London: Save the Children.

Ennew, J. & Miljeteig, P. (1996). Indicators for children's rights: Progress report on a project. *The International Journal of Children's Rights, 4*, 213–236.

Miljeteig, P. (1997). The international effort to monitor children's rights. In A. Ben-Arieh & H. Wintersberger (Eds.), *Measuring and monitoring the state of children—Beyond survival* (55–62). Vienna: European Centre for Social Welfare Policy and Research.

North American Congress on Latin America (NACLA). (1994). Report on children's health. *NACLA Report on the Americas, 17*(6), 35–40.

September, R. (1996). Possible sources for knowing the state of the child—The South African experience: Using the *Convention on the Rights of the Child* and the National Plan of Action as a framework to establish goals, implement and monitor them. In A. Ben-Arieh & H. Wintersberger (Eds.), *Monitoring and measuring the state of children—Beyond survival* (309–321). Vienna: European Centre for Social Welfare Policy and Research.

# Appendix: *Convention on the Rights of the Child*

ADOPTED BY THE GENERAL ASSEMBLY OF THE UNITED NATIONS ON 20 NOVEMBER 1989

PREAMBLE

*The States Parties to the present Convention,*

*Considering* that in accordance with the principles proclaimed in the Charter of the United Nations, recognition of the inherent dignity and of the equal and inalienable rights of all members of the human family is the foundation of freedom, justice and peace in the world,

*Bearing in mind* that the peoples of the United Nations have, in the Charter, reaffirmed their faith in fundamental human rights and in the dignity and worth of the human person, and have determined to promote progress and better standards of life in larger freedom,

*Recognizing* that the United Nations has, in the Universal Declaration of Human Rights and in the International Covenants on Human Rights, proclaimed and agreed that everyone is entitled to all the rights and freedoms set forth therein, without distinction of any kind, such as race, colour, sex, language, religion, political or other opinion, national or social origin, property, birth or other status,

*Recalling* that, in the Universal Declaration of Human Rights, the United Nations has proclaimed that childhood is entitled to special care and assistance,

*Convinced* that the family, as the fundamental group of society and the natural environment for the growth and well-being of all its members and particularly children, should be afforded the necessary protection and assistance so that it can fully assume its responsibilities within the community,

*Recognizing* that the child, for the full and harmonious development of his or her personality, should grow up in a family environment, in an atmosphere of happiness, love and understanding,

*Considering* that the child should be fully prepared to live an individual life in society, and brought up in the spirit of the ideals proclaimed in the Charter of the United Nations, and in particular in the spirit of peace, dignity, tolerance, freedom, equality and solidarity,

*Bearing in mind* that the need for extending particular care to the child has been stated in the Geneva Declaration on the Rights of the Child of 1924 and in the Declaration of the Rights of the Child adopted by the United Nations in 1959 and recognized in the Universal Declaration of Human Rights, in the International Convenant on Civil and Political Rights (in particular in articles 23 and 24), in the International Covenant on Economic, Social, and Cultural Rights (in particular in its article 10) and in the statutes and relevant instruments of specialized agencies and international organizations concerned with the welfare of children,

*Bearing in mind* that, as indicated in the Declaration of the Rights of the Child adopted by the General Assembly of the United Nations on 20 November 1959, "the child, by reason of his physical and mental immaturity, needs special safeguards and care, including appropriate and legal protection, before as well as after birth,"

*Recognizing* that in all countries in the world there are children living in exceptionally difficult conditions, and that such children need special consideration,

*Taking due account* of the importance of the traditions and cultural values of each people for the protection and harmonious development of the child,

*Recognizing* the importance of international cooperation for improving the living conditions of children in every country, in particular in the developing countries,

*Have agreed* as follows:

PART 1

Article 1

For the purposes of the present Convention a child means every human being below the age of 18 years unless, under the law applicable to the child, majority is attained earlier.

Article 2

1. The States Parties to the present Convention shall respect and ensure the rights set forth in this Convention to each child within their jurisdiction without discrimination of any kind, irrespective of the child's or his or her parent's or legal guardian's race, colour, sex, language, religion, political or other opinion, national, ethnic or social origin, property, disability, birth or other status.

2. States Parties shall take all appropriate measures to ensure that the child is protected against all forms of discrimination or punishment on the basis of the status, activities, expressed opinions, or beliefs of the child's parents, legal guardians, or family members.

Article 3

1. In all actions concerning children, whether undertaken by public or private social welfare institutions, courts of law, administrative authorities or legislative bodies, the best interests of the child shall be a primary consideration.

2. States Parties undertake to ensure the child such protection and care as is necessary

for his or her well-being, taking into account the rights and duties of his or her parents, legal guardians, or other individuals legally responsible for him or her, and, to this end, shall take all appropriate legislative and administrative measures.

3. States Parties shall ensure that the institutions, services and facilities responsible for the care or protection of children shall conform with the standards established by competent authorities, particularly in the areas of safety, health, in the number and suitability of their staff as well as competent supervision.

Article 4

States Parties shall undertake all appropriate legislative, administrative, and other measures, for the implementation of the rights recognized in *this* Convention. In regard to economic, social and cultural rights, States Parties shall undertake such measures to the maximum extent of their available resources and, where needed, within the framework of international cooperation.

Article 5

States Parties shall respect the responsibilities, rights, and duties of parents or, where applicable, the members of the extended family or community as provided for by the local custom, legal guardians or other persons legally responsible for the child, to provide, in a manner consistent with the evolving capacities of the child, appropriate direction and guidance in the exercise by the child of the rights recognized in the present Convention.

Article 6

1. States Parties recognize that every child has the inherent right to life.

2. States Parties shall ensure to the maximum extent possible the survival and development of the child.

Article 7

1. The child shall be registered immediately after birth and shall have the right from birth to a name, the right to acquire a nationality, and, as far as possible, the right to know and be cared for by his or her parents.

2. States Parties shall ensure the implementation of these rights in accordance with their national law and their obligations under the relevant international instruments in this field, in particular where the child would otherwise be stateless.

Article 8

1. States Parties undertake to respect the right of the child to preserve his or her identity, including nationality, name and family relations as recognized by law without unlawful interference.

2. Where a child is illegally deprived of some or all of the elements of his or her identity, States Parties shall provide appropriate assistance and protection, with a view to speedily re-establishing his or her identity.

Article 9

1. States Parties shall ensure that a child shall not be separated from his or her parents against their will, except when competent authorities subject to judicial review determine, in accordance with applicable law and procedures, that such separation is necessary for the best interests of the child. Such determination may be necessary in a

particular case such as one involving abuse or neglect of the child by the parents, or one where the parents are living separately and a decision must be made as to the child's place of residence.

2. In any proceedings pursuant to paragraph 1, all interested parties shall be given an opportunity to participate in the proceedings and make their views known.

3. States Parties shall respect the right of the child who is separated from one or both parents to maintain personal relations and direct contact with both parents on a regular basis, except if it is contrary to the child's best interests.

4. Where such separation results from any action initiated by a State Party, such as the detention, imprisonment, exile, deportation or death (including death arising from any cause while the person is in the custody of the State) of one or both parents or of the child, that State Party shall, upon request, provide the parents, the child or, if appropriate, another member of the family with the essential information concerning the whereabouts of the absent member(s) of the family unless the provision of the information would be detrimental to the well-being of the child. States Parties shall further ensure that the submission of such a request shall of itself entail no adverse consequences for the person(s) concerned.

Article 10

1. In accordance with the obligation of States Parties under Article 9, paragraph 1, applications by a child or his or her parents to enter or leave a State Party for the purpose of family reunification shall be dealt with by States Parties in a positive, humane and expeditious manner. States Parties shall further ensure that the submission of such a request shall entail no adverse consequences for the applicants and for the members of their family.

2. A child whose parents reside in different States shall have the right to maintain on a regular basis save in exceptional circumstances personal relations and direct contacts with both parents. Towards that end and in accordance with the obligation of States Parties under Article 9, paragraph 2, States Parties shall respect the right of the child and his or her parents to leave any country, including their own, and to enter their own country. The right to leave any country shall be subject only to such restrictions as are prescribed by law and which are necessary to protect the national security, public order (*ordre public*), public health or morals or the rights and freedoms of others and are consistent with other rights recognized in the present Convention.

Article 11

1. States Parties shall take measures to combat the illicit transfer and non-return of children abroad.

2. To this end, States Parties shall promote the conclusion of bilateral or multilateral agreements or accession to existing agreements.

Article 12

1. States Parties shall assure to the child who is capable of forming his or her own views the right to express those views freely in all matters affecting the child, the views of the child given due weight in accordance with the age and maturity of the child.

2. For this purpose, the child shall in particular be provided with the opportunity to be heard in any judicial and administrative proceedings affecting the child, either directly,

or through a representative or an appropriate body, in a manner consistent with the procedural rules of national law.

Article 13

1. The child shall have the right to freedom of expression; this right shall include freedom to seek, receive and impart information and ideas of all kinds, regardless of frontiers, either orally, in writing or in print, in the form of art, or through any other media of the child's choice.

2. The exercise of this right may be subject to certain restrictions, but these shall only be such as are provided by law and are necessary; (a) for respect of the rights or reputations of others; or (b) for the protection of national security or of public order (*ordre public*), or of public health or morals.

Article 14

1. States Parties shall respect the right of the child to freedom of thought, conscience and religion.

2. States Parties shall respect the rights and duties of the parents and, when applicable, legal guardians, to provide direction to the child in the exercise of his or her right in a manner consistent with the evolving capacities of the child.

3. Freedom to manifest one's religion or beliefs may be subject only to such limitations as are prescribed by law and are necessary to protect public safety, order, health, or morals or the fundamental rights and freedoms of others.

Article 15

1. States Parties recognize the rights of the child to freedom of association and to freedom of peaceful assembly.

2. No restrictions may be placed on the exercise of these rights other than those imposed in conformity with the law and which are necessary in a democratic society in the interests of national security or public safety, public order (*ordre public*), the protection of public health or morals or the protection of the rights and freedoms of others.

Article 16

1. No child shall be subjected to arbitrary or unlawful interference with his or her privacy, family, home or correspondence, nor to unlawful attacks on his or her honour and reputation.

2. The child has the right to the protection of the law against such interference or attacks.

Article 17

1. State Parties recognize the important function performed by the mass media and shall ensure that the child has access to information and material from a diversity of national and international sources, especially those aimed at the promotion of his or her social, spiritual and moral well-being and physical and mental health. To this end, States Parties shall:

   (a) Encourage the mass media to disseminate information and material of social and cultural benefit to the child and in accordance with the spirit of Article 29;

   (b) Encourage international cooperation in the production, exchange and dissemination of such information and material from a diversity of cultural, national and international sources;

(c) Encourage the production and dissemination of children's books;

(d) Encourage the mass media to have particular regard to the linguistic needs of the child who belongs to a minority group or who is indigenous;

(e) Encourage the development of appropriate guidelines for the protection of the child from information and material injurious to his or her well-being bearing in mind the provisions of Articles 13 and 18.

Article 18

1. State Parties shall use their best efforts to ensure recognition of the principle that both parents have common responsibilities for the upbringing and development of the child. Parents or, as the case may be, legal guardians, have the primary responsibility for the upbringing and development of the child. The best interests of the child will be their basic concern.

2. For the purpose of guaranteeing and promoting the rights set forth in this Convention, States Parties shall render appropriate assistance to parents and legal guardians in the performance of their child-rearing responsibilities and shall ensure the development of institutions, facilities, and services for the care of children.

3. States Parties shall take all appropriate measures to ensure that children of working parents have the right to benefit from child care services and facilities for which they are eligible.

Article 19

1. States Parties shall take all appropriate legislative, administrative, social, and educational measures to protect the child from all forms of physical or mental violence, injury or abuse, neglect or negligent treatment, maltreatment or exploitation including sexual abuse, while in the care of parent(s), legal guardian(s) or any other person who has care of the child.

2. Such protective measures should, as appropriate, include effective procedures for the establishment of social programmes to provide necessary support for the child and for those who have the care of the child, as well as for other forms of prevention and for identification, reporting, referral, investigation, treatment, and follow-up of instances of child maltreatment described heretofore, and as appropriate, for judicial involvement.

Article 20

1. A child temporarily or permanently deprived of his or her family environment, or in whose own best interests cannot be allowed to remain in that environment, shall be entitled to special protection and assistance provided by the State.

2. States Parties shall in accordance with their national laws ensure alternative care for such a child.

3. Such care could include, *inter alia*, foster placement, Kafala of Islamic law, adoption, or if necessary placement in suitable institutions for the care of children. When considering solutions, due regard shall be paid to the desirability of continuity in a child's upbringing and to the child's ethnic, religious, cultural and linguistic background.

Article 21

States Parties which recognize and/or permit the system of adoption shall ensure that the best interests of the child shall be the paramount consideration and they shall:

(a) ensure that the adoption of a child is authorized only by competent authorities who determine, in accordance with applicable law and procedures and on the basis of all pertinent and reliable information, that the adoption is permissible in view of the child's status concerning parents, relatives, and legal guardians and that, if required, the persons concerned have given their informed consent to the adoption on the basis of such counselling as may be necessary;

(b) recognize that intercountry adoption may be considered as an alternative means of child's care, if the child cannot be placed in a foster or adoptive family or cannot in any suitable manner be cared for in the child's country of origin;

(c) ensure that the child concerned by intercountry adoption enjoys safeguards and standards equivalent to those existing in the case of national adoption;

(d) take all appropriate measures to ensure that, in intercountry adoption, the placement does not result in improper financial gain for those involved in it;

(e) promote, where appropriate, the objectives of this article by concluding bilateral or multilateral arrangements or agreements, and endeavour, within this framework, to ensure that the placement of the child in another country is carried out by competent authorities or organs.

Article 22

1. States Parties shall take appropriate measures to ensure that a child who is seeking refugee status or who is considered a refugee in accordance with applicable international or domestic law and procedures shall, whether unaccompanied or accompanied by his or her parents or by any other person, receive appropriate protection and humanitarian assistance in the enjoyment of applicable rights set forth in this Convention and in other international human rights or humanitarian instruments to which the said States are Parties.

2. For this purpose, States Parties shall provide, as they consider appropriate, cooperation in any efforts by the United Nations and other competent intergovernmental organizations or non-governmental organizations co-operating with the United Nations to protect and assist such a child and to trace the parents or other members of the family of any refugee child in order to obtain information necessary for reunification with his or her family. In cases where no parents or other members of the family can be found, the child shall be accorded the same protection as any other child permanently or temporarily deprived of his or her family environment for any reason, as set forth in the present Convention.

Article 23

1. State Parties recognize that a mentally or physically disabled child should enjoy a full and decent life, in conditions which ensure dignity, promote self-reliance, and facilitate the child's active participation in the community.

2. States Parties recognize the right of the disabled child to special care and shall encourage and ensure the extension, subject to available resources, to the eligible child and those responsible for his or her care, of assistance for which application is made and which is appropriate to the child's condition and to the circumstances of the parents or others caring for the child.

3. Recognizing the special needs of a disabled child, assistance extended in accordance

with paragraph 2 shall be provided free of charge, whenever possible, taking into account the financial resources of the parents or others caring for the child, and shall be designed to ensure that the disabled child has effective access to and receives education, training, health care services, rehabilitation services, preparation for employment and recreation opportunities in a manner conducive to the child's achieving the fullest possible social integration and individual development, including his or her cultural and spiritual development.

4. States Parties shall promote in the spirit of international co-operation the exchange of appropriate information in the field of preventive health care and of medical, psychological and functional treatment of disabled children, including dissemination of and access to information concerning methods of rehabilitation education and vocational services, with the aim of enabling States Parties to improve their capabilities and skills and to widen their experience in these areas. In this regard, particular account shall be taken of the needs of developing countries.

Article 24

1. States Parties recognize the right of the child to the enjoyment of the highest attainable standard of health and to facilities for the treatment of illness and rehabilitation of health. States Parties shall strive to ensure that no child is deprived of his or her right of access to such health care services.

2. States Parties shall pursue full implementation of this right and, in particular, shall take appropriate measures:

   (a) to diminish infant and child mortality;

   (b) to ensure the provision of necessary medical assistance and health care to all children with emphasis on the development of primary health care;

   (c) to combat disease and malnutrition including within the framework of primary health care, through *inter alia* the application of readily available technology and through the provision of adequate nutritious foods and clean drinking water, taking into consideration the dangers and risks of environmental pollution;

   (d) to ensure appropriate pre- and post-natal health care for mothers;

   (e) to ensure that all segments of society, in particular parents and children, are informed, have access to education and are supported in the use of, basic knowledge of child health and nutrition, the advantages of breastfeeding, hygiene and environmental sanitation and the prevention of accidents;

   (f) to develop preventive health care, guidance for parents, and family planning education and services.

3. States Parties shall take all effective and appropriate measures with a view to abolishing traditional practices prejudicial to the health of children.

4. States Parties undertake to promote and encourage international co-operation with a view to achieving progressively the full realization of the right recognized in this article. In this regard, particular account shall be taken of the needs of developing countries.

Article 25

States Parties recognize the right of a child who has been placed by the competent authorities for the purposes of care, protection, or treatment of his or her physical or mental health, to a periodic review of the treatment provided to the child and all other circumstances relevant to his or her placement.

Article 26

1. States Parties shall recognize for every child the right to benefit from social security, including social insurance, and shall take the necessary measures to achieve the full realization of this right in accordance with their national law.

2. The benefits should, where appropriate, be granted taking into account the resources and the circumstances of the child and the persons having responsibility for the maintenance of the child as well as any other consideration relevant to an application for benefits made by or on behalf of the child.

Article 27

1. States Parties recognize the right of every child to a standard of living adequate for the child's physical, mental, spiritual, moral and social development.

2. The parent(s) or others responsible for the child have the primary responsibility to secure, within their abilities and financial capacities, the conditions of living necessary for the child's development.

3. States Parties in accordance with national conditions and within their means shall take appropriate measures to assist parents and others responsible for the child to implement this right and shall in case of need provide material assistance and support programmes, particularly with regard to nutrition, clothing and housing.

4. States Parties shall take all appropriate measures to secure the recovery of maintenance for the child from the parents or other persons having financial responsibility for the child, both within the State Party and from abroad. In particular, where the person having financial responsibility for the child lives in a State different from that of the child, States Parties shall promote the accession to international agreements or the conclusion of such agreements, as well as the making of other appropriate arrangements.

Article 28

1. States Parties recognize the right of the child to education, and with a view to achieving this right progressively and on the basis of equal opportunity, they shall, in particular:

(a) make primary education compulsory and available free to all;

(b) encourage the development of different forms of secondary education, including general and vocational education, make them available and accessible to every child, and take appropriate measures such as the introduction of free education and offering financial assistance in case of need;

(c) make higher education accessible to all on the basis of capacity by every appropriate means;

(d) make educational and vocational information and guidance available and accessible to all children;

(e) take measures to encourage regular attendance at schools and the reduction of drop-out rates.

2. States Parties shall take all appropriate measures to ensure that school discipline is administered in a manner consistent with the child's human dignity and in conformity with the present Convention.

3. States Parties shall promote and encourage international co-operation in matters relating to education, in particular, with a view to contributing to the elimination of ignorance and illiteracy throughout the world and facilitating access to scientific and technical knowledge and modern teaching methods. In this regard, particular account shall be taken of the needs of developing countries.

Article 29

1. States Parties agree that the education of the child shall be directed to:

(a) the development of the child's personality, talents and mental and physical abilities to their fullest potential;

(b) the development of respect for human rights and fundamental freedoms, and for the principles enshrined in the Charter of the United Nations;

(c) the development of respect for the child's parents, his or her own cultural identity, language and values, for the national values of the country in which the child is living, the country from which her or she may originate, and for civilizations different from his or her own;

(d) the preparation of the child for responsible life in a free society, in the spirit of understanding, peace, tolerance, equality of sexes, and friendship among all peoples, ethnic, national and religious groups and persons of indigenous origin;

(e) the development of respect for the natural environment.

2. No part of this article or article 28 shall be construed so as to interfere with the liberty of individuals and bodies to establish and direct educational institutions, subject always to the observance of the principles set forth in paragraph 1 of this article and to the requirements that the education given in such institutions shall conform to such minimum standards as may be laid down by the State.

Article 30

In those States in which ethnic, religious or linguistic minorities or persons of indigenous origin exist, a child belonging to such a minority or who is indigenous shall not be denied the right, in community with other members of his or her group, to enjoy his or her own culture, to profess and practice his or her own religion, or to use his or her own language.

Article 31

1. States Parties recognize the right of the child to rest and leisure, to engage in play and recreational activities appropriate to the age of the child and to participate freely in cultural life and the arts.

2. States Parties shall respect and promote the right of the child to fully participate in cultural and artistic life and shall encourage the provision of appropriate and equal opportunities for cultural, artistic, recreational and leisure activity.

Article 32

1. States Parties recognize the right of the child to be protected from economic exploitation and from performing any work that is likely to be hazardous or to interfere

with the child's education, or to be harmful to the child's health or physical, mental, spiritual, moral or social development.

2. States Parties shall take legislative, administrative, social and educational measures to ensure the implementation of this article. To this end, and having regard to the relevant provisions of other international instruments, States Parties shall in particular:

(a) provides for a minimum age or minimum ages for admissions to employment;

(b) provide for appropriate regulation of the hours and conditions of employment; and

(c) provide for appropriate penalties or other sanctions to ensure the effective enforcement of this article.

## Article 33

States Parties shall take all appropriate measures, including legislative, administrative, social and educational measures, to protect children from the illicit use of narcotic drugs and psychotropic substances as defined in the relevant international treaties, and to prevent the use of children in the illicit production and trafficking of such substances.

## Article 34

States Parties undertake to protect the child from all forms of sexual exploitation and sexual abuse. For these purposes States Parties shall in particular take all appropriate national, bilateral and multilateral measures to prevent:

(a) the inducement or coercion of a child to engage in any unlawful sexual activity;

(b) the exploitative use of children in prostitution or other unlawful sexual practices;

(c) the exploitative use of children in pornographic performances and materials.

## Article 35

States Parties shall take all appropriate national, bilateral and multilateral measures to prevent the abduction, the sale of or traffic in children for any purpose or in any form.

## Article 36

States Parties shall protect the child against all other forms of exploitation prejudicial to any aspects of the child's welfare.

## Article 37

States Parties shall ensure that:

(a) No child shall be subjected to torture or other cruel, inhuman or degrading treatment or punishment. Neither capital punishment nor life imprisonment without possibility of release shall be imposed for offences committed by persons below 18 years of age;

(b) No child shall be deprived of his or her liberty unlawfully or arbitrarily. The arrest, detention or imprisonment of a child shall be in conformity with the law and shall be used only as a measure of last resort and for the shortest appropriate period of time;

(c) Every child deprived of liberty shall be treated with humanity and respect for the inherent dignity of the human person, and in a manner which takes into account the needs of persons of their age. In particular, every child deprived of liberty shall be separated from adults unless it is considered in the child's best interest not to do so and shall have the right to maintain contact with his or her family through correspondence and visits, save in exceptional circumstances;

(d) Every child deprived of his or her liberty shall have the right to prompt access to legal and other appropriate assistance as well as the right to challenge the legality of the deprivation of his or her liberty before a court or other competent, independent and impartial authority and to a prompt decision on any such action.

Article 38

1. States Parties undertake to respect and to ensure respect for rules of international humanitarian law applicable to them in armed conflicts which are relevant to the child.

2. States Parties shall take all feasible measures to ensure that persons who have not attained the age of 15 years do not take a direct part in hostilities.

3. States Parties shall refrain from recruiting any person who has not attained the age of 15 years into their armed forces. In recruiting among those persons who have attained the age of 15 years but who have not attained the age of 18 years, States Parties shall endeavour to give priority to those who are oldest.

4. In accordance with their obligations under international humanitarian law to protect the civilian population in armed conflicts, States Parties shall take all feasible measures to ensure protection and care of children who are affected by an armed conflict.

Article 39

States Parties shall take all appropriate measures to promote physical and psychological recovery and social re-integration of a child victim of: any form of neglect, exploitation, or abuse; torture or any other form of cruel, inhuman or degrading treatment or punishment; or armed conflicts. Such recovery and re-integration shall take place in an environment which fosters the health, self-respect and dignity of the child.

Article 40

1. States Parties recognize the right of every child alleged as, accused of, or recognized as having infringed the penal law to be treated in a manner consistent with the promotion of the child's sense of dignity and worth, which reinforces the child's respect for human rights and fundamental freedoms of others and which takes into account the child's age and the desirability of promoting the child's re-integration and the child's assuming a constructive role in society.

2. To this end, and having regard to the relevant provisions of international instruments, States Parties shall, in particular, ensure that:

(a) No child shall be alleged as, be accused of, or recognized as having infringed the penal law by reason of acts or omissions which were not prohibited by national or international law at the time they were committed;

(b) Every child alleged as or accused of having infringed the penal law has at least the following guarantees:

(i) to be presumed innocent until proven guilty according to the law;

(ii) to be informed promptly and directly of the charges against him or her, and if appropriate through his or her parents or legal guardian, and to have legal or other appropriate assistance in the preparation and presentation of his or her defence;

(iii) to have the matter determined without delay by a competent, independent and impartial authority or judicial body in a fair hearing according to law, in the presence of legal or other appropriate assistance and, unless it is considered not to be in the best interest of the child, in particular, taking into account his or her age or situation, his or her parents or legal guardians;

(iv) not to be compelled to give testimony or to confess guilt; to examine or have examined adverse witnesses and to obtain the participation and examination of witnesses on his or her behalf under conditions of equality;

(v) if considered to have infringed the penal law, to have his decision and any measures imposed in consequence thereof reviewed by a higher competent, independent and impartial authority or judicial body according to the law;

(vi) to have the free assistance of an interpreter if the child cannot understand or speak the language used;

(vii) to have his or her privacy full respected at all stages of the proceedings.

3. States Parties shall seek to promote the establishment of laws, procedures, authorities and institutions specifically applicable to children alleged as, accused of or recognized as having infringed the penal law and, in particular:

(a) the establishment of a minimum age below which children shall be presumed not to have the capacity to infringe the penal law;

(b) whenever appropriate and desirable, measures for dealing with such children without resorting to judicial proceedings, providing that human rights and legal safeguards are fully respected.

4. A variety of dispositions, such as care, guidance and supervision orders; counselling; probation; foster care; education and vocational training programmes and other alternatives to institutional care shall be available to ensure that children are dealt with in a manner appropriate to their well-being and proportionate both to their circumstances and the offence.

Article 41

Nothing in this Convention shall affect any provisions that are more conducive to the realization of the rights of the child and that may be contained in:

(a) the law of a State Party;

(b) international law in force for that State.

PART II

Article 42

States Parties undertake to make the principles and provisions of the Convention widely known by appropriate and active means, to adults and children alike.

Article 43

1. For the purpose of examining the progress made by States Parties in achieving the realization of the obligations undertaken in the present Convention, there shall be established a Committee on the Rights of the Child, which shall carry out the functions hereafter provided.

2. The Committee shall consist of 10 experts of high moral standing and recognized competence in the field covered by this Convention. The members of the Committee shall be elected by States Parties from among their nationals and shall serve in their personal capacity, consideration being given to equitable geographical distribution as well as to the principal legal systems.

3. The members of the Committee shall be elected by secret ballot from a list of persons nominated by States Parties. Each State Party may nominate one person from among its nationals.

4. The initial election to the Committee shall be held no later than six months after the date of the entry into force of the present Convention and thereafter every second year. At least four months before the date of each election, the Secretary-General of the United Nations shall address a letter to States Parties inviting them to submit their nominations within two months. The Secretary-General shall subsequently prepare a list in alphabetical order of all persons thus nominated, indicating States Parties which have nominated them, and shall submit it to the States Parties to the present Convention.

5. The elections shall be held at meetings of States Parties convened by the Secretary-General at United Nations Headquarters. At those meetings, for which two-thirds of States Parties shall constitute a quorum, the persons elected to the Committee shall be those who obtain the largest number of votes and an absolute majority of the votes of the representatives of the States Parties present and voting.

6. The members of the Committee shall be elected for a term of four years. They shall be eligible for re-election if re-nominated. The term of five of the members elected at the first election shall expire at the end of two years; immediately after the first election the names of these five members shall be chosen by lot by the Chairman of the meeting.

7. If a member of the Committee dies or resigns or declares that for any other cause he or she can no longer perform the duties of the Committee, the State Party which nominated the member shall appoint another expert from among its nationals to serve for the remainder of the term, subject to the approval of the Committee.

8. The Committee shall establish its own rules of procedure.

9. The Committee shall elect its officers for a period of two years.

10. The meetings of the Committee shall normally be held at the United Nations Head-quarters or at any other convenient place as determined by the Committee. The Committee shall normally meet annually. The duration of the meetings of the Committee shall be determined, and reviewed, if necessary, by a meeting of the States Parties to the present Convention, subject to the approval of the General Assembly.

11. The Secretary-General of the United Nations shall provide the necessary staff and facilities for the effective performance of the functions of the Committee under the present Convention.

12. With the approval of the General Assembly, the members of the Committee established under the present Convention shall receive emoluments from the United Nations resources or such terms and conditions as the Assembly may decide.

Article 44

1. States Parties undertake to submit to the Committee, through the Secretary-General of the United Nations, reports on the measures they have adopted which give effect to the rights recognized herein and on the progress made on the enjoyment of those rights:

(a) within two years of the entry into force of the Convention for the State Party concerned;

(b) thereafter every five years.

2. Reports made under this article shall indicate factors and difficulties, if any, affecting the degree of fulfillment of the obligations under the present Convention. Reports shall also contain sufficient information to provide the Committee with a comprehensive understanding of the implementation of the Convention in the country concerned.

3. A State Party which has submitted a comprehensive initial report to the Committee need not in its subsequent reports submitted in accordance with paragraph 1(b) repeat basic information previously provided.

4. The Committee may request from States Parties further information relevant to the implementation of the Convention.

5. The Committee shall submit to the General Assembly of the United Nations through the Economic and Social Council, every two years, reports on its activities.

6. States Parties shall make their reports widely available to the public in their own countries.

Article 45

In order to foster the effective implementation of the Convention and to encourage international cooperation in the field covered by the Convention:

(a) The specialized agencies, UNICEF and other United Nations organs shall be entitled to be represented at the consideration of the implementation of such provisions of the present Convention as fall within the scope of their mandate. The Committee may invite the specialized agencies, UNICEF and other competent bodies as it may consider appropriate to provide expert advice on the implementation of the Convention in areas falling within the scope of their respective mandates. The Committee may invite the specialized agencies, UNICEF and other United Nations organs to submit reports on the implementation of the Convention in areas falling within the scope of their activities;

(b) The Committee shall transmit, as it may consider appropriate, to the specialized agencies, UNICEF and other competent bodies, any report from States Parties that contain a request, or indicate a need, for technical advice or assistance along with the Committee's observations and suggestions, if any, on these requests or indications;

(c) the Committee may recommend to the General Assembly to request the Secretary-General to undertake on its behalf studies on specific issues relating to the rights of the child;

(d) the Committee may make suggestions and general recommendations based on information received pursuant to articles 44 and 45 of this Convention. Such suggestions and general recommendations shall be transmitted to any State Party concerned and reported to the General Assembly, together with comments, if any, from States Parties.

PART III

Article 46

The present Convention shall be open for signature by all States.

Article 47

The present Convention is subject to ratification. Instruments of ratification shall be deposited with the Secretary-General of the United Nations.

Article 48

The present Convention shall remain open for accession by any State. The instruments of accession shall be deposited with the Secretary-General of the United Nations.

Article 49

1. The present Convention shall enter into force on the thirtieth day following the date of deposit with the Secretary-General of the United Nations of the twentieth instrument of ratification or accession.

2. For each State ratifying or acceding to the Convention after the deposit of the twentieth instrument of ratification or accession, the Convention shall enter into force on the thirtieth day after the deposit by such State of its instrument of ratification or accession.

Article 50

1. Any State Party may propose an amendment and file it with the Secretary-General of the United Nations. The Secretary-General shall thereupon communicate the proposed amendment to States Parties with a request that they indicate whether they favour a conference of States Parties for the purpose of considering and voting upon the proposals. In the event that within four months from the date of such communication at least one-third of the States Parties favour such a conference, the Secretary-General shall convene the conference under the auspices of the United Nations. Any amendment adopted by a majority of States Parties present and voting at the conference shall be submitted to the General Assembly of the United Nations for approval.

2. An amendment adopted in accordance with paragraph (1) of this article shall enter into force when it has been approved by the General Assembly of the United Nations and accepted by a two-thirds majority of States Parties.

3. When an amendment enters into force, it shall be binding on those States Parties which have accepted it, other States Parties still being bound by the provisions of this Convention and any earlier amendments which they have accepted.

Article 51

1. The Secretary-General of the United Nations shall receive and circulate to all States the text of reservations made by States Parties at the time of ratification or accession.

2. A reservation incompatible with the object and purpose of the present Convention shall not be permitted.

3. Reservations may be withdrawn at any time by notification to this effect addressed to the Secretary-General of the United Nations who shall then inform all States. Such notification shall take effect on the date on which it is received by the Secretary-General.

Article 52

A State Party may denounce this Convention by written notification of the Secretary-General of the United Nations. Denunciation becomes effective one year after the date of receipt of the notification by the Secretary-General.

Article 53

The Secretary-General of the United Nations is designated as the depository of the present Convention.

Article 54

The original of the present Convention, of which the Arabic, Chinese, English, French, Russian, and Spanish texts are equally authentic, shall be deposited with the Secretary-General of the United Nations.

IN witness thereof the undersigned plenipotentiaries, being duly authorized thereto by their respective governments, have signed the present Convention.

# Index

# About the Contributors

**Arlene Bowers Andrews** is director of the Division of Family Policy at the University of South Carolina Institute for Families in Society and Associate Professor of Social Work. A social worker and community psychologist, she is the author of *Victimization and Survivor Services* (1992) and several articles and book chapters regarding family violence prevention and community systems development. She recently authored the handbooks *Helping Families Survive and Thrive, Strong Neighborhoods—Strong Families*, and *Promoting Family Safety and Nurture*. Dr. Andrews was the founding executive director of community programs for victims of domestic violence and child maltreatment and has served as a consultant and volunteer with numerous developing community organizations. Her work has included drafting legislation, monitoring child and family policy and program effectiveness, and participating in an international scholarly work group to monitor the state of the child beyond survival.

**Frank D. Barry** is a senior extension associate at Cornell University's Family Life Development Center, where he assists local communities in creating strong neighborhood environments for raising children. Prior experience includes eight years in Latin America community development work. More recently he served on the U.S. Advisory Board on Child Abuse and Neglect and coauthored the board's major policy recommendations in 1993. He also coauthored *Protecting Children from Child Abuse and Neglect* with Dr. Gary Melton in 1994. Recent publications include several chapters and articles on the effect of community environment on child rearing and social problems.

**Asher Ben-Arieh** is director of the Center for Research and Public Education at the National Council for the Child in Israel and a faculty member of the Paul Baerwald School of Social Work at the Hebrew University in Jerusalem. Since 1988 he has been the project director and editor of the annual *State of the Child in Israel—A Statistical Abstract*. Mr. Ben-Arieh has been involved in several research projects regarding child protection, juvenile offenders, childhood deprivation, and children's services evaluation. He is a member of the Israeli Knesset committee for Early Childhood Development. His publications include articles on deprived and immigrant families. Recently he initiated and chaired the international work group on "Measuring and Monitoring Children's Well-Being Beyond Survival."

**María Luisa Blanco** is a Spanish attorney at law who qualified at the Complutense University of Madrid, the Inter-American Institute for Human Rights in Costa Rica, and the International Institute for Human Rights in France as a specialist of human rights and, in particular, childrens' rights. She was appointed president of the European Law Student Association in Spain, after which she moved to Brussels where she was director for human rights at the International Board. In 1995 she served as a human rights observer and electoral observer in the U.N. Mission in Haiti. She has an M.A. in International Studies from the University of South Carolina and is presently a Ph.D. student at the UNED University of Madrid. Her published research includes *The Analysis of Human Rights as Seen by Law Students in Europe*.

**Malfrid Grude Flekkøy** is a Norwegian psychologist who qualified at the University of Oslo and the Norwegian Association of Psychologists as a specialist in child and adolescent psychology. From 1981 to 1989 she served as the first ombudsman for children in Norway (indeed, the first in the world). She was then appointed Senior Fellow at the UNICEF International Child Development Center in Florence, Italy, where she wrote a book about her experiences as ombudsman (*A Voice for Children*) and studied methods of fulfilling children's rights. Long active in national and international organizations for child mental health, Dr. Flekkøy was secretary-general of the International Association for Child and Adolescent Psychiatry and Allied Professions and has served as an elected municipal official. She is coauthor of *The Participation Rights of the Child* and has published in such journals as the *Journal of the China Law Society, Transational Law and Contemporary Problems, International Journal of School Psychology*, and *Child Rights Journal*. She is currently chief psychologist at Nic Waals Institute in Oslo.

**Robert E. Greenberg** is professor of pediatrics emeritus, University of New Mexico School of Medicine. After ten years on the faculty at Stanford University, he became the first chairman of pediatrics at the Martin Luther King Jr. General Hospital/Charles R. Drew Medical School in the Watts district of Los

Angeles, created in response to the 1965 Watts riots. A wide spectrum of community-based child health and educational services were developed. In 1976, he moved to New Mexico, where he became professor and chairman of pediatrics at the University of New Mexico for the ensuing decade. He has authored many articles in professional journals. He is a past-president of the Society for Pediatric Research and the Western Society for Pediatric Research. He received a National Institute of Health Research Career Development Award. In 1996, he retired from the active faculty in order to develop a research program in the social determinants of child health within the New Mexico Advocates for Children and Families.

**Patricia Y. Hashima** is a developmental psychologist specializing in social cognitive development in young children. Her research interests include children's developing sense of justice, prevention of child victimization, and cultural influences on family socialization. Currently, she is a research associate at the Family Research Laboratory at the University of New Hampshire.

**Natalie Hevener Kaufman** is a political scientist specializing in international law and the politics of gender. She is professor of government and international studies at the University of South Carolina and director of the Office of Families and Democracy at the USC Institute for Families in Society. She is a member of the study group on Measuring and Monitoring Children's Well-Being Beyond Survival. In the area of international law her books include *Human Rights Treaties and the Senate, International Law and the Status of Women*, and *The Participation Rights of the Child* (with Malfrid Flekkøy). Her articles have appeared in *International and Comparative Law Quarterly, Child Rights Journal, Human Rights Quarterly*, and *Harvard Women's Law Journal*.

**Robin Kimbrough** is an associate director of the Institute for Families in Society at the University of South Carolina. She is also the director of the institute's Division on Justice Studies and the Family and an adjunct professor of law. Working in state governments and national professional associations, Ms. Kimbrough has long been active in service system reform in juvenile justice, criminal justice, education, social services, substance abuse services, and the courts.

**Jiři Kovařík** is a leading figure in child research and policy in the Czech Republic. He is a senior researcher at the Research Institute of Labour and Social Affairs in Prague. He has a particular interest in the evolving conditions for children and families in the Czech Republic and has specialized in the study of children living in different situations, including out-of-home care.

**Susan P. Limber** is assistant director of the Institute for Families in Society at the University of South Carolina, and associate research professor of neuropsychiatry and behavioral sciences at USC. Her graduate training is in developmental psychology and law. Before coming to the Institute for Families, she was the James Marshall Public Policy Fellow for the Society for the Psychological Study of Social Issues. Her research and writing have focused on legal and psychological issues related to youth violence, child protection, and children's rights.

**Gary B. Melton** is professor of neuropsychiatry and behavioral science and adjunct professor of law, pediatrics, and psychology at the University of South Carolina, where he directs the Institute for Families in Society. A former president of the American Psychology-Law Society and the American Psychological Association Division of Child, Youth, and Families Services, he served on the American Bar Association's Working Group on the *Convention on the Rights of the Child*. Professor Melton is president of Childwatch International, a global network of child research centers and a research fellow in the Centre for Behavioural Science at the University of the Free State in South Africa. He has served on several national work groups, including the U.S. Advisory Board on Child Abuse and the national board of Parents Anonymous. The author of more than 250 publications and a consulting editor of eighteen journals and monograph series, he has lectured or conducted research in twenty countries and territories. Dr. Melton has received multiple awards for distinguished contributions.

**Barbara Morrison-Rodriguez** is research professor and director of the division on Families of Africa and the African Diaspora at the University of South Carolina Institute for Families in Society. Dr. Morrison-Rodriguez's prior positions have included the I. DeQuincey Newman Endowed Chair in Social Work at USC, faculty positions at Hunter College, State University of New York at Albany, and Mt. Sinai School of Medicine, and associate commissioner of Mental Health and director of Long Term Care for the New York State Office for Aging. She is currently research fellow at the Centre for Behavioural Sciences at the University of the Free State, Republic of South Africa. Dr. Morrison-Rodriguez has published in the areas of ethnicity and family services, minority aging, and child welfare. She has a special interest in strengthening the role of fathers in families.

**Virginia Murphy-Berman** is research director and research professor at the Center on Children, Families and the Law at the University of Nebraska, Lincoln. Dr. Murphy-Berman is a clinical/personality psychologist who has special interests in program evaluation and applied policy research. She has published numerous articles on issues that concern children and families, and she has served as the director of numerous federal and state funded grants to evaluate different types of social programs.

**Allen M. Parkman** is the regents' professor of management at the University of New Mexico where he teaches microeconomics and macroeconomics to graduate business students. His research involves the application of economic analysis to the law with an emphasis on public policy issues, especially those affecting the family. He is the author of *No-Fault Divorce: What Went Wrong?* (1992) and his articles have appeared in numerous journals including the *American Economic Review*, the *Review of Economics and Statistics*, and the *American Bar Association Journal*. During 1981–1982 he was a senior staff economist on the president's Council of Economic Advisors in Washington, D.C.

**Leroy H. Pelton** is professor and former director of the School of Social Work, University of Nevada, Las Vegas. He is also professor emeritus of the School of Social Work at Salem State College in Massachusetts and former special assistant to the director of the New Jersey Division of Youth and Family Services. Dr. Pelton has written numerous journal articles and other publications in psychology, social work, child welfare, and social policy. He is the editor of *The Social Context of Child Abuse and Neglect* (1981) and the author of *The Psychology of Nonviolence* (1974), *For Reasons of Poverty* (1989), and *Doing Justice* (1999).

**Jens Qvortrup** is a sociologist and head of the Department for Social and Health Studies, South Jutland University Centre, University of Copenhagen, Denmark. His main interest is sociology of childhood, about which he has published widely. He was director for the sixteen-country study on Childhood as a Social Phenomenon, 1987–1992, which produced a series of national reports and the book *Childhood Matters* (1994). He is past president of ISA's Research Committee 53 on Sociology of Childhood and board member of ASA's section Sociology of Childhood.

**Brandy Randall** is a doctoral student in developmental psychology at the University of Nebraska. Her research interests include faith development and religious identity in adolescence, and the significance of early attachment relationships for later development.

**Francis E. Rushton** is a private pediatrician who has practiced pediatrics in Beaufort, South Carolina, for the past fifteen years. He is the senior member of Lowcountry Pediatrics, P.A., a specialty pediatric practice. Dr. Rushton is associate professor of pediatrics and on the faculty of the Institute for Families in Society at the University of South Carolina. Dr. Rushton has served as president of the South Carolina chapter of the American Academy of Pediatrics and as a member of numerous state and national organizations concerned with maternal and child health. He currently promotes innovative health care delivery in his rural community as director of Well Baby Plus, a program that provides care to adolescent mothers and their infants on a school campus in a group format, with a home visitation component. Dr. Rushton is also currently the CATCH (Community Access to Child Health) coordinator for the South Carolina chapter of the American Academy of Pediatrics.

**Ross A. Thompson** is professor of psychology at the University of Nebraska, where he has an appointment at the College of Law and was formerly with the interdisciplinary Center on Children, Families, and the Law. His psycholegal research interests span the intersection of child development, families, and the law, and include divorce and child custody, child maltreatment, grandparents' rights, and research ethics. He also contributes to research on infant-parent attachment, early sociopersonality development, and the growth of emotional understanding.

**Judith Torney-Purta** is professor of human development in the College of Education at the University of Maryland in College Park and codirector of the Developmental Sciences Specialization. She also serves as chair of the International Steering Committee for the IEA Civic Education Study.

ISBN 0-275-96265-2

9 780275 962654

HARDCOVER BAR CODE